racing
while
black

racing
while
black

HOW AN AFRICAN-AMERICAN
STOCK-CAR TEAM MADE ITS
MARK ON NASCAR

LEONARD T. MILLER

with

ANDREW SIMON

Seven Stories Press

NEW YORK

A SEVEN STORIES PRESS FIRST EDITION

Seven Stories Press
140 Watts Street
New York, NY 10013
www.sevenstories.com

In Canada: Publishers Group Canada, 559 College Street, Suite 402, Toronto, ON M6G 1A9

In the UK: Turnaround Publisher Services Ltd., Unit 3, Olympia Trading Estate, Coburg Road, Wood Green, London N22 6TZ

In Australia: Palgrave Macmillan, 15–19 Claremont Street, South Yarra, VIC 3141

College professors may order examination copies of Seven Stories Press titles for a free six-month trial period. To order, visit www.sevenstories.com/textbook or send a fax on school letterhead to (212) 226-1411.

Book design by Jon Gilbert

Library of Congress Cataloging-in-Publication Data

Miller, Leonard T.
 Racing while black : how an African-American stock-car team made its mark on nascar / Leonard T. Miller with Andrew Simon.
     p. cm.
 ISBN 978-1-58322-896-8 (hardcover)
  1. Automobile racing drivers—United States—Biography. 2. African American automobile racing drivers—Biography. I. Simon, Andrew. II. Title.
 GV1032.M44 2010
 796.720922
 [B]
                                    2009037885

Printed in the United States of America

9 8 7 6 5 4 3 2 1

Contents

Foreword

I have been watching more and more racing lately, and am keenly aware of the important part NASCAR and its stars play in advertising. How else would I have heard of Jeff Gordon, Tony Stewart or Dale Earnhardt Jr.?

My expertise is in the multi-million-dollar business of sports. I know how crucial motorsports are in my field. I also know how minimal the role of blacks is in the business of sports generally, and of motorsports in particular. While blacks dominate on the playing field in many sports, their role in the front office is still limited. In motorsports, the limitations are not only in the front office, but also on the field of play.

In this day and age, any sector of society in which the television viewership, live gate, and sponsorship packages are so large that billions of dollars are associated with it, clearly lacks something when the powers behind the business are not diverse. The arguments for diversity range from business justifications as a way of broadening the customer base, to the social goal of looking more like America, rather than only white America. I should be clear that my primary concern is racial diversity. Other issues are important, including the international aspect, gender, and sexual orientation, but race in America plays a special, historic role—particularly in motorsports.

A good friend of mine, an African-American, is a former government official of the state of Indiana. He grew up in Indianapolis, where he attended public schools. While we were in college, he and his brother would always talk about going to *the*

500 as children. What could that be all about? I wondered. Every now and then there'd be a flurry about something black in racing, like Willy T. Ribbs, or George Mack starting a team, but I didn't know any black racing fans personally—not until I met these guys.

For at least twenty years, my friend and his brother invited me to go with them to the Indianapolis 500: to attend the parade the day before, to hear Jim Nabors and Florence Henderson sing the opening songs, to hear the same old guy say, "Gentlemen, start your engines." They spoke about the day and about race week with such passion. I didn't get it.

Finally, in 2005, I took them up on their offer and brought my family along. Pretty quickly I understood what it was all about. All that hyperbole about being the greatest sports spectacle on earth, the history of the race, the pride of the people who put on the event. It all came across in an incredibly powerful way.

On race day I found myself with a few hundred thousand other people, rising up in the stands cheering on Danica Patrick as she became the first woman to hold the lead in Indy history. I didn't miss a second of the irony of me sitting with a row full of black folks in a track filled with white folks, caught up in the excitement. Every face I saw was cheering for the underdog girl. I did wonder whether the crowd would have had the same reaction if this had been the first black driver in this position. *Racing While Black* will give you a better understanding of the issues to evaluate before making that call.

Why didn't I know more about this whole motorsports world? Why hadn't I been before? Why had no one in my social or business orbit been? By attending that one event, I began to understand the pull of motorsports. But I also realized that this was only one type of car. I still had little clue about NASCAR, ARCA, NHRA, F1, CART, and all the other abbreviations and acronyms of the motorsports world.

I grew up in Los Angeles. Occasionally in high school and on visits home from college, while roaming around town on a Friday or Saturday night, my buddies and I would wander into Beverly Hills or Hollywood and cruise looking for a secret night club no one else knew about. Every now and then we'd walk into a place that had shrimp on ice, champagne, and cracked crab laid out. Before we were chased out, we'd soak it in and say to each other, yeah, there is a world going on here that we know nothing about.

Years later on *Saturday Night Live*, Eddie Murphy did a skit where he disguised himself as a white man. In his voiceover, he described all that he usually encountered as a black man, and how much easier life was as a white man. Things he traditionally paid for were free; he didn't have to fill out forms for transactions. On a bus, a party broke out when the last black man got off and only whites (and the disguised Murphy) remained on board. Murphy delivered dry comedy and biting social commentary at its best.

All of this my friends and I have come to call "secrets from the black man"—a phrase that sounds like an old headline from *Muhammad Speaks*, the old paper of the Black Muslims.

Well, here's a book that takes you into a world that is almost a complete secret from the black man. We don't have an Eddie Murphy—type guide who can clandestinely provide us with all the insights one could get only as a true white insider. But *Racing While Black* gives you something more. This is the story of a family, and of the businesses and individuals associated with them, who have strived for NASCAR success, and uncovered many secrets along the way.

Not only does *Racing While Black* depict the little-known efforts of these African-Americans in racing but, in doing so, it takes you through the greater history of blacks in motorsports. So look forward to learning about a great business, look forward to learning the secrets of motorsports, and look forward to getting the guidance one needs to be successful in a business that now plays a powerful role in the global economy. Fasten your shoulder harness.

Kenneth L. Shropshire
David W. Hauck Professor at the Wharton School
Director, Wharton Sports Business Initiative
Wharton School
University of Pennsylvania
Philadelphia, Pennsylvania
January 2010

For Lauren C. Miller, my legacy.

Acknowledgments

LEONARD T. MILLER

I would first like to honor Leonard W. Miller, my father and author of *Silent Thunder: Breaking Through Cultural, Racial, and Class Barriers in Motorsports*, the genesis of this work. I was privileged to grow up by his side, witnessing one of the most prominent eras in American motor racing. I'll never forget my visits to Watkins Glen, New York and Lime Rock, Connecticut in the 1970s, being around famous drivers such as Mario Andretti, Jody Sheckter, Mark Donohue, Al Unser, Peter Revson, David Hobbs, and Sam Posey. I watched my father's Brown & Williamson Tobacco–sponsored Black American Racers team compete with driver Benny Scott against the best in the world in Formula Super Vee and Formula 5000. The Black American Racers Association allowed me to meet legendary African-American racecar drivers such as Wendell Scott, Malcolm Durham, Sumner "Red" Oliver, and Mel Leighton, as well as the famous African-American auto-racing photographer Ace Lane Jr.

I could never thank Steve Lanier enough for introducing me to Ethan Casey in 1999. Steve knew I needed an editor who would be passionate about my story. I gained two lifelong friends that day.

Thanks to Ethan Casey, who edited this work from the other side of the North Atlantic. I enjoyed the frequent trips to London, where I hand-carried papers, notes, pictures, and computer disks. I'll cherish visiting all the pubs and restaurants, from Wimbledon to Hyde Park to Brixton. I'll never forget the train rides from Waterloo Station for home-cooked meals in Ethan's home.

Ethan Casey helped put me in touch with journalists and authors who have already communicated my story around the globe. I appreciate his diligence in continuing to edit my work while traveling on other assignments in South Africa, Burma, Pakistan, and all over America.

Jeanne Humphrey typed reams of handwritten pages and put them in an electronic format under ambitious deadlines. Her painstaking work will remain in my memory forever.

ANDREW SIMON

Special thanks to Mom, Dad, Matt, and EJ. Shout-out to Seven Stories Press, *Complex*, *ESPN The Magazine*, and Bittersweet in Brooklyn.

Like Father . . .

Auto racing is in my blood.

Some of my earliest childhood memories are of my father, Leonard W. Miller, drag racing at local strips in New Jersey and southeastern Pennsylvania. (Drag racing is head-to-head competition, two cars racing against each other on a straightaway track.) In the summer of 1965, when I was four years old, my father and my Uncle Dexter brought me along to places like Atco Raceway, Englishtown Raceway Park, and Vargo Dragway, which were all a short drive from our home in Lawrenceville, New Jersey. I wasn't old enough to be in the pit area, but my dad would let me sit in the driver's seat of his modified Volvo P-1800 as it was flat-towed around the outskirts of the tracks. From the bleachers, I cheered for my dad every time he shot off the starting line. I was drawn to the ear-piercing clamor, the cottony trains of exhaust, and the smell of rubber being singed by the asphalt.

I took an early interest in taking things apart, too. Under my dad's close supervision, I learned how to dismantle body and engine parts, and then put them back together. I became handy with screwdrivers and wrenches. Sometimes I'd even help out in the shop by removing hard-to-reach interior insulation with my small arms and hands, which lightened the car for racing. I'd ride along with my father and Uncle Dexter to junkyards that had rare parts. I'd take trips to an auto repair shop on Olden Avenue in Trenton, New Jersey that was owned by a gentleman named Tony Hill, an immigrant from England who ordered and machined all of the parts. My dad, Uncle Dexter, and Tony spent hours fine-tuning the P-1800. The hard work paid off, as my father sped to victory often.

At Atco, Englishtown, and Vargo, I witnessed the coming together of a small yet vibrant community of African-American racers. With the black power movement in full force, black drivers had splashy cars with hip names like Soul Shaker and Black Knight. I'll never forget Warlock, a mean Dodge Barracuda Hemi owned by a guy named Sol Walker. Warlock was deep purple and had an ornate painting of a flame that morphed into a naked African-American woman on its hood. Altered for drag racing, Warlock had tires three times as wide as street tires. Sol had a big Afro, wore a black leather jacket, and kept a hair pick with red, black, and green trim peeking out of his back pocket. There was an overall atmosphere of rebelliousness and camaraderie in the black drag racing community of that era. Fresh off of the Civil Rights Act of 1964, the niche of black teams was just beginning to feel comfortable expressing its Afrocentricity and love of racing.

In 1968, my dad met two black drivers that would inspire him to turn his love of racing into more than a hobby. One was Malcolm Durham, the country's best and most popular African-American drag racer. Malcolm grew up on a farm in Goldsboro, North Carolina, and started racing locally in the late '50s. He later relocated to the Washington, DC, area where, in 1963, he zipped Strip Blazer, his Z-11 Impala, past regional favorites Dave Strickler and Bill Jenkins. The news of a dominant black driver began to spread throughout drag racing circles. Many of Malcolm's white opponents were uneasy with the idea of a black rival, others were downright enraged. But as he continued to win, he drew more and more spectators. Pretty soon, Malcolm realized that he could use his dark complexion to his advantage. "We encountered some problems in the South because those people didn't want to accept us," Malcolm recalls on nhra.com, where he's listed as one of the Top 50 drivers in the National Hot Rod

Association's (NHRA) first fifty years. "But for me, being black was actually a plus because it made me unique, and I tried to capitalize on it as much as possible. During the late 1960s, I averaged $800 per appearance, and that made me one of the highest paid drivers in the business." As he and my father grew friendlier, Malcolm suggested that my dad consider forming a team. Malcolm noticed that a lot of African-American drag racers in the DC-area circuit had talent, but lacked the resources that my father had going for him: mechanical skills, steady income, and focus.

My father had been working on cars since he was a teenager. During his college days, in the mid-1950s, he customized a 1940 Ford convertible into a hot rod. He used to idle the rambunctious beast out on the roads of the Mainline of Philadelphia, where he grew up. As my grandparents tell it, the noise generated by the dual Stromberg 97 carburetors and Smitty muffler made neighbors run to their windows. My father honed his handiwork when he served in the US Third Army's 45 Ordnance Battalion's Direct Automotive Field Support Unit at Fort Bragg, where he trained to fix Army vehicles alongside other servicemen who shared his love of racing. By the mid-'60s, he held a steady job as a senior social research scientist at New York University's Graduate School of Social Work. Malcolm thought my father could do bigger and better things than just race. "Malcolm said racers must decide whether they are going to race for fun or to win," writes my father in his book, *Silent Thunder*. "He thought too many black racers ran for fun and were more interested in betting on or against each other's cars than in understanding the art and science of racing." Malcolm and my dad discussed bringing together other black drivers and crew members for a concerted racing effort, i.e. a team.

The other driver that steered my father's racing ambitions was Wendell Scott. My father met Wendell at a National Association for Stock Car Auto Racing (NASCAR) race in Trenton. In the '50s and '60s, Wendell was one of the only black stock-car drivers to race at the NASCAR level. Unlike drag racing, which had small havens of other African-American participants, the stock-car racing community was vastly white, Southern, uneducated, and bigoted. But the prejudice and isolation didn't deter Wendell. In 1963, the same year Malcolm bested Strickler and Jenkins, Wendell narrowly beat out NASCAR forefather Buck Baker in a 100-mile Grand National series race in Jacksonville, Florida, becoming the first African-American to win on NASCAR's highest level. However, track officials handed the trophy to Baker in the winners' circle. They gave Wendell a convoluted explanation, saying that he indeed had won the race but was not awarded the trophy due to a scoring error. Still, Wendell pressed on. In 1966, he finished sixth in the Grand National series standings, just 1,250 points shy of third-place finisher Richard Petty, one of the greatest NASCAR drivers of all time.

My father knew that what Wendell Scott experienced at Jacksonville was nothing new to black racecar drivers. In 1910, boxing legend Jack Johnson raced against Barney Oldfield—among the country's best white drivers at the time—in one of the first documented car races involving an African-American driver. The American Automobile Association (AAA), then the governing body of the country's major motorsports events, did not allow blacks to participate in its events and refused to sanction the highly publicized Johnson-Oldfield showdown, which was held at a track in Sheepshead Bay, Brooklyn.

The AAA's segregationist policy led some black drivers, like 1920s racer Dewey "Rajo Jack" Gatson, to compete in roving "outlaw" circuits. During the early days of the Indianapolis 500, Charlie Wiggins, a black racer and mechanic from Evansville, Indiana, repeatedly tried to enter his self-built "Wiggins Special" ride, but the AAA turned him away. In 1924, Wiggins decided to take matters into his own hands. With the help of local African-

American businessman William Rucker, Wiggins started an annual racing event exclusively for African-American drivers called the Gold and Glory Sweepstakes. Some 12,000 black racing fans made the annual pilgrimage to the one-mile dirt track at the Indiana State Fairgrounds in Indianapolis for fireworks, parades, stunt shows, and hotly contested races. "It became the Indianapolis 500 for the black population," says racing historian Joe Freeman in PBS's For Gold & Glory TV special, which first aired in 2003. In the 1920s, many of Indiana's state officials were affiliated with the Ku Klux Klan. Wiggins and his fellow drivers had to fend off marches, beatings, and threats of lynching. Despite the presence of the KKK, the Gold and Glory Sweepstakes became a beacon of hope for black drivers, including Joie Ray, who in 1946 became the first black driver to earn an AAA license, and Sumner "Red" Oliver, who in 1973 would become the first black mechanic in the pits of the Indianapolis 500.

Down south in the late 1940s, a group of black drivers formed their own version of the Gold and Glory Sweepstakes: the Atlanta Stock Car Club (ASCC). Members Richard "Red" Kines, twin brothers Ben and George Muckle, and Charlie Scott were just a few of the African-American racers who towed their cars to tracks across Georgia and the Southeast. According to an August 8, 2004 article in The Atlanta Journal-Constitution entitled "Racing's Black Pioneers," the club organized transportation on race days from downtown Atlanta to tracks in the countryside and set up beauty contests, food vendors, and music: "It was like a picnic, a big party," recalls Ben Muckle's wife, Dorothy. Founded around the time when Daytona Beach track impresario and race promoter William H.G. France formed NASCAR, the ASCC in its prime drew thousands of fans to events. Like its white, Floridian counterpart, the ASCC's competition was rigorous, and helped one driver in particular cross over into France's league—albeit for merely a moment. In 1956, Charlie Scott finished nineteenth out of seventy-two drivers in a NASCAR race held at France's Daytona Beach road course. However, it was Scott's one and only NASCAR appearance. Without adequate finances, Scott and the rest of his ASCC brethren could not afford to sustain their personal racing efforts or their organization, which dissolved by the late '50s. Still, the ASCC, like the Gold and Glory Sweepstakes before it, established havens for African-Americans to enjoy racing as both participants and spectators.

Inspired by the experiences of Malcolm, Wendell, Charlie Scott, and others, my father and Uncle Dexter founded a team in 1969. Their goal: Assemble a small group of African-American drag racers who shared their ambitions of winning. They purchased a 1955 Chevrolet station wagon from a junkyard and modified it for NHRA competitions. They named the Chevy wagon Mr. Diplomat, after the car's sketching of an English top hat, cane, and pistol on the doors. Mr. Diplomat was bright yellow and had two bold blue stripes running across the hood. Underneath the hood, they gave Mr. Diplomat a six-cylinder Corvette motor that met the requirements of the NHRA's V-Stock class, a level at which they could compete and remain within budget for an entire season. My father enlisted Kenny Wright, a childhood friend who was a Philadelphia-area auto body repair specialist and a drag racer in his spare time, to drive Mr. Diplomat. By now, my father was more interested in cultivating the team than driving. The Miller Brothers Team—as my father and uncle coined the effort—got off to a fast start and never looked back. Kenny reached the winner's circle dozens of times during the '69–'71 seasons.

Looking to build on the success they were having in drag racing, my father set his eyes on open-wheel racing, specifically the Indianapolis 500. (Open-wheel racing involves single-seat vehicles that have all four wheels exposed. Open-wheel racecars are driven in series like Formula 1, IndyCar, and Champ Car, on either oval or road courses.) At the time, the Indianapolis 500 was the country's most hallowed racing event. It was the race most drivers had dreamed about winning since they were kids. Wendell Scott and Malcolm Durham had already cracked open a window of opportunity for broader African-American participation in motorsports. A black driver in the Indy 500 had the potential to bust the window wide open.

My father figured that the same principles netting the team's success in drag racing could apply to an open-wheel effort. At any level of auto racing, a team is only as good as its crew and its finances. The Miller Brothers Team's newest crew members, Alex Baynard and Ollie Volpe, improved on the solid nucleus of mechanical expertise. When it came to budgeting, my father and his teammates knew how to stretch money for an entire season. All too often my father watched local professional drag racers either race in a class they weren't financially equipped to handle, or blow the bulk of their funds at the beginning of a season, leaving hardly anything for regular upkeep and crash repairs.

Such an open-wheel effort would require a significant amount of money, exponentially more than it took to drag race. Even in those days, IndyCar team budgets ran in the millions. By the time the '70s rolled around my father ran a manpower consulting firm in Trenton that grossed $18 million a year. The healthy revenue stream could cover some costs, but he would need the help of corporate sponsors if he was going to sustain an IndyCar program. His buddy Ron Hines was a thriving mechanical engineer for General Motors and immediately expressed interest in helping out any way he could. In my father's office, which was on the second floor of a brownstone directly across from the New Jersey State Capitol, I used to sit in on meetings where he and Ron devised marketing plans, driver development programs, and pitches for potential sponsors. Ron always scribbled notes furiously on his yellow pad.

In 1971, my father received a call from his friend Mel Leighton about an African-American open-wheel driver in California named Benny Scott. Mel, a former sprint-car driver who in 1949 attempted to enter the Indianapolis 500 but was turned away due to his skin color, met Benny on the Los Angeles racing circuit. (Sprint cars are midsize racers with a high power-to-weight ratio. They are typically run in quick heats or short races. The modern versions sport a large "aerodynamic wing" atop the roll cage.) Mel saw a world of potential in Benny. Benny's father, Bill "Bullet" Scott, raced in California during the '30s. Benny shared his father's passion and devotion, racing cars while he simultaneously worked toward a PhD in psychology. When my father met him, Benny said he had barely enough money to continue racing. The lack of funding forced him to be resourceful. He built competitive cars from second-hand parts and learned invaluable mechanical skills on his own. My father and Ron brought Benny on board as a driver and set a goal of entering him in the Indy 500 by 1977. In order to meet this goal, my father and Ron wanted to partner with an existing Indianapolis driver, someone who could mentor Benny and help recruit sponsors. Through a business contact, my dad met Indy driver John Mahler, who agreed to partner with Benny. Shortly thereafter, my father brought together three primary investors (Brig Owens, former safety for the Washington Redskins; Richard Deutsch, president of Harbor Fuel Oil; and Paul Jackson, owner of one of the largest African-American–operated construction companies) to help launch Vanguard Racing, Inc., an open-wheel team featuring John Mahler and Benny Scott as its drivers.

In 1972, Mahler finished twenty-second at the Indy 500. From the pits, Benny studied Mahler's maneuvering and also helped the crew work on the car. Later in the year, Benny started entering and winning lower-level Sports Car Club of America (SCCA) Formula A races in the South Pacific Division. After winning a race in Denver, a rival driver was heard saying, "Can you imagine a baboon has won the first-place Formula A trophy?" Benny was shocked. It was the first time he had heard such a remark directed toward him. My father reminded Benny of all the bigotry Jackie Robinson had to face when, in 1947, he became Major League Baseball's lone African-American player. It was the price Benny would have to pay for being a pioneer.

Satisfied with the success of Vanguard Racing, my father joined Wendell Scott, Ron Hines, and Malcolm Durham in founding the Black American Racers Association (BARA) in 1973. The goal of BARA was to organize African-American drivers in all types of racing—stock-car, open-wheel, drag—and pave the way for greater successes. BARA also wanted to introduce racing fans to African-Americans' rich, underrepresented history in motorsports. BARA would publish an annual yearbook and hold a Black American Racers Day at Englishtown Raceway Park. Black American Racers, Inc., a team operated by some of BARA's members, built a racing program revolving around Benny Scott. My father, Ron, and Wendell subsidized all racing expenses until they could find a primary sponsor. They drafted proposals and tapped my father's business contacts to help shop the sponsorship proposals to companies that already marketed toward motorsports fans. It didn't take long for the Brown & Williamson Tobacco brand Viceroy to bite. At the time, Viceroy was sponsoring racing legends Mario Andretti and Al Unser in the Formula 5000 series. Solidifying the money wasn't easy. My father had to plead with folks at Brown & Williamson to get an amount of money that was on par with what the company's white teams received—$24,000 as opposed to the $12,000 they offered him. He finally got it. The following year, Black American Racers, Inc., entered Benny in the inaugural Long Beach Grand Prix. In Long Beach, fans pulled Benny and my father aside and asked them questions about BARA. The media started paying attention, too, as newspaper articles about BARA surfaced in both the US and Europe.

In 1976, my father and Benny Scott were acknowledged for

their hard work by being inducted into the Black Athletes Hall of Fame. They were honored at a lavish ceremony at the Hilton in New York City. Tagging along with the BARA crew, I was awestruck by all of the celebrities in the room. Bill Cosby paraded around with a long cigar in his mouth. Sports commentators Howard Cosell and Frank Gifford rubbed shoulders with New York Knicks legend Earl "The Pearl" Monroe and Buffalo Bills superstar O.J. Simpson. The Godfather of Soul, James Brown, was in the house. I ran around asking the stars to scribble autographs on my program. During the award presentation, my father and Benny Scott spoke about their shared dream of making it to the Indianapolis 500. The crowd gave them a rousing ovation.

Sadly, the Indianapolis 500 dream fizzled. Viceroy's sales plummeted, and in 1975 labor unions pressured executives at Brown & Williamson Tobacco to eliminate motorsports budgets in order to avoid more layoffs. The onset of affirmative action initiatives during the Carter administration, which benefited African-American businesses in industries like computer technology and construction, actually had an adverse effect on my father's search for a new sponsor. Fortune 500 CEOs, who could barely stomach having to dole out money to African-Americans in the first place, balked at the idea of allocating additional dollars to a black racing team. My father would tell stories at the dinner table about meetings with white corporate executives whose faces turned red at the very mention of "African-American" and "motorsports sponsorship" in the same sentence. Benny Scott, who was on the brink of becoming the Jackie Robinson of IndyCar, returned to Pasadena and waited for my father to call when more money came in. My father never made that call.

In 1978, my father hit one of the lowest points in his racing career. He had just recruited a black open-wheel racer from nearby Somerset, New Jersey, named Tommy Thompson. Tommy showed a high aptitude for driving and quickly worked his way up to the

United States Auto Club (USAC) Mini-Indy Formula Super Vee Touring Series. He was so dedicated to the effort that he invested $25,000 of his own money to keep the car in operation. Tommy climbed to number twelve in the national Mini-Indy Series rankings, and spirits were high going into the September 23 race at Trenton Speedway. On the last lap of the race, Tommy ricocheted off of a competitor at turn four. The car flipped into the air, shattering into three heaps of disfigured metal. As he was rushed off to the hospital and put on life support, an onlooker was heard saying, "That's one less nigger we have to worry about."

Two days later, Tommy was pronounced dead.

Tommy's death took a lot out of my father, as well as his cohorts. Kenny Wright said he was quitting racing for good. Ron Hines, who had lost a friend on the track a few years prior, took a leave of absence. Were it not for a local twenty-year-old African-American racer named Bruce Driver, Black American Racers, Inc., might have folded for good.

My dad had recently switched his focus to stock cars when Bruce contacted him about racing. (Stock-car racing has its roots in competitions featuring vehicles made for general consumers, as opposed to open-wheel cars, which are built for the sole purpose of racing. During the '60s, however, automakers started making faster, more aerodynamic models of stock cars specifically for competition.) By 1976, NASCAR's Winston Cup Series, the league's top division, had the highest attendance numbers in motorsports worldwide—upwards of 1.5 million a year. Bruce, who came up racing go-karts in the Trenton area, heard my dad was looking for a driver to race at local dirt tracks; dirt-track racing, geared toward amateurs, was a common stepping stone for more competitive stock-car racing. Bruce shared an interest in climbing the NASCAR ranks and volunteered to go in on a dirt-track racing program with my father.

For the 1980 season, Bruce Driver raced at Flemington

Speedway in the Chevrolet-powered Sportsman stock car that he and my father had built. At the time, Flemington was the most competitive dirt track in New Jersey. Ron Hines returned from his sabbatical and helped maintain the car. On break from Morehouse College, I made it to most of the races that summer and watched Bruce from the grandstands. Bruce won five times that summer. We never had much time to celebrate, though. Fans sitting around me yelled, "Those niggers from Trenton have to be cheating!" and "There's no way those niggers can beat us!" and "That nigger Bruce has a white girlfriend!" When it was time for Bruce, my father, Ron, and crew member Mark Blackwell to pose for pictures during the trophy ceremony, shouts of "nigger" rained down from the bleachers.

Sitting out in the grandstands at Flemington that summer, hearing the racial epithets, knowing all the struggles my father and his partners had to go through just to make it to the winner's circle, I was disturbed and disappointed. Guys like Charlie Wiggins, Mel Leighton, and Wendell Scott had all confronted such bigotry in their uncompromising dedication to racing. My family's roots were in racing, my father *belonged* in racing, and he was still being treated as an outsider based on the color of his skin. With every mounting taunt I could see the exasperation and deflation in his face.

That summer at Flemington, something awakened within me. I could no longer sit on the sidelines and watch the same, decades-old mistreatment of African-Americans in racing without doing something about it. I was an adult now, and I could see all that my father and Bruce Driver were up against. I wanted to learn the ins and outs of building an African-American team from the ground on up. I wanted to find the Jackie Robinson of stock-car racing. I wanted to enact change.

It was in my blood.

Finding Jackie 2

Stock-car racing has always been about defiance: defying rules, defying mortality, defying the odds. Many of the sport's first drivers were moonshine runners of the post-Prohibition American South, outlaws who modified their automobiles in order to out-speed authorities. Some of these daring bootleggers entered their getaway cars into the first stock-car races. The treacherous, half-regulated competitions were typically held on makeshift dirt and red-clay tracks in Virginia, the Carolinas, Georgia, and Florida. Fans bet on favorites and reveled in the cheap thrills. One of NASCAR's first celebrity drivers, Junior Johnson, came directly out of the bootlegging tradition. Johnson ran liquor for his father in Wilkes County, North Carolina, during the 1940s, and invoked the same wit and fearlessness that he used to outrun cops against his opponents on the racetrack, amassing fifty wins in his NASCAR career.

While Dale Earnhardt did not begin his path toward stardom under the same unlawful circumstances, NASCAR's working-class hero did represent the ethos of the growing stock-car fan base: gritty, hard-working, and family-oriented. Earnhardt grew up in the textile-producing town of Kannapolis, North Carolina, without much education or money. Though he displayed exceptional driving talent as a teenager, Earnhardt, who was married with a child by the age of eighteen, postponed his NASCAR dream in favor of making enough money to support his family. Eventually, Earnhardt and his four siblings scraped together whatever they had to put him back in the driver's seat. On his ascent to

NASCAR's elite Winston Cup series, Earnhardt's reckless driving style led to wrecks, injuries, debt, and angry rivals. But he always managed to race another day. In 1980, Earnhardt won the first of his seven Cup series titles, and for the next decade and a half virtually dominated the sport.

When a nineteen-year-old kid named Jeff Gordon first broke onto the circuit in 1992, not many expected him to be the heir to Earnhardt's throne of NASCAR greatness. He was too small, too young, and too clean-cut. Plus, he was from just about as far away from the South as you can go in the continental US: California. But his skill quickly trumped all doubt, as the pretty boy from Vallejo won four series championships between 1995 and 2001, claiming over $30 million in winnings during that stretch.

If my father and I were to break a black driver into the Winston Cup series, our effort would need to start with someone ready to face a different set of challenges. Wendell Scott, the first black driver to win a major NASCAR race, came up through the stock-car ranks in the Civil Rights era. Many track officials turned him away when he tried to enter races. When he did race, prejudiced rivals made every attempt to decimate his car, bumping and attacking his car, the memorable No. 34. Crash repairs were costly, and Wendell, an auto mechanic and former moonshine runner in his native Danville, Virginia, often didn't have enough money to aptly fix his car. He pieced together worn parts and enlisted his sons to help with labor. He managed to remain competitive, and in the process showed the NASCAR community that a black driver could not only hang with the big boys, he could win. When he finally did eek out that first major victory in 1963, NASCAR officials stole his shine by awarding the trophy to a white driver. Junior Johnson, Dale Earnhardt, and Jeff Gordon had to go through their own struggles, but none of them ever had a victory taken away because of his skin color.

Wendell retired in 1973 after a near-fatal crash in Talladega,

Alabama, the same year African-American driver Randy Bethea beat out stalwart Darrell Waltrip to qualify for first at a NASCAR race in Nashville, Tennessee. It was Wendell who called my father to tell him the news. In turn, my father recruited Randy to take a stab at open-wheel racing in my father's Formula Super Vee. The experiment didn't go so well, as Randy struggled through a handful of races. Randy and my father parted ways soon after. Randy returned to stock cars, but he never received enough support from sponsors and peers. After competing in one Winston Cup race in the 1975 World 600 in Charlotte, North Carolina, where he finished thirty-third out of forty cars, Bethea dropped out of the NASCAR circuit.

While Wendell and Randy helped pave the way for a black driver in NASCAR, the incident with Bruce Driver at Flemington showed me that the road to a more permanent integration was still rocky. Our driver was going to have to show the utmost patience, courage, and focus if he was to make a lasting mark on the sport. This was a big burden to bear. In 1947, when Jackie Robinson integrated the sport of baseball, he was more than just a baseball player with exceptional talent. He was a symbol of courage and hope for African-Americans still pushed to the margins from Jim Crow laws, and he represented a seismic shift not only in sports but also in society at large. Within a few years of Jackie playing baseball, black players steadily became more accepted into the sport. We were looking for a driver who could help open up the same doors in NASCAR, which was still entrenched in the deep South, family legacy, and an overwhelmingly white fan base, well into the '90s.

Plus, our driver would serve as the face of our business. My father and I had aspirations of drawing an entirely new audience into NASCAR. We envisioned Miller Racing, which my father and I founded in 1994, as the gatekeeper to an untapped wealth of potential fans who just might start paying attention to

NASCAR if a driver who looked like them, spoke like them, and went through similar life struggles emerged as a champion. Besides winning, Johnson, Earnhardt, and Gordon all had something else in common: They found ways to parlay their personas and fan appeal into bona fide brands. After retiring from driving in 1966, Johnson became a team owner and backed drivers Cale Yarborough and Darrell Waltrip on their respective runs to NASCAR championships. Writer Tom Wolfe's 1964 article about Johnson in *Esquire* magazine was re-adapted for the eponymous 1973 movie *The Last American Hero*, starring Jeff Bridges. (The same article also introduced the phrase "good ol' boy" into the literary canon.) Dale Earnhardt marketed his No. 3 Goodwrench Service car any way he and his corporate sponsors knew how. T-shirts, hats, bumper stickers, key chains, die-cast cars—wherever there was an opportunity to emblazon the No. 3 for a merchandising buck, Earnhardt found it and exploited it. The well-spoken, good-looking Gordon was a lightning rod for companies looking to jump into NASCAR's swelling popularity in the '90s. Gordon's appeal to women and to the more affluent broadened NASCAR's overall fan base, and helped him nab lucrative endorsement deals from Pepsi, TAG Heuer, and numerous other brands. My father and I thought we could build a sound, profitable business around a black driver with the right mix of talent, inner strength, and fan appeal.

Toward the end of the '80s, we learned that Bruce Driver was not that driver. A struggling economy kept BARA out of commission for much of the decade. Reaganomics strapped a lot of black businesses for cash, and my father's consulting firm was no exception. In 1984, he had to liquidate all of his racing assets in order to make up an increasing amount of debt. Six years passed with no racing activity. In the meantime, I finished up my business degree at Morehouse College and worked toward earning a commercial pilot's license. In order to pay for flight training at

Trenton Mercer County Airport, I moved back home with my parents and took a job with Frito-Lay as a route salesman.

In the winter of '88, my father received a phone call out of the blue from Bruce Driver, who hadn't raced since BARA folded in 1981. Bruce said he was building a NASCAR Modified racer near his home in Pennington, New Jersey. (Modified is a subdivision of NASCAR whose races take place primarily in the Northeast. The cars, by design, are part open-wheel, part stock-car.) My father phoned his friend Herb Jones, who volunteered to invest in our program whenever we landed a driver. Herb earned his keep with a prosperous steel contracting business. On a brisk winter morning, my father, Herb, and I met Bruce in a barn overlooking a massive cornfield. Bruce said he had the Modified half-complete and just needed money to finish it. Herb agreed to chip in, and within weeks he and my father were writing checks in five-digit amounts. Once the car was completed, we entered Bruce in a lower-level series at Shangri-La Speedway in Owego, New York. It was a good three-hour drive to Shangri-La from where we were then living in eastern Pennsylvania, but my father was adamant about racing at a NASCAR-sanctioned track. Budding teams and drivers learned the ropes of NASCAR at small tracks like Shangri-La, then a fixture of the northeastern stock-car circuit. Just as baseball has the minor leagues, NASCAR has lower-level competitions at such mini-speedways. Shangri-La taught me how teams operated on the grassroots level: how much money was needed, how the rules and the nuances of the sport differed from drag racing and Indy racing, how the skill level of other drivers and crew members stacked up.

Shangri-La also schooled me on how crudely and abrasively some of the folks at smaller tracks could treat a black team. Just like at Flemington, the fans at Shangri-La heckled us and called us "nigger." One night, angry competitors surrounded our team in the infield and swung wrenches in our direction. They accused

Bruce of causing an accident. It was tiring driving three hours to the events, putting up with racial slurs, then driving home, often alone, to crawl into bed at three o'clock in the morning. The NASCAR Modified effort in Oswego lasted for just the '89 season, after which my father and Bruce walked away from each other. My father wanted to hire a chief mechanic who could set up the chassis better than Bruce, but Bruce wanted to do everything his way. As quickly as it was resurrected, the Bruce Driver Miller Racing team folded.

Beginning in 1990, I made it my mission to find a driver. I started randomly calling asphalt stock-car tracks in North and South Carolina to inquire about any African-American drivers who were racing locally. After about fifty calls, I stumbled upon a driver named Tom Rice, who was racing at the Old Dominion Speedway in Manassas, Virginia, just ten miles from my current home of Centreville. At the time, I was piloting commercial flights out of the DC area as my day job. I got a hold of Tom on the phone and gave him the quick history of my family and its involvement in racing. Tom wanted to work his way up to NASCAR's Winston Cup series, but barely had enough money to stay competitive in the speedway's Sportsman class. We agreed to meet the following Saturday at Old Dominion.

I arrived about an hour early. Racecar trailers were filing into the pit area in the center of the 3/8-mile oval track. At the time, Old Dominion Speedway was the most run-down, unprofessional, dirty, antiquated auto-racing facility I had ever seen. It was like a junkyard that happened to have some cars racing around its center. I thought to myself, What other African-Americans would have the nerve to get out of their vehicles at a place like this? (A decade later, new management realized no race fans appreciated the mess, and worked rigorously to make Old Dominion one of the more well-appointed tracks in the South.) Before long, I noticed a black official in the parking lot. I introduced myself and told the official that I was looking for Tom Rice. The gentleman's name was Eric Stewart. He had cornrows and a big potbelly. During the week, he was an electrician. A lot of people smiled at Eric as they passed by and came up to shake his hand. I was happy to see him in an officiating capacity. At some of the smaller racetracks, the occasional African-American on the premises was often an older, hard-on-his-luck gentleman sitting on a stool in the restroom collecting coins in a pie dish. Such scenes always made me wonder if this is precisely how most white racing fans preferred to see African-Americans at the racetrack: hapless, relegated to barely noticeable corners, scraping by with loose change.

"Tom is struggling," Eric said. "He doesn't have enough money to compete. Do you have a million bucks?"

As I chatted more with Eric, another dark-skinned man started making his way across the parking lot toward me. When he got closer, I noticed a white woman trailing behind him.

"Are you Lenny Miller?" he asked in a Southern drawl with his hand extended in front of mine. Tom introduced himself and his wife, Crystal.

Hundreds of good ol' boys and their families were lined up in the parking lot waiting to enter the speedway. I had a feeling we would be the center of attention, and I fought back an urge to run back to my car and speed home to Fairfax County. Tom told me how he and Crystal usually sat near the fourth turn because it was less crowded, which was fine by me. Many African-American drivers had white wives, and interracial couples often didn't sit well with the track clientele. I learned that once at Flemington, when the sight of Bruce Driver's white girlfriend upset some fans in the grandstands. They called me a nigger and threatened my life, just for being affiliated with the mixed couple.

It was a long walk to that fourth turn. We passed plenty of rebel-flag T-shirts, railroad hats, and people spitting chewing tobacco. We found an open spot in the rickety, splinter-infested bleacher seats. Crystal took her usual position: she sat one row in front of Tom to help conceal the fact that they were there together. Tom and I started to discuss the money and time commitment it would take for him to race every week. Crystal handed me an envelope with pictures of their racecar, which had No. 34 on the sides. Tom had chosen No. 34 in honor of Wendell Scott. I immediately had a good feeling about Tom and Crystal. They were a close, loving couple who shared our dream of breaking the color barriers in NASCAR. Like my father and others, they had confronted all too many road-blocks. "We're stuck in a rut," Tom said. They talked about how they'd been racing at Old Dominion for years with no financial support, how other teams rejected them when they asked for any sort of assistance with parts or labor. They financed their effort solely on the money they made from their tractor-trailer repair business. Crystal worked in the front office while Tom did the mechanic work in the back. She never referred to him as her husband in front of customers. Crystal was also an outstanding mechanic. She could weld, cut sheet metal, and change clutches. It wasn't uncommon to see her slide out from beneath a car, covered in thick grease from her elbows to her wrists.

That evening I called my father and Herb Jones to see what we could do for Tom and Crystal. For starters, Tom needed a good engine, which cost $10,000, and he would need another $10,000 for tires and crash repairs. The three of us figured we could pull together $10,000–$15,000 in cash for a start-up budget. Plus, my father had enough money to build an engine on account with R&W Engines, the trusty Lancaster, Pennsylvania–based father-son team my dad had been going to for years. Tom and Crystal were elated when they found out we were going to back them. They even volunteered to drive the five hours up to eastern Penn-sylvania to pick up the new engine themselves. Tom said no one had ever helped him out this much.

A month and a half later, Miller Jones Racing entered Tom Rice in about fifteen races at Old Dominion. He usually finished in the middle of the pack. It quickly became evident that Tom's limited crew help was preventing him from moving up in the standings. While Crystal was doing as much work as she could handle, his pit crew began and ended with her. In order to find additional support, I wanted to find a local small business that could pitch in some dollars. On the local level of stock-car racing, it was common for an auto dealership to sponsor a car, so I called a few minority-owned auto dealers within an hour of Manassas. Some people hung up on me, others yelled in disgust. The friendlier folks politely declined. The only dealer who expressed interest was Mike Nelms, a former Washington Redskins player who owned Champion Chevrolet in Culpeper, Virginia. I mentioned my idea of placing a Champion discount coupon ad featuring Tom and the car in the *Old Dominion Driver*, the speedway's weekly program. He said he was interested and asked me to come down for a meeting.

A week later, I showed up for our meeting dressed in a business suit, ready to present a sponsorship plan that was tailored for his business. The showroom's general manager paged Nelms and asked me to kindly wait. Forty-five minutes passed without any word from Nelms. Finally, Nelms responded to the general manager's call, but said he would be another two hours. He had totally forgotten the appointment. After killing time in the town's tiny center, I met Mike back at his office, which was lined with photos of his NFL playing days. He pulled out a golf club from a closet and practiced his swing as he listened to my pitch. He said he could do something in the way of engine parts. He called in his service manager, a diehard NASCAR fan, and asked him to show me the General Motors Performance Parts Catalog. I circled what we needed—enough parts for two engines—and Mike told me to come back next week with Tom.

When we arrived the following week, Tom had barely outstretched his hand before Mike said, "Look, gentlemen, we priced all the parts you guys need, and the parts are too expensive." He wished us the best of luck and left to play golf. Afterward, Nelms's service manager pulled us aside and offered some words of support. He told us a Champion-backed, African-American team at Old Dominion would net the dealership more visibility. Mike was unfamiliar with stock-car racing, he said, and didn't want to try anything new. In the end, my father, Herb Jones, and I decided to press on without a sponsor and agreed to subsidize expenses for the season ourselves.

A few African-American drag racers were milling about Tom's shop at Old Dominion when the engine arrived. They were impressed with R&W's fine work and the fact that Miller Jones Racing was supporting him, but they had huge reservations about Tom racing at Old Dominion. "Tom, you're crazy messing with those rednecks up in Manassas," they said. "You should go drag racing, where at least you see more of us." When Tom's white friends discovered he had a top-notch engine that had been serviced and tested on a dynamometer (or "dyno," as it's more commonly called), they abruptly stopped visiting and volunteering their assistance. This wouldn't be the last time I noticed such a paradox went it came to an African-American driver on the rise. Black cohorts shy away from helping any further because they foresee the eventual struggles; whites stop helping because a promising African-American driver poses a competitive threat to their car-racing livelihoods. One-time "friends" would turn their backs and say things like "That nigger must be cheating" and "This is the only sport we have left!" When an African-American was running in last place, he was a nice black guy doing his best to get by. Everyone at the racetrack accepted that.

Before we could enter the new vehicle for racing, I had to get the team a NASCAR-approved competitor's license. An official was distributing applications from the hood of an old, rusty pickup.

"You're not gonna drive a racecar here, are you?" he asked.

"I'm not here to apply for a fishing license," I replied.

The old rebel ripped off an application, told me to fill out the appropriate areas, and asked me to make out a check to NASCAR.

"Oh, you're not going to drive!" the official said with great relief when he noticed I checked the crew member box. "You must be with Tom Rice."

Tom Rice competed in the 1991 season at Old Dominion Speedway and did better than any other season in his career.

Sadly, though, by the '92 season, we didn't have enough resources to support Tom and Crystal. We had no other choice but to pull out of the Old Dominion program, leaving Tom and Crystal by themselves again.

The following summer, another couple of drivers came out of my litany of phone calls to Southern tracks. Brothers David and Jeff White were competing regularly at Summerville Speedway, located in the Charleston area of South Carolina. In the summer of 1993, I hopped a plane down to Charleston to check out a Saturday night of racing—and hopefully find the Whites.

When I arrived, it was a hot, humid summer afternoon. After taking in the towering pines and palmettos on the serene drive from the motel to the speedway, I arrived at Summerville to the loud rumble of cars revving up for the night's races. I made my way to the main office to inquire about the Whites. As I approached the wooden staircase leading up to the office, I noticed three middle-aged women sitting inside, each wearing a Summerville Speedway uniform. One of them asked politely if she could help me. The other two looked petrified. I took only one step up, so I wouldn't scare them any further, and told the first woman I had flown down from Virginia to meet the Whites. In a thick drawl, she told me Jeff drove a four-cylinder modified Pontiac Sunbird. The other two women dispersed. I guessed they were going to spread the word that an unknown black man was on the premises.

I sat high up in the grandstands so I could see the entire track and pit area. At least three thousand people were already in attendance, and fans were still filing through the gate. I noticed only one other African-American in the stands. He was wearing bib overalls and a railroad engineer's hat. When practice ended, I still saw no sign of the Whites or their Sunbird. Then qualifying races started. Still no sign.

I walked down the steep grandstands toward the fourth turn, where about twenty cars were waiting at a gate to cross the track and enter the pit area. I observed them all closely, but I didn't notice any African-American drivers. During a break in qualifying I approached the woman operating the gate to tell her I was looking for the Whites.

"I heard you was here," she said. She pointed to where the Whites usually parked their truck and trailer, adding how junky and run-down their equipment was.

It was dark now, and I didn't see the Whites anywhere in the pits. During another break in qualifying, I walked back toward the gate to enter the grandstands. The woman at the gate said, "If they're not here by now, they probably won't show up tonight. Qualifying is almost over. But if I see 'em, I'll tell 'em you're lookin' for 'em." I sat in the grandstands again for about thirty minutes and watched a close race in the four-cylinder modified division. This was the division in which the Whites raced. Still no sign of them. I headed back to the main office and spoke to the same woman from earlier in the evening. This time around, we introduced ourselves to each other. She was Zandra Powell, one of the owners of Summerville.

"Did you find Jeff White?" Mrs. Powell asked.

I told her that I'd had no luck, and that I wanted to leave a message for them to contact me at home in Virginia.

"Before we do that, let me page him over the public address

system," she replied. "Sometimes if they can't afford to race, they come and watch."

She grabbed a two-way radio on the desk and told the track announcer to page Jeff White. Over the scream of engines, I heard, "Jeff White, please report to the office," repeated three times. While we waited, Mrs. Powell told me that her sons raced at Myrtle Beach and used to race at Summerville, where one had been a track champion. They were trying to enter one son in the NASCAR Busch series, the division just below Winston Cup.

"It takes a few cents to compete in the big leagues," I remarked.

"It takes more dollars than cents," she said with a laugh.

David White burst through the office door, gasping for air as if he had jogged ten miles to get there.

"David, how come you guys aren't racing tonight?" asked Mrs. Powell.

"We were late preparing the car from last week's crash," he said with a thick Gullah accent. "We just couldn't get here on time."

David shook my hand and told me his brother, Jeff, used to race at Summerville, but Jeff had recently joined the military on the West Coast. David was now racing the family's four-cylinder modified, and his father, Leroy, was the mechanic. David led me to his father, who had their truck, trailer, and racecar—which had the phone number of David's mother's beauty shop on its side—parked outside the fourth-turn gate.

The car was a death trap on wheels. The body was badly dented. The tires were bald. The roll cage was rusty. The dashboard was crooked. The seat didn't even have a cushion; it was just a fiberglass shell with metal bolts exposed to the driver's body.

"How can you drive this car?" I asked David. "It must feel like you're sitting on a bed of nails."

"This is all we have to run," he said.

When Leroy opened the side door of their old cube van to get a pen and pad, rusty spark plugs, old tools, hunks of torn metal, and filthy rags poured onto the ground. Their dream, Leroy said as he cleared the debris, was to move to Charlotte and compete in Winston Cup. But the Whites, like the Rices, had neither the money nor the help. Leroy told me how their African-American friends dismissed the sport, scoffing at the idea of spending a Saturday night around a bunch of white boys at the racetrack. He told me how competitors were friendly when they had a terrible night, but gave his family the silent treatment when they did well. We also talked about the enormous advantage the Powells' sons had growing up in a racing family. It was fairly common for the offspring of racetrack owners to win races at the local levels and advance relatively fast to Winston Cup. The kids got free, unlimited practice on the track and were funded by revenues generated from the speedway itself. And, of course, there were the little advantages, like breezing past the eyes of the technical inspector, who was on the family payroll and had a vested interest in overlooking any minor form of cheating.

Overall, I thought David showed promise. He was aggressive, athletic, and his family was passionate about racing. With good equipment and half a chance, David probably would have made it to the big leagues years earlier. I flew home the next morning, tired from the short trip, but happy to have made inroads with the Whites. My father, Herb, and I had already exhausted our money on the Rices and simply couldn't afford to back the Whites. Still, I figured I might try finding a local sponsor for David. I returned to Summerville and started pitching car dealerships and other local businesses marketing plans with David as the centerpiece. No one expressed interest. Competing with about $1,000 in their pockets for the entire year—short of the thousands it took to compete even at the four-cylinder Modified level— David's career eventually stagnated.

Another driver that caught our attention was a kid up in Massachusetts named Chris Woods. Racing promoter Joe Gerber, a friend of my father's, was coordinating the Race of Champions qualifying night at Riverside Park Speedway in Agawam and called my father as soon as Chris started winning races. When my father and I flew up to meet Chris, we were immediately struck by his personable attitude, good looks, thick New England accent, and uncanny driving ability. A prominent local racing family, the Fullers, had taken Chris under its wing. The Fuller brothers brought Chris along with them to various events in the Northeast, which gave Chris the opportunity to experience the ins and outs of competitive stock-car racing firsthand. Recognizing the world of potential, my father enrolled Chris in the Buck Baker Driving School at the North Carolina Motor Speedway in Rockingham, where he proved to be a quick learner. Chris was ecstatic when we told him about our aspiration to find a black driver who could work his way up the NASCAR ranks and eventually compete in Winston Cup. He said he was willing to relocate down South to start the process.

In Chris, we felt like we had our driver, someone who was experienced and could likely give us a return on any investment. The next step was moving our operation down to stock-car country: North Carolina.

3

Concord

Charlotte, North Carolina, was the heart of NASCAR. The local fans lived and breathed stock-car racing. The media outlets covered the overflowing fount of up-and-coming short-track drivers right up to the big boys at Charlotte Motor Speedway. North Carolina's biggest, most bustling metro area also functioned as NASCAR's commercial center, housing the corporate headquarters of major teams as well as powerful PR and marketing agencies. Agawam, Shangri-La, and Summerville were all competitive places to race, but they were fairly isolated from the national spotlight. Racing and winning in the Charlotte area would garner headlines in the *Charlotte Observer* and catch the attention of NASCAR's influential corporate executives. One particular bigwig we hoped to eventually track down was H.A. Humpy Wheeler, the president of Charlotte Motor Speedway. Back in the early '80s, Wheeler started publicly advocating for a black driver to enter NASCAR. At the time, the sport was looking to expand its fan base, and Humpy Wheeler knew that a successful black driver in NASCAR would stir enough publicity to attract more eyes, both white and black, to the sport. Humpy Wheeler also followed through on his talk, helping black Indy driver Willy T. Ribbs get sponsorship in the late '80s. My father and I considered Humpy Wheeler the Branch Rickey of auto racing. (Branch Rickey was the executive of the Brooklyn Dodgers who, in 1945, signed Jackie Robinson to the team.)

In the spring of '94, I started our transition southward with Tom Cotter. Cotter was the president of Cotter Communications, which was on its way to becoming the most successful public relations and marketing firm in stock-car racing. I first heard about Cotter back when he was a lieutenant at the Charlotte Motor Speedway under Humpy Wheeler. At the time, he was helping Willy T. Ribbs and his African-American manager, former Miller Brewing sports executive Sam Belnavis, get sponsorship. I wrote a short letter to Cotter explaining our effort and how he might be able to help my father and me. When I called a week later to follow up, he said he was interested in hearing more.

My father and I flew to Charlotte armed with a Miller Jones Racing profile that highlighted the competitive African-American drivers of my father's day: Benny Scott, Tommy Thompson, Randy Bethea, Wendell Scott, Malcolm Durham. We also had a book by racing author Andrew Schupack that listed Black American Racers, Inc., as one of the top sixty auto-racing teams in the world during the mid-1970s. When it came to selling the idea of breaking a black driver in NASCAR, my father and I felt it was important to establish a timeline of black participation in motorsports. It was news to most folks, black and white, that African-Americans had raced cars formally since the '20s. We wanted potential business partners to see the history of success and exclusion for themselves. In our minds, anyone who joined forces with us would be part of rewriting the history of racism in motorsports. Who *wouldn't* want to be a part of that?

Cotter Communications resided on Hudspeth Road in Harrisburg, just a stone's throw from Charlotte Motor Speedway. In the center of the reception area, a shiny racecar glistened under the office lights. We later learned that the display vehicle was regularly rotated in and out of the office, depending on what client was scheduled to visit. If reps from Mercedes-Benz were in town, Cotter placed a Benz gull-wing front and center. If John Deere had an appointment, a familiar green and yellow tractor greeted guests. Over the next few years, my father and I would see show cars in the reception area sporting the names and logos of Sears Die-Hard, Maxwell House Coffee, Black Flag, French's Mustard, Western Auto Stores, and ACDelco.

Cotter was the kind of executive you would find on Madison Avenue:tall, thin, clean-cut, and upbeat. We had sent him one of the best pitch letters he had ever read, he said. For a good fifteen minutes, my father and I described our background in auto racing and, particularly, our intent to market African-American drivers. Cotter listened closely and talked about his experience working alongside Willy T. Ribbs. After an hour, Cotter offered to show us around the Charlotte Motor Speedway and take us out to lunch.

The speedway was a massive complex. We went in through the VIP entrance and passed plush couches, a gift shop, and portraits of stock-car legends en route to the elevators. We got off on the seventh floor and headed to the upscale Speedway Club restaurant, where we gazed down upon the enormous grandstands surrounding the mile-and-a-half oval. Looking around at the white clientele, some of whom were staring my father and me down like they had never seen a black person before, I couldn't help but think about the lingering segregation in certain parts of the United States. Here we were, in a metropolitan area that consisted of nearly 20 percent black folks, inside a venue that housed the country's fastest growing sport, and I suddenly felt like my father and I might have been the first people of color to ever set foot in the speedway.

After the racetrack, we headed over to a restaurant called The Construction Company. The building had three authentic stock cars perched atop its roof. Inside, NASCAR paraphernalia adorned the walls, tables, and everywhere in between. There were hoods, fenders, bumpers, mini-models of stock cars in glass cases, drivers' uniforms, autographed artwork, and checkered-flag tablecloths. As we walked through the restaurant, a string of people stopped

Cotter to talk business or just say hello. While we ate, Cotter agreed that we should move our operation to the Charlotte area and suggested that we start racing Chris Woods at nearby Concord Motor Speedway—home to minor-league stock-car racing, as soon as possible. Chris would get a chance to hone his skills against the country's preeminent crop of amateur drivers. If we one day advanced to the Busch Series, having Concord victories on our resume would show that we earned our racing stripes at the grass-roots level. According to Cotter, evidence of us coming up through the ranks was important when it came to earning the respect of our racing peers and, more importantly, sponsors.

Cotter recalled when, in 1978, Humpy Wheeler lobbied to bring open-wheel driver Willy T. Ribbs down to Charlotte. Wheeler thought Willy, who came from a racing pedigree, might be able to stir up a little buzz in NASCAR country. Willy's grand-father Henry Ribbs raced motorcycles all over California. His father, William "Bunny" Ribbs, was an amateur sports-car racer in the '50s and '60s. Willy's older brother Phil competed in For-mula Atlantic cars in the 1970s. After graduating from high school in 1975, Willy moved to Europe to race in the Formula Ford series and won the Dunlop Championship in his first year of competing. Wheeler helped set up Willy in owner Will Cronkite's No. 96 Ford for the 1978 World 600 race at Charlotte Motor Speedway. Many in the stock-car racing community fumed at Wheeler's idea, as they felt Willy was getting a free pass to the higher levels of competition just because he was black. It was the height of the affirmative action debate in the US, and those who viewed NASCAR as a strict meritocracy did not accept an African-African whom they felt didn't pay his dues. Willy's abra-sive, cocky nature didn't help him make any friends, either. "This is stock-car racing. It's just turning left over and over," Willy said to his rivals in the days leading up to the World 600. "I'm a road racer. With the same amount of resources, I'm gonna clean your clock." During the summer of 1978, Black American Racers, Inc., actually had a run-in with Willy at an Ontario Mini-Indy race. Willy hung around the team's garage area and taunted Tommy Thompson, poking fun at his driving ability. In the days leading up to the World 600, Willy reportedly turned the wrong way down a one-way street and subsequently tried to outrun police. News of the incident led to track officials disqualifying him from the event. Cronkite filled the seat in the No. 96 Ford with a local hot shoe by the name of Dale Earnhardt. Cotter's anecdote about Willy also stressed how crucial it was for us to uphold an air of professionalism. "Maintain your car with a devoted, savvy crew," he said. "Keep your shop neat and orderly at all times, order uniforms for all of the crew members, and do your best to avoid conflicts in the pits." Such steps would help preclude the inevitable racist chatter about how we didn't belong.

Back at the office, Cotter set up a dinner appointment for us with a local African-American ophthalmologist named Dr. Anderson. The eye doctor had recently approached Cotter about starting his own stock-car team. The only catch, Cotter said, was that Dr. Anderson, who was fifty years old and had minimal racing experience, wanted to be the driver. Cotter bid us goodbye and told us to keep in touch.

Cotter's referral to Dr. Anderson raised my eyebrows. I wondered if Cotter recommended Dr. Anderson on the age-old presumption that blacks are better off "sticking together." Since we were breaking into a business that was dominated by white executives, this type of logic would ultimately lead us nowhere. I also shared Cotter's concern about Dr. Anderson wanting to be the driver. I wondered if he was having some sort of midlife crisis and was looking for a new hobby to keep him occupied. If this were true, the meeting would be a waste of our time. Nonetheless, my father and I decided to take the two-hour drive west to Asheville to see him.

After weaving our way through the Great Smoky Mountains, we arrived at the Grove Park Inn in Asheville. Dr. Anderson was waiting for us in the lobby. He was dressed in khakis and penny loafers. We introduced ourselves and sat at a table on the outdoor terrace overlooking the mountains. Dr. Anderson started the conversation by telling us about the Porsche he raced as part of a private racing club. (Club racing is, in a nutshell, rich folk driving expensive sports cars around a rented racetrack.) My father asked him if he wanted to become a partner in our forthcoming effort at Concord Motor Speedway. The doctor insisted that he wanted to be behind the wheel. We explained that our priority was getting Chris Woods on a path toward Winston Cup, and that a consolidated effort could result in more racing opportunities for all of us down the road. The doctor, while cordial and courteous, was not interested in such collusion if he wasn't going to drive. We exchanged information at the end of dinner, and my father and I headed back to the Hilton in Charlotte.

A few days later, I told Chris we were prepared to start his move down South. At the time, Chris was an auto repair service writer for a Honda dealership. I figured he would be able to find similar work near Charlotte. I used the directory for the National Association of Minority Auto Dealers (NAMAD) to call half a dozen dealerships in the Charlotte area see if anyone was hiring. A few of the dealers I contacted wanted a résumé faxed. Chris told me he'd never had a résumé in his life, nor did he have a clue how to develop one. Over the phone I asked him questions about his background and eventually created one for him. Archie Kindle, owner of Plaza Ford and a NASCAR fan, called me back and sounded very enthusiastic. I also received a call back from Stan Carter, owner of All American Ford Mercury in Mocksville. Tom Cotter suggested I call Jimmy Johnson, general manager at Hendrick Motorsports. Rick Hendrick owned more than eighty dealerships, including several Honda dealers in the Charlotte area.

The following week I received a call from Tom Blocker, vice president of fixed operations for the entire Hendrick Automotive empire. I told Blocker we could be down in Charlotte for an interview in two weeks. I figured Hendrick might be the best situation for Chris. If he worked hard at the dealership and impressed at Concord, Chris was likely to catch the eye of someone at Hendrick Motorsports, which boasted some of the most competitive cars and drivers in the sport. I envisioned Chris working his way up to being a crew member with Hendrick Motorsports while driving for Miller Jones Racing on Saturday nights at Concord.

My next call was to Henry and Yvonne Furr, owners of Concord Motor Speedway. The listed number for the speedway ended up being the Furrs' home phone. Such was the charm of many smaller racetracks in the South. Yvonne, in her sugary, Southern voice, answered the phone. I told her that I was a part owner of Miller Jones Racing and that we had an African-American stock-car driver who was ready to compete with the best of the best at Concord. She was both surprised and excited. There had never been an African-American driver in the history of the track, she said, and Concord might attract more fans with one. We talked about how current NASCAR drivers had gone through Concord on their way to stardom—people like Dale Earnhardt Jr., Bobby Labonte, and Ernie Irvan—and how Chris could be the next big name on this list. A week later, after mailing Yvonne a team profile, we spoke again. This time she asked if we needed a race shop. Yes, I said, and we needed tools, equipment, and a mechanic. She said she would help us out any way she could. We agreed to meet at the track in the coming days.

The day before he had his interviews at the dealerships, Chris and I met at his arrival gate at Charlotte Douglas International Airport. It was the first time we had met in person in two years. On the drive to the Charlotte Holiday Inn, I went over the next day's itinerary: Tom Blocker of Hendrick Automotive Group at 9 a.m., Archie Kindle of Plaza Ford in Lexington at 11:30, and Stan Carter of All American Ford Mercury in Mocksville at 2 p.m. Chris told me he needed to go to K-Mart to buy a necktie. Over the phone I had asked him to make sure he brought a new pair of dress slacks, shirt, tie, and shoes. Apparently he didn't listen, so we picked up a five-dollar polyester tie.

Chris's grooming wasn't the greatest. The next morning, as we were dressing, I noticed him putting on a dingy, wrinkled white dress shirt with a noticeable stain on the collar. He didn't have a belt, and his pants were crumpled up and infested with lint balls. He slipped on a pair of old, cracked dress shoes with no socks, pulled out his K-Mart tie, and knotted it loosely around his neck. Perfect, I thought to myself. We can kiss the Hendrick job good-bye.

At Hendrick, a receptionist who looked like a fashion model greeted us. She escorted us down a short hallway that was lined with oil paintings toward Tom Blocker's executive office. Chris commented on her looks as she walked away in her designer skirt. I started to consider the reality that Chris might very well get involved with a white woman down in North Carolina. I thought of Bruce Driver and the altercations stemming from his involvement with a white girlfriend, and the Rices, who had worked so carefully to conceal their relationship. I started to think about the turmoil and hatred an interracial relationship might generate at this small track in the middle of North Carolina. I started to tense up.

Chris was visibly uncomfortable during the interview with Blocker. He answered questions with flat, one-word responses. I started jumping in to answer questions for him. Blocker listened intently, but eventually told us that Hendrick Automotive Group tended to promote its employees internally. It was a polite brush-off. Blocker walked us to the entrance and said he would call us if a job opportunity opened up.

As we headed north on I-85 to Plaza Ford, Chris spoke excitedly about packing his belongings in Agawam. It was clear he was starting to get comfortable with the idea of moving down South. While I was happy that Chris was embracing his new home, I also wondered how he would adjust. He had lived in Massachusetts his entire life, and for years associated with liberal-leaning white folks who didn't pay his skin color much mind. My father and I learned this when we started spending time with him and the Fullers, the white racing family that helped raise him. When the Fullers found him, Chris was in wretched circumstances. Around the age of twelve, his parents divorced and neither parent wanted custody. For a short stretch he was living in a basement, by himself, alongside the family dog that had recently passed. The Fullers, who lived in a postcard New England town with only a handful of other African-Americans, took Chris into their household and introduced him to the family business. He learned everything quickly, especially the driving. By 1991, he started winning at Agawam regularly. During this time period, when my father and I started visiting Agawam, we noticed how he didn't react much to the subtle racism around him: the cold or confused stares, the snickers, the offhand jokes. We would hear the occasional "nigger" from fans and other crew members. Chris didn't acknowledge the epithets much. It was almost as if they were talking to someone else. There was one instance, though, he couldn't ignore. He had just won one of the evening's earlier races and parked his car in the trailer, leaving his tools and helmet lying in the driver's seat. After the last race of the night, Chris ran up to my father and me and showed us his helmet. It was filled with urine. But Chris brushed it off and continued to win races— chasing down white girls the entire time. When I first spoke to him about moving down to North Carolina, I told him that urine in his helmet might be the least of his troubles. Here, I told him, winning races and wooing white women with his JFK-like accent might be enough for rival drivers to wreck him and, possibly, kill him. Chris seemed pretty unfazed by my caveat, which wasn't surprising. Chris, like most racers, possessed a fearlessness. It was this same gusto that pushed him to compete in such a dangerous sport day in and day out.

It had gotten much hotter outside by the time we reached Plaza Ford. An African-American salesman came up to us in the lot and gave us a sales pitch. Once we introduced ourselves, he smiled and asked which of us was the stock-car driver. It felt good to know that word of our arrival had spread at the dealership. The salesman guided us to Archie Kindle's office and told us to wait while he looked for Archie. Chris loosened his tie. By now, his shirt was even more wrinkled, and for the first time I noticed the dry, flaky skin on his sockless ankles. I sighed and picked up the *Black Pages* booklet on the desk. I leafed through listings of African-American businesses and services in the Greensboro-Lexington area, looking for potential barbershops for Chris. Archie Kindle walked in with his white service manager, a man named Bob Reed. Archie wore a thousand-dollar suit and had a thick roll of dollar bills peering out of his front pocket. Everyone within a ten-mile radius of Archie's dealership treated him like a king. He drove around in a restored maroon 1965 Ford Galaxy 500. He ate lunch almost daily at the Golden Corral restaurant, where the staff always addressed him as "Mr. Kindle." He started telling us how he enjoyed attending Busch Grand National events in South Boston, Virginia, and Charlotte Motor Speedway every year. He used tickets he got through Ford Motor Company. Ford Winston Cup show cars sometimes appeared at Plaza Ford to help drive showroom traffic, he said. Archie acknowledged how financially difficult it was to maintain a team and told Chris he was doing the right thing by moving down to the Charlotte area. Bob Reed chimed in to lecture Chris about driving, as Reed himself had raced when he was younger. Reed asked Chris if he could discipline himself to balance all the hours he devoted toward racing with a 9–5 job at the dealership.

Chris would have to stay up late to work on the racecar, many nights until 2 a.m.

Chris remained quiet and nodded his head. I jumped right into questions of pay and benefits. Kindle explained the pay formula, which included a base salary and commission. Judging from Chris's experience, they said he was perfect for an assistant service manager job. I told them the offer sounded good and that Chris could start in four to six weeks. Archie asked us to check in with him every two weeks. He even offered to lease Chris a condo that he owned in Greensboro for a reasonable rate.

We scrambled to make the last interview at All American Ford Mercury, which was fifteen miles away. Like Lexington, Mocksville was one of those Southern towns that looked like it hadn't changed much since World War II. Chris and I pulled into the dealership, which, compared to Plaza Ford, looked like a mom-and-pop used-car lot. When he met us, Stan Carter wasn't smiling. Before we could say much, the retired Navy admiral told us he had reviewed Chris's résumé and that Chris wasn't qualified to work at the dealership. When I broached the subject of Chris racing at Concord, Carter got enraged and told us that wasn't what we were here to talk about. Carter then brought in his white service manager, who reiterated Carter's thoughts so closely that it was almost as if their routine had been rehearsed. The service manager then told us about a mechanic who worked at All American and raced at nearby Bowman Gray Stadium Speedway. All-American had invested money in the stock-car, he said, and the mechanic/driver had helped their dealership win five trophies, all on display in a case on the showroom floor. When I later found out that the All American driver was white, it made sense to me why Carter and his service manager were against hiring Chris. They already had a face for their small racing endeavor, one that was white and safe. If Chris joined All American as a driver, he would threaten to disrupt the secure position the dealership had already built up in the racing community.

Near the end of the conversation, I asked Carter if he by chance knew a colleague of mine, African-American Navy test pilot Stan Campbell. Carter changed his demeanor and excitedly said, yes, he knew Stan Campbell well. Stan had landed on his aircraft carrier several times. Carter asked if I had Stan's telephone number. He had heard that Stan was selling large volumes of truck chassis to the government, and he wanted to get involved in the lucrative project. It was funny witnessing Carter's complete change in attitude once he discovered *he* could benefit from the meeting. This wouldn't be the last time I was involved in such a scenario, where an African-American business contact could so unequivocally reject our ideas yet still seek our help. It was always infuriating. On such occasions, I wondered how this type of self-interest would affect not only our personal goals, but how much it would prevent the progress of other African-Americans looking to advance through peers in corporate America.

I gave Stan Campbell's number to Carter, thanked him for his time, and walked out with Chris.

"What a jerk," said Chris as we drove back toward Charlotte to catch our evening flights home. All in all, though, the whirlwind day turned out to be a success. We ended up accepting Plaza Ford's offer and told Archie Kindle that Chris could start work on August 1.

Next, we needed to secure a racecar and a garage at Concord.

When I told Yvonne Furr that we were prepared to set up shop at Concord, she was elated. She asked me to come down to Concord as soon as possible. In the meantime, she would look into where I could buy a racecar and have an engine built. Within a week, I found myself back on the bucolic roads of North Carolina, passing old farmhouses, churches, and fruit stands toward Concord Motor Speedway. The track was nestled in a lush clearing of trees about 1/4 of a mile off the main road. Henry Furr gave me a warm welcome. He was tall, lanky, and spoke with a Carolinian accent so thick that it was difficult, at times, for me to understand. He gave me a tour of the facility, starting with the ladies' restrooms. He bragged about how impeccable they were, pointing out that if the bathrooms weren't clean, especially the ladies' room, casual racing fans would not come back to the track. It was important to keep the premises as family-friendly as possible, he said. Next, we hopped in a brand-new Ford pickup that had a Concord Motor Speedway logo on its doors and drove through the underground tunnel that connected the exterior of the speedway with the pit area inside the oval. The tunnel was a first-rate feature. At many small racetracks, personnel, racecars, and trailers are often confined to the interior of the course's oval until the end of the night because there is not enough time in between races for teams to traverse the track with all of their equipment. If, say, your team drops out of an early race due to mechanical problems or a crash, you're pretty much stuck in the infield until the last race ends, which could easily be midnight or later. The tunnel allowed teams to come and go as they pleased.

The pit area was impressive, too. The tire shop had columns of freshly made Goodyear racing tires, as well as tire changers and racing wheels. Henry and Yvonne's son Tim and wife Avette operated the tire business. Avette handled inventory and accounting, while Tim and two employees mounted tires. Like many other small tracks across the country, Concord was a family business through-and-through. Henry, a former excavator and heavy equipment operator, developed the entire fifty-acre facility, literally from the ground on up. Judging from what I already saw of the speedway, I would have guessed that the Furrs' net worth was well into seven figures; the speedway was probably worth $5 million alone.

After walking around the 15,000-seat grandstands and the air-conditioned VIP suites, we got back into the pickup and drove around the track at about 70 mph. Even at that moderate speed, the force of the oval's 23-degree turns made me feel like I might slide out of my seat and shoot right through the door. At the rear of the facility was a separate, quarter-mile go-kart track outfitted with its own grandstands and an announcer's booth. (Competitive go-kart racing is geared toward entry-level and junior drivers. The cars are small and light with engines typically running at 5 to 30 horsepower. Juniors can start racing go-karts around five years old.) Go-kart drivers raced on Thursday nights throughout the summer months.

Lastly, Henry showed me the ins and outs of the 20,000-square-foot race shop complex. The nicer garages had 3,000 square feet of floor space, fourteen-foot-high doors, and were equipped with heat, air conditioning, and air lines to operate power tools. Henry then introduced me to Nick Smith, who owned an on-site chassis repair business in shop No. 11. Nick and his wife Pam, a Southern belle wearing skimpy shorts, had been told I was coming and appeared happy to see a potential customer. Pam and the Smiths' liver-colored dog milled about the shop as Nick described the process of building a car that met the speedway's requirements. Nick could fabricate, weld, and, boy, could he talk up a storm. I listened and took notes. Nick also mentioned that he was from Connecticut. He, like many others, had relocated to the Charlotte area to cash in on NASCAR's boom. By 1990, it was common to see aspiring drivers from all over the country hanging around Concord, Charlotte Motor Speedway, and area race shops. Helmet bags in hand, they were looking for whatever work they could find. Fast-talking businessmen from New York popped up at the Speedway Club to broker million-dollar deals. Working-class folks like Nick Smith brought their mechanical expertise down south with the hopes of doubling their earnings from back home. The influx was met with bitterness from some of the locals, good ol' boys who felt like their jobs and livelihoods were being threatened. But bigger-business types, like the Furrs, saw the long-term economic potential and welcomed the transplants with open arms. Other locals did as well, those who simply loved stock-car racing more than anything in the world and were happy to see more and more people sharing their passion.

Before we left Nick and Pam's shop, I showed them a photo of Chris Woods standing in the winner's circle. Stock-car folks gossiped like anyone else in a tight-knit community, and I wanted to strike up a little bit of a buzz. Henry then walked me over to his son's maintenance area. Tim was talking on the phone at an old desk while an older man in overalls was working with the tire equipment. Once he hung up, Tim shook my hand and mentioned that he knew a driver who had a chassis for sale, for cheap, because his wife didn't want him to race anymore. The wife was threatening divorce if her husband didn't sell everything. Henry, Tim, and the old-timer all agreed that the chassis was like brand new and well worth the forty-five-minute drive out to Denton for an inspection. The driver wanted $7,000 for it, not including the engine. This was half the price of a new chassis, which could take eight weeks to build. Tim called a friend of the owner to find out if I could look at it right away, and then gave me directions to a repair garage on Route 49 North.

Along Route 49, I passed rebel flags, trailer homes, and country stores. When I pulled up to the ramshackle structure that was the repair garage, I could hear a radio tuned to country music. Rusty tools and old tires were strewn about. The door to the office was open.

"Is anyone home?" I shouted.

After a few seconds, a young man dressed in greasy mechanic's trousers walked in through a back door.

"Are you the guy wantin' to look at the racecar?" he asked.

He washed his hands and told me we would need to take a

short drive over to where the chassis was located. The door to the mechanic's raggedy 1965 Ford Falcon creaked when I opened it. As I sat down, I saw a hole in the floor nearly a foot in diameter. I straddled the hole and watched the pavement below zip by as the mechanic headed north on Route 49. He chatted away about how every Saturday night he worked on the car we were about to see. It was owned and driven by a friend of his. His friend's wife was tired of her husband devoting all his time and hard-earned money to racing. She even went as far as taking the engine out and hiding it. After the car was sold, she would reveal the whereabouts of the engine, which he would have to sell, too.

We turned off of Route 49 and bounced along a dirt and gravel driveway toward a trailer home. The mechanic stopped in front of a small wooden barn, which had a few cows and goats grazing around its periphery. He removed two wooden stakes and opened the double doors. The white fiberglass Chevrolet Camaro body looked like it was in good condition, and the car appeared to have all its integral parts (with the exception of the pillaged engine). The mechanic told me to look it over and, if I was interested, he would give me his friend's phone number to make a deal.

"Are you from out of town?" he asked on the way out.

I told him I lived in Virginia.

"I knew you weren't from these parts," he replied. "You don't sound like you're from Virginia either."

When I got back to Concord, I noticed a gentleman talking to Nick and Pam in shop No. 11. He was Dave Tomczak, a driver from Milwaukee who operated next-door in shop No. 10. Tomczak, who was gangly and had an ostrich-like gait, faced a similar dilemma as the owner of the stock car I had just seen: His wife, who was still in Milwaukee, wanted a divorce. Even though Tomczak planned on returning to Concord in six months to compete again, he had to unload his racing assets quickly in order to get his finances straightened out. This meant everything in the shop—

including an immaculate, school bus–yellow Chevy Lumina with No. 21 on its sides, a trailer, two engines, tools, and light machinery—was currently for sale at bargain-basement prices. It also meant that shop No. 10 was available for lease. There were no other vacant shops at the speedway, Tomczak said, and the waiting list was several months long. Shop No. 10 was clean and appeared to be in top working condition. Tomczak even offered to sublet his apartment in the historic section of Concord to Chris Woods.

It was almost too good to be true. If we operated out of shop No. 10 we could practice at the track frequently. Crash repairs could be done next door at Nick Smith's—a wooden door joined the two areas and locked on both sides—and we could tap Concord's pool of volunteer mechanics to assemble our own on-site pit crew. When I told Tomczak I would have to think about it, he blurted out an offer of $10,000, which would cover the car—minus the engine—plus all of the shock absorbers, coil springs, axles, fuel jugs, radiators, and extra body sections on hand. I told him I'd get back to him right away.

Henry and Yvonne pulled up to shop No. 10 in the speedway pickup to say goodbye. Their farewell was as warm as their welcome. Yvonne rolled down the window and said, in the same hospitable voice I had heard over the phone a few weeks prior, "It was a pleasure to meet you, Mr. Miller." Chic and sporting enough jewelry to open a store at the mall, Yvonne assured me that shop No. 10 was ours if we wanted it and that I could contact her at home if I needed anything. "Welcome to the Concord Motor Speedway, honey." She and Henry pulled away on the rocky surface outside of the garages, smiling and waving goodbye.

That night my father and I calculated exactly how much money we would need to get things started at Concord. Ten thousand dollars for Dave Tomczak's stock car and parts; $17,000 for an engine from R&W; $4,800 for the twelve-month shop lease;

$8,000 for Goodyear racing tires; $4,000 for tools; and, last but not least, $10,000 for crash damage and mechanical failures. Based on past experiences, my father figured the likelihood of crash damage for Chris was at least 50 percent higher than average. If we didn't properly factor crash damage into the budget, we would risk Chris missing future races while we waited for money to come in. Fewer races meant fewer opportunities to accumulate points and move up in the standings. Such setbacks would impede any progress toward wins, visibility, and, ultimately, sponsorship money.

We accepted Tomczak's offer. Over the phone, Tomczak and I created a detailed list of all the items Miller Jones Racing would receive. He said he would also ship some items he had hiding away in his father's garage in Milwaukee. He wanted cash.

When I returned to the Hilton where I usually stayed, the many African-American staffers who recognized me by now began asking questions about my line of work. When I told them my father and I had just leased a race shop at Concord Motor Speedway, and that an African-American driver would soon be racing there, they all got excited and asked more questions. Some of the women behind the check-in counter lived within fifteen minutes of Concord but had never even heard of the track. A bellhop overheard our conversation and pulled me aside, away from some pretty white ladies he was assisting in the lobby.

"You have a brother that can run with those rednecks down here?" he asked.

"Not only can he run, he can win," I told him.

"Bro, if you guys can pull it off, this town will never be the same. These crackers kill each other over racing cars down here. You guys got nerve. You have my support."

When I arrived at shop No. 10 to complete the deal with Tomczak, a couple of mechanics were dismantling the exhaust on the car. At first, they thought I was the driver. No, I explained, a young guy from Massachusetts named Chris Woods would be behind the wheel.

"Is he your brother?" one of them asked.

"You don't sound like you're from around here," the other one followed.

They were itching for information. I directly answered their questions but didn't volunteer any additional information. This led each of them to half-nod in faux approval and go back to working on the car for another few minutes, only to come back and ask me another question. It was a competitive ploy on my part. I wanted the news of Chris's arrival to whirr around the rumor mill, but I didn't want to reveal too many of the details about our equipment, the class we would be entering at Concord, or our eventual plan for sponsorship. If I did, I'd be opening doors for our future rivals to sabotage us. The fickle question-and-answer session ran the length of time it took for the mechanics to remove the engine: three hours.

In the meantime, Tomczak and I laid out hundreds of parts on the shop floor. He had the look of someone who was being evicted. Tomczak was leaving his home-away-from-home and had to make snap decisions about the financial worth of items he had worked so arduously and thoroughly to compile. It was bitter-sweet for me, inheriting the fragments of another man's vision in order to jumpstart my own.

"Do you have the cash?" he whispered as our inventory run-through came to a close. I peeled off $10,000 in hundred-dollar bills, asked Tomczak for a handwritten receipt, and double-checked the itemized list of everything Miller Jones Racing had just purchased. I changed the locks on all the doors and gave one last glance at the shiny saffron chassis before cutting the lights. It was just after midnight. One of the mechanics uttered to the other, "I have to come down on Saturday nights to see this." The two mechanics hopped into their pickups and disappeared into the darkness.

4
Starting Our Engine

"You're at this hotel more than I am," joked the bellhop at the Hilton when Chris and I approached the check-in counter. It was the first week of June, 1994, and our goal was to start racing by the end of July. Now that we had a shop and a car, we needed to build an engine. R&W Engines could build an engine for us in four to five weeks, but it would be expensive to transfer it all the way down to North Carolina, not to mention the extreme care with which it would need to be secured for the long trip. Also, should the engine have any mechanical problems during race season, it would be more convenient to have the engine builder nearby for maintenance.

"So you're the driver that's going to run at Concord?" the bellhop asked Chris.

"I'm the one," responded Chris. "We'll turn some heads." Two of the African-American women behind the desk smiled at Chris and asked for his autograph.

"Let us know the schedule at Concord and we'll be there," they said.

We dumped our belongings in the room and headed over to Concord. It was a weekday afternoon, and besides a few speedway employees walking around the pit area the track was deserted. Chris and I headed up to the top of the grandstands. For a racing fan, looking down upon a quiet, lifeless track is always somewhat surreal. My mind started filling in the blanks: bleachers packed with fans in trucker hats and flannel shirts, pit crews getting parts on and off the cars, the track announcer calling out positions, cars blasting in and around each other in furious symbiosis, and the ear-splitting drone of manned machines running on pure adrenaline. A babyfaced, twenty-two-year-old Jeff Gordon had just won his first major race, the Coca-Cola 600, down the road at Charlotte Motor Speedway in May, and Dale Earnhardt would spend the summer gunning for his seventh championship. There was an overall feeling of promise, excitement, and anticipation surrounding NASCAR. With the program we were assembling, I could just begin to taste the possibilities in front of us.

We made our way over to shop No. 10. I pulled the keys out of my jeans, opened the locks, and flicked on the fluorescent lights. Chris's eyes opened wide.

"Nice. I think we'll be all right down here," he said, beaming at the No. 21. "Do you think we should put a rebel flag on it so we blend in a little bit?"

It must have been about 90 degrees in the shop. Before long, Henry Furr walked in and, smiling from ear to ear, introduced himself to Chris. Then, switching his tone, he put on the hat of stern track impresario. He began lecturing us on the basic rules and expectations for drivers at Concord. He conducted the mandatory drivers' meetings around 5 p.m. on Saturday nights, where he laid down the law on both racing and pit-area conduct. While his post during races was in the VIP suite underneath the announcer's booth, he was in constant contact via two-way radio with the flagman in the crow's nest, the track announcer, the tow-truck drivers, the technical inspector, the VIP hosts, and the front gate. He called the shots at Concord, and he wasn't afraid to grip *anyone* by the neck over his walkie-talkie. He suggested that we recruit serious crew members, not a bunch of beer and whiskey drinkers or folks willing to cut corners. "Don't cheat," he said, "because everyone gets caught, and it can ruin your reputation and career." And lastly, no fighting. Drivers can get worked up over who causes a wreck, he explained. On one occasion a driver pulled a gun on another driver. Henry now had deputies monitoring the pits.

Reverting back to his usual, affable demeanor, Henry said to call him if we needed any help. As he pulled away in his pickup, Chris snickered at the Southern sermon we had just received.

"Who knows what's going to happen to us down here," he said. "We don't know anyone. We may face a shotgun in the pits. But let me tell you, I am not giving those rebels one inch on the track. They can kiss my black ass!" Chris's brio, while caustic, was somewhat welcome. I figured the swagger might help him rise above whatever taunts and altercations he experienced on race days. Like any successful driver, he had to firmly believe that he was better than his competitors. Focus was also paramount for Chris: focus out on the track, focus while maintaining the car. In auto racing, even the slightest diversion can cost a driver his position in the race, and, in worse cases, it can lead to a wreck, injury, or even death. I imagined the forthcoming jeers from rivals, good ol' boys brought up with the same bigoted mindset of their ancestors. When Jackie Robinson dug in at home plate, he had to block out vulgarities and epithets cascading down from the bleachers, death threat letters, the snubbing of teammates and competitors alike. Through it all, Jackie remained composed, enough to knock the ball out of the park and eventually change the way sports fans—and society at large—perceived skin color. Chris's patience under duress would not only affect our team's chase toward the winner's circle, it had the potential to steer the collective progress of African-Americans in auto racing.

Nick Smith referred us to an engine builder named Sy Earnhardt out in Mt. Pleasant (no relation to Dale Earnhardt). After passing a bean farm and turning onto a windy road that cut through a thicket of pine trees, we pulled into the gravel parking area outside of Earnhardt's garage. Inside, two men were working on an engine block with an apparatus that had several gauges and dials. The high-tech machine was pumping some kind of fluid. For an engine shop, the place was spotless. The two men, one older and one in his twenties, noticed Chris and me walking toward them from about forty feet away. They stared at us as we drew closer. Chris became dead quiet. When I smiled and said hello, the bearded older gentleman returned the hello, cautiously, while the younger man leaned against a doorframe and nodded only once. I told them we needed a winning engine for a Late Model Stock car at Concord Motor Speedway. The young man, who was rail thin, backed off of the doorframe, stood up straight, and tossed the hat he was wearing onto another piece of machinery. The older man wiped the fluid off his hands and shut down the apparatus, all the while maintaining eye contact with us. As the titanic mechanism settled down like a turbine jet engine after landing, I thought to myself, We're about to get into a fist fight with these guys.

The younger man looked us over from head to toe and asked, "Have you guys ever raced on an oval track before?" Chris replied that he had been racing for four years in New England and had visited victory lane several times. Then came the deluge of questions: "Where are you from? Are both of you going to drive? Where are you going to work on your car? How did you get here? Do you know how tough Concord is? Who's your sponsor?" He fired off so many so quickly that we couldn't possibly answer them all.

The older man was Sy Earnhardt. When I asked him how much time and money it would require for him to build an engine for us, he said he was too busy and would not be able to do it. Once Earnhardt rejected us, the younger man loosened up and introduced himself as A.J. Sanders, a Late Model Sportsman driver at Concord. Sanders referred us to Automotive Specialists in Concord, who, as he put it, built some of the best stock-car engines around. He added, "I'll see you around Concord and see how you do." In the months to come, we would indeed see Sanders, as he was one of the more talented drivers at Concord. He didn't have enough money to sustain his car, though. The rumor around the track was that his family helped chip in, to the point where they were taking "bread, butter, and milk off the dinner table for him to race," as someone once put it. Sanders's father, who wore eyeglasses twice the thickness of the bottom of a Coke bottle, was always on hand to cheer on his son. Sanders was also one of the riskiest drivers at Concord. He totaled his equipment many times, and had to be taken off on a stretcher at least twice. He may have been brash, but the kid had as much desire to win as anyone I had ever seen.

"Sorry I couldn't help you boys," said Sy as we made our way out. We got about halfway to the parking lot when I realized I had no idea where Automotive Specialists was. When I re-entered the garage, Sy and Sanders eyed me like I had come back to rob them. I told them I needed directions. "That would help," they replied in unison. Sy wrote directions and a phone number on a pad and told me that the guy to talk to was Dale Earnhardt's brother, Randy.

In the wake of the Sy Earnhardt experience, Chris asked me on the way to Randy Earnhardt's, "Do you really think we're going to get a top-notch engine from him?"

"After we pay top dollar, it'll be top-notch for a few laps, then blow up," I replied. My skepticism was not solely based on the idea that we might get a subpar engine because of our skin color. Randy Earnhardt's nephews Kerry and Dale Jr. and niece Kelley had all recently entered the division in which we would be racing, Late Model Stock. For competitive reasons, each respective Earnhardt clan had both financial and family ties to another team in the area, which meant they had incentive to give us a substandard engine. This is why, at the higher levels of NASCAR, a team will either have its own in-house engine builder or contract a private engine builder. That way, the potential for a conflict of interest is minimized.

Still, we had to head back north on Route 601 toward Concord anyway and figured we didn't have much to lose by seeing what Automotive Specialists had to offer. Sy Earnhardt's directions ended up being confusing. We stopped in an old country store to see if anyone had heard of Roberta Road or Automotive Specialists. It was like I had stepped back in time forty or fifty years. The hardwood floors were patchy and worn-down. A rickety freezer vibrated and hummed as if it were about to explode. The whole place smelled of fresh produce. The couple told me we were five minutes away and directed us back on course.

We arrived at an old, bright-white concrete building that, like Sy Earnhardt's shop, had no storefront or sign. We pulled the car up to an old man in overalls to ask if we were at the right place. He said yes and then walked inside. When we reached the door of the building, we noticed the old-timer talking to a second gentleman. Both had distressed looks on their faces. Slowing our walk and keeping our eyes on the front door, Chris and I stepped inside and went directly to a little office near the front. Randy Earnhardt shot up from behind his desk and asked, "What can I do for you?" I told him we needed an engine for a Late Model Stock car.

"Is it for a NASCAR Late Model or a Concord Late Model?" he asked.

"Concord," I said.

He was nervous. I asked him for an itemized parts list for a Late Model engine and what it would cost. He said he had an engine that was already built for his nephew Kerry who, for unexplained reasons, didn't need it anymore. "It's brand new, and you could have it for $17,000," he said. I took his business card and said that if we were interested we would give him a call.

Our last stop of the day was Summer Lake Apartments. I

wanted to find Chris a place to stay as soon as possible. A young, pretty white woman in the office told us a one-bedroom was going to be available in two weeks. The rent was only $400 a month. She showed us a prototype unit, the laundry area, and the rec room. Picking up on Chris's accent, she asked where he was from and what he was doing down in Concord. When Chris said he was going to race, she perked up with girlish glee and told him she loved car racing. She said she wanted to hold a picnic to welcome him to the apartment complex and show off the No. 21. Chris asked for a lease immediately. Once more, I had flashes of Bruce Driver and the Rices, but Chris had old habits. They agreed to work out the details of the lease over the phone while Chris was back in Massachusetts preparing for the move. "All right, Chris, call me," she said with enough flirtatiousness to make most men smile. "And welcome to the Carolinas." Back at the Hilton, the ego trip for Chris continued. The African-American woman behind the counter asked about our day and wanted to know what Chris was doing later that evening. It started to feel like Chris was a prince in the making.

My father and I decided to have R&W build the engine. Despite the logistical difficulties of getting it down south, we knew that R&W would deliver an engine on par with any at Concord. My father had known the owners, Ron Whitney and his son Ron Jr., since the early '70s. The first engine my father purchased from R&W was for Bruce Driver's stock car at Flemington, the engine that helped Bruce get to the winner's circle eight times between 1980 and 1981. Ron and his son ran their two-man operation out of an unmarked building near Lancaster, Pennsylvania, and relied solely on word-of-mouth for new business. They built drag-racing engines, special-order engines for custom-car aficionados, sports-car engines—they could even re-construct Rolls-Royce engines for show cars. Their research & development (R&D) was unparalleled. If they needed a rare part, they would call distributors around the world until they found it. If they couldn't find it, they would get the necessary engineering books and fabricate the part to a tee, right down to the original material and specs. Down the road, they would compare some carburetors we bought from a local shop with carburetors a rival bought at the same shop and discover that ours were not the same quality. Ron and his son understood what we were up against and they wanted to be a part of any success that we achieved. If we made it to NASCAR and the Charlotte Motor Speedway, Ron later told me, R&W would move down south and serve as our in-house engine builders. They not only looked past our skin color, they grasped the business potential that could trickle down to them if our effort took off.

A few weeks later, my father, Herb Jones, and I flew down to Charlotte to meet Tom Cotter for lunch. Cotter wanted to introduce us to his new business partner, Todd Moore, who had just resigned from a position at the Daytona International Speedway. My father and Herb Jones also wanted to visit Concord and take in a Saturday night of racing. The three of us met at the Avis car rental counter at the airport where, just as at the Hilton, the black employees were becoming familiar with me. I'd show them photographs of Chris Woods and tell them we hoped to be racing by the end of the summer. As the weeks went by, they grew more and more enthusiastic and started asking me for status reports. When I was the only passenger on the shuttle bus, the drivers would often become candid. A female driver once told me, "I know those redneck crackers hate you guys. That redneck racing is all they have left that doesn't include blacks." When we got to the Hilton, the questions and words of encouragement continued. The manager on duty, a tall, blonde Southern woman, welcomed us back and gave us complimentary breakfast tickets, now a routine gesture from the staff. Our Hilton friends also started giving us discounts and helped squeeze us in when the place was overbooked. It was as if the Avis and Hilton employees identified with our plight as the underdogs. They knew we had to scratch and claw our way up the racing ranks, and they were rooting for us.

We met Cotter and Moore at the Construction Company. They walked in sporting high-priced khakis, leather shoes, and golf shirts. Todd, who was as polished and as enthusiastic as Cotter, talked about his job at Daytona and asked us about our experiences. Cotter once again spoke about the Willy T. Ribbs experiment-gone-wrong in Charlotte. He wanted to reiterate to everyone at the table how countless drivers, businesspeople, and fans would jump on any opportunity to derail us, and that we would, in turn, need to conduct ourselves with the utmost professionalism and focus. I thought of Chris's brash comments at Concord a few weeks back. Ribbs had probably, without trying, set African-American integration into NASCAR back a few years. On top of the other challenges, Chris would have to work hard to eradicate the memory of Willy's actions at Charlotte.

It was warm and sticky outside when my father, Herb, and I got to Concord. I showed them the grandstands, the tunnel, the pit area, the garage complex, shop No. 10, and the No. 21 Lumina. They liked what they saw, but the day quickly took an unexpected turn. When my father broached the subject of how we were going pay for the engine, tools, and spare parts, Herb told us he was leaving the team. While the Concord endeavor encouraged him, the meeting with Cotter and Moore left him feeling deflated. "I'm older, you're older," he said, pointing to my father. "We go into these meetings and look like old men trying to hang on." Over the course of seven years, Herb had invested close to half a million dollars in the team, and he felt like we were still a ways away from locking down sponsorship help. Between running his steel company and trying to get a race team off the ground, he was just plain worn out. He congratulated me on what I had accomplished down at Concord so far and wished us the best. I understood where Herb was coming from. For decades, he had been fighting racism in the steel trade in order to grow his business into a $30-million-a-year powerhouse. The additional prejudice in the car-racing world caused Herb to reach his breaking point.

Five o'clock that evening, we returned to Concord for the Saturday night races. Two-dozen trailers, strapped with stock cars and equipment, waited to enter the tunnel. About forty people were in line at the pit-pass shack. As we parked, all eyes were on us. Yvonne Furr waved to us through the glass window of the shack. She opened the side door and yelled out, "Come on inside where it's cool!" She gave me a big hug and welcomed my father and Herb. "Henry Furr, please report to the rear entrance," she said into her two-way radio. While we waited for Henry, she gave us free VIP suite passes for the evening. She told us over and over to give her a week's notice if we had any potential sponsors, family members, or others who wanted to visit the speedway, and she would take care of them, on the house.

Henry walked in and introduced himself to my father and Herb, telling them that Chris was a nice young man and that he should do well at the speedway. By the time we exited the pit-pass shack, the line for credentials had gotten longer and the equipment trailers were starting to pass through the tunnel. I could hear cars blasting around the track on practice runs and smell the aromas of Southern fried chicken, country ham sandwiches, hamburgers, and French fries wafting over from the concession stand. Once again, all eyes fixated on the black threesome. It felt like some of the good ol' boys, chewing tobacco in their Civil War–era beards and grimy work clothes, were looking right through us, brooding about what agenda we might possibly have at their little racing enclave. I started to envision the riot that might break out once we unleashed Chris in the No. 21. Glancing over at the sheriff deputies stationed near the pit-pass shack, I hoped they would never have to leave their post during our nights of racing.

We stopped back at shop No. 10 before heading up to the VIP

suites. There, we bumped into our neighbor in shop No. 9 for the first time. Wally Bell was a stocky, clean-cut drag racer in his fifties who leased a shop at the speedway but did not race there. My father recognized him by name. Wally was a popular drag racer in the 1960s and competed against many of the great African-American drag racers of that era, including Malcolm Durham. Wally spoke a mile a minute and was constantly cracking jokes. He later proved to be a huge asset to us, too. He was a Northerner who knew about some of the resistance we were going to face being outsiders. He told us who cheated, who lied, who did shoddy work, and who would have problems dealing with African-Americans. In time, when my father and I weren't around to watch over Chris, Wally took it upon himself to mentor him and advise him on how to handle himself. Wally's cleanliness and attention to detail were exemplary. I hoped some of that would rub off on Chris. He also periodically called my father and me to update us on important happenings at Concord, telling us when Chris had some "hangers-on he doesn't need around" and informing us when someone tried to break into our shop. Wally saved us a lot of headaches.

Our other neighbor, Nick Smith, was busy doing some last-minute chassis work on the yellow No. 11 Ford driven by Jody Starnes. The Starnes family was always on hand Saturday nights. The mother was the head janitor at the track, while the pot-bellied father, who was a gravedigger at a nearby cemetery, drove their trailer to the speedway. As the three of us approached the No. 11, the Starneses eyed us with caution. Nick got asked if we were going to hang out in the pits that night. We told him we were going to watch from the VIP suite, prompting him to make a comment suggesting we were big spenders. We wished the Starneses good luck and headed over to the main entrance, where we were met by an older woman whose leathery skin looked like it had taken in the late afternoon North Carolina sun for decades. Her hair was short, gray, and disheveled, and she had two teeth missing behind her stoic lips. She ran that front gate like a dictator, too. Hand her your ticket and keep the line moving. Lord help you if you didn't have a ticket. My father and I eventually started calling her the wooden soldier. Some of our northern African-American friends who would later visit the track were so intimidated by characters like the wooden soldier—one friend once said, "What was that?"—and the Starneses that they never came back. It was frustrating to hear the elitist attitude of our well-to-do friends and colleagues toward the working-class fans at Concord and other small tracks. The "trailer trash" comments emanated their own form of prejudice, a prejudice that would only fortify the racial divide in car racing. For, if African-Americans who had the money and resources to help integrate the sport chose not to because they saw the sport as "too redneck" and "too Southern"—and if the majority of white folks involved in the sport were to thwart us—how were things ever going to change?

A thin, older gentleman in Wrangler jeans, cowboy boots, a freshly pressed dress shirt, and a cap with a racing logo welcomed us into the VIP suites. His name was Paul Wilson. Paul was a native of Concord who had raced stock cars when he was younger, both locally and at tracks up north, including Flemington. Like Wally Bell, Paul was a talker. Before my father and I could sit down, he whispered to us that earlier in the week the flagman had told him there was "no room for a nigger in this sport." By now the races had started, and as cars zipped past our field of vision, shaking the glass of the suites with every lap, Paul gave us some background on every driver who had the potential to make it to NASCAR, who had money, who was hotheaded, and who cheated. He recommended engine builders, pit crew personnel, chassis experts, and truck drivers. He even offered to cut our grass if we moved to Concord and volunteered to drive our trailer if we ever took the team on the road.

The sun was just beginning to set, and the Street Stock class was finishing its twenty-five-lap race. There were five classes at Concord: the entry-level four-cylinder Modified; the intermediate Street Stock, Pro Stock, and Late Model Stock; and the premier class, Late Model Sportsman. The four-cylinder Modifieds had basic racing engines. The doors were welded and had window netting, the chassis might have had stock-car trim or a spoiler, and the bodies could vary from a Pontiac Sunbird to a foreign model, like a Datsun. The four-cylinders were the cheapest to maintain and could be driven by someone with minimal racing experience. The Street and Pro Stock had Plexiglass windows, a racing seat, a roll cage, a V8 engine, racing suspension, and specialized tires and wheels. A Pro Stock engine had about 25 percent more engine modifications than a Street Stock. Moving up to Late Model Stock, for which Chris was skilled enough to drive, the rules for both the exterior and interior were more standardized. While four-cylinder, Street, and Pro Stock specs varied from track to track across the country, the Late Model classes at Concord and other Southern tracks usually conformed to a rulebook that came directly from the NASCAR offices in Daytona. Late Model bodies were, ideally, custom-built and had expensive components, a more tubular chassis, and enough engine modification to generate 300 to 350 horsepower (as opposed to 200 to 250 for Pro). Finally, for Late Model Sportsman, the body specs, chassis, suspension, and tires were exactly the same as Late Model Stock, and the engine was tailored to reach 450 to 500 horsepower. Late Model Sportsman cars went around the track so fast that on turns the brakes would glow like fire embers. Annual budgets ranged from $5,000 for four-cylinder up to more than $150,000 for Late Model Sportsman. Saturday night purses ranged from $700 for four-cylinder up to $5,000 for a Big 10 Series Late Model Sportsman race, which would also be broadcast on local cable television to 500,000 households.

Track announcer Doug Smith shouted out car positions like he was calling a heavyweight title fight. The crowd of eight thousand cheered their favorite drivers and hissed at others. Word had spread that three black guys were up in the VIP area, as various track personnel and other curious parties started dropping into our section to check us out. A woman sat behind us and tried to sell us an ad in a new stock-car newspaper she was starting. A former NASCAR Winston Cup queen pushing forty, she was holding onto her seductive looks via skintight white pants, a skimpy see-through blouse, and spiked heels. The woman said she might like to interview Chris for a cover story. Herb Jones and I listened in as my father negotiated ad prices and told her he wanted to hold off on any story until Chris had raced half a dozen times. After reviewing a prototype of the newspaper, he wrote a check for fifty dollars for a yet-to-be-determined ad. We saw the woman periodically after that, but the newspaper never materialized, and we never did get our fifty dollars back.

Another woman walked into our suite holding a freshly baked pound cake. She was Paul Wilson's wife. They had met about fifteen years back in New Jersey, her home state. When she learned that my father and I had lived a large part of our lives in the Garden State, she took an immediate liking to us and promised to bake a pound cake every time we came to town. Mrs. Wilson and her husband started bouncing Yankee and rebel jokes back and forth. Even though she was a Yankee, she once said, she could out-bake any Southern woman.

Before the Sportsman race started, a farmer-like gentleman walked into the suite with a coffee can taking bets. Herb asked him who he was pulling for in the final race and bet ten dollars based on the gentleman's tip. The man gave Herb a slip of paper and said he would be back after the race if Herb won. In the end, Herb lost his bet.

After the final race, we said our goodbyes to the Wilsons and others and headed back to the Hilton. On the drive back, we commented on the two other African-Americans we noticed at the track. One was in the stands sitting by himself, the other was a crew member on the Late Model Sportsman car driven by Terry Brooks. The guy working on Brooks's car had big amber-colored glasses and a Jheri-curl 'do that dripped hair oil all the way down the back of his shirt. He seemed fairly accepted around the pits, but I wondered if this was because he was relegated to a service position. Historically, the pits were a slightly more tolerant place than the actual racetrack. After decades of racing at the Gold and Glory Sweepstakes and other local tracks, the closest Sumner "Red" Oliver could get to the Indianapolis 500 was as a mechanic in 1973. We hoped to push participation one step further.

We had a few weeks until R&W completed our engine. To bide my time, I enrolled in a four-day stock-car chassis-setup course in Mooresville. Located about 25 miles north of Charlotte, Mooresville was a hub for the race shops of big-league stock-car teams. When I got into town, I took some time to check out the national race-shop headquarters of Roush, Penske South, Bahari, Ricky Rudd, Penske-Kranefuss, and Sabco, which were all located in one industrial park. Some of these facilities were like small college campuses. The grounds had fountains and manicured lawns out front, with marble floors and comfortable couches in the lobbies. The garage areas spanned 50,000 to 100,000 square feet, which was enough space to house an in-house parts department and rows of racecars. The floors of the climate-controlled work areas were coated with an epoxy paint that cost $20,000 per 4,000–5,000 square feet. The mechanics had access to the best computers and technical equipment money could buy. A far cry from the cluttered, grease-ridden cubicles of Concord, these grand edifices were constructed to help their tenants compete at the highest levels of NASCAR, and the fiscal backbone for all of them was corporate sponsorship. As I left the industrial park and headed east toward the chassis school, I imagined a day when we would house our own fleet of shiny stock cars in such top-notch digs.

The chassis course was held at the Motorsports Performance Center near the historic part of Mooresville. The scenery reminded me of the stories my grandparents used to tell at Thanksgiving about the old South. Railroad tracks ran through the center of town; a steady flow of customers came in and out of old brick buildings with faded wooden signs; and townspeople stopped to chat with one another in the warm Carolina sun. The students in the class were mostly a mixture of stock-car drivers and mechanics. There was also one road racer from California. At lunch breaks, we organized into small groups and carpooled to a local barbecue restaurant. Like the Construction Company in Charlotte, the restaurant had photos, some dating back to the 1950s, of race teams and drivers plastered all over the walls. The waitresses were on a first-name basis with the clientele and there was a constant buzz of stock-car conversation. At the table, I positioned myself next to one of the instructors, Skip Pope. Skip had won at Charlotte Motor Speedway in the old Sportsman class but couldn't afford to maintain his car anymore. Like so many others in the racing community, Skip was now divorced. His wife couldn't tolerate his obsession anymore. Without financial and family support, he now lived in a small room in the back of an abandoned gas station on Route 601 in Concord. The facility had a washer and dryer in the back room, a closet for his clothes, and two repair bays that held his pair of Sportsman cars. He didn't need a fancy place just to sleep, he told me. When he wasn't sleeping or teaching a chassis class, he worked on his cars. As he gnawed on a barbecue sandwich and slaw, I pumped Skip for additional chassis-setup pointers and asked him if he had any interest in helping us out at Concord. He agreed to work on our chassis for a reasonable price. I figured the combination of an

R&W engine, Chris Woods, and a chassis expert like Skip gave us a great foundation.

After finishing up the intensive class, which entailed waking up at 6 a.m. and going to bed at 11 p.m. for four days straight, I decided to stop by Concord before going back home to Virginia. I wanted to speak to Nick Smith about what we would need if Skip were to perform chassis setups in-house. Nick gave me a list of all the necessary shop machinery, tools, spare parts, metals, and chemicals and told me where to buy everything.

"Now that you know how to put this whole thing together, you just need a million bucks," joked Nick as he locked up his shop for the night.

5

"Do all these places accept MasterCard?"

In 1972, driver Richard Petty inked a $250,000 a year sponsorship with auto motor oil company Scientifically Treated Petroleum, better known as STP. It was the first deal of its kind. Previously, stock-car drivers and their families would pay for the majority of a team's racing expenses themselves, with occasional financial help from local mechanic shops, retail stores, and, if you were good enough, race winnings. "Up until that time you lived off what you made at the race track," says Petty—in a July 12, 2008 interview with the *Los Angeles Times*—of how drivers stayed afloat before the sponsorship era. STP had already found success in open-wheel racing by sponsoring Mario Andretti, who had cruised to victory three years earlier at the Indianapolis 500 in an "STP Oil Treatment Special"–branded car. Looking to make a similar splash in NASCAR, STP approached Petty, a driver with nearly 150 victories to date, racing lineage (his father, Lee Petty, raced against Junior Johnson, Buck Baker, and others in NASCAR's formative years, winning three series championships between '54 and '59), and a larger-than-life smile. STP's foray into motorsports netted instant results, to the tune of an $11 million jump in sales between 1968 and 1973. Petty raced in the now iconic red and blue No. 43 STP car right up until his retirement in 1992, setting the record for series championships at seven in 1979 and making the oval STP logo ubiquitous along the way.

In the early '80s, other big-name companies picked up on how STP was successfully integrating marketing and motorsports.

Pretty soon, a winning car's sponsor became as integral to its identity as the driver and car number. Darrell Waltrip not only won Cup titles in '81 and '82 in his No. 11 Mountain Dew Buick, he found a way to spin fans' disapproval of his aggressive driving style into brand recognition for his sponsor. In the winner's circle after one race, he sloughed off a showering of boos by announcing, "They were saying Dew!" In 1985, Wrangler Jeans parlayed Dale Earnhardt's brash image into a full-fledged ad campaign, labeling him "One Tough Customer." In '86 and '87, Earnhardt raced his No. 3 Wrangler Jeans Monte Carlo to consecutive Cup championships. (Beginning with the '88 season, Earnhardt partnered with GM Goodwrench for a long, prolific run.) By the '90s, megabrands like Kellogg's Corn Flakes and Proctor & Gamble's Tide poured millions into their teams' Winston Cup pursuit.

Two weeks into June of '94, I would have settled for a few thousand dollars to help keep our fledgling Concord effort on track. I had already withdrawn nearly $20,000 from my personal bank account—money that was supposed to have been the down payment on a single-family home—for expenses that were quickly piling up. A successful Concord program, we hoped, was our ticket to landing a corporate sponsor. Until then, we had to finance things ourselves. I tapped friends, colleagues, and family members for financial assistance. For the most part, I faced ambivalence or sheer disbelief. People would ask why I was spending my own hard-earned money on stock-car racing. Immediate family members looked upon our NASCAR vision as a hand grenade, a suicide mission into the country's deepest pockets of racism. At uppity African-American cocktail parties I sometimes attended with my father, guests couldn't understand why we would invest thousands of dollars into something that could be destroyed in a moment's notice. We impressed upon folks that we were interested in more than just having someone drive around in circles: We were trying to break black drivers into the fastest growing sport—and one of the fastest growing businesses—in the country. This was our American dream. But to partygoers, swaddled in their expensive fur coats and fancy Mercedes-Benzes, it sounded like a nightmare. My father and I resorted to making business calls in dark corners of the house, slanting the truth to loved ones, asking associates to send us ambiguously worded faxes. We even spoke in code over the phone. We had a few closet African-American benefactors who gave us money here and there, small amounts of cash that would go unnoticed by their wives. On one occasion, a prominent physician in Philadelphia showed up to an event with hundred-dollar bills pinned inside his tuxedo. While the amounts from these secret benefactors were small, such contributions helped keep our spirits up. They reminded us that we weren't alone in our undertaking.

Chris and I met again in Charlotte to take in a Big 10 series race at Concord and follow-up at Summer Lake Apartments. The competition at Big 10 series races was always stiff, and some repeat winners ended up making it to NASCAR. After meeting at the airport on Friday afternoon and making the requisite stop at the Hilton, we headed over to the speedway for qualifying night. On Big 10 weekends, people flooded Nick's shop for last-minute chassis work. Racers, crew members, girlfriends, and spectators socialized and talked about Saturday night's race. The area became a bit of a hangout. Some drivers took advantage of the commotion by sliding in to borrow Nick's tools and asking him for free technical advice. Nick never said anything to the freeloaders, though. One character we met that evening was a flamboyant, smooth-talking driver nicknamed Hollywood. Hollywood's hallmark was a twenty-two-foot-long stretch limousine that had purple neon lights underneath. The gaudy craft looked like it was part-spaceship. Hollywood often pulled up in the limo accompanied by a local stripper. He had a reputation for sleeping with the wives and girlfriends of some of the drivers and crew members, which rubbed many the wrong way. Hollywood didn't bother me too much. In fact, I found his shtick amusing. I was more concerned with the scene as a whole. I wondered how it would affect work in our shop. It was noisy, Chris was flirting with the pretty white women, and a throng of curious spectators, many of them guys with Confederate flag tattoos and yellow teeth, stood right in front of our shop doors.

Before leaving Concord for the evening, we stopped by the pit-pass shack to say hello to Yvonne, who slipped us a couple of VIP tickets for the weekend, and checked in with Paul Wilson at the VIP suites. Paul filled us in on all the gossip: who was in town for the weekend, who was about to quit racing, who was on the way toward NASCAR. As promised, Mrs. Wilson walked in with a pound cake.

On Saturday morning, Chris and I drove to Summer Lake Apartments. Dressed in high heels and a skirt that hugged her hips, the sultry manager was just finishing a phone call when we arrived. She grabbed a set of keys from a locked cabinet and offered to show us Chris's new apartment. She warned us that they had not finished cleaning it. She wasn't lying. A family of flies swarmed over a pool of water outside the front door. Inside, the apartment looked like a dungeon. There were ashes in the fireplace, the carpet was filthy, the walls were stained, and there was hardly any natural light. The manager reassured us that the cleaners weren't finished. Chris, unfazed by the dinginess, said he was satisfied and was prepared to write a check for the deposit and first month's rent. Once we left Summer Lake, Chris said that he would love for the manager to stop by his place every night. We ate lunch at the Construction Company and spent the rest of the afternoon visiting a long list of parts suppliers. By the time we reached Concord for the evening races, my head was throbbing from all the running around.

"How you boys doin' today?" asked the wooden soldier at the front gate. Before we could make small talk, a young boy trying to sneak into the grandstands stole her attention. Inside we ran into Henry Furr, who invited us to the 5 p.m. drivers' meeting that was about to start. More than a hundred drivers squeezed into a metal structure adjacent to the pit-pass shack for the mandatory meeting. Flanked by an entourage of grizzled, rotund officials, Henry laid down all of the speedway's rules. He covered technical inspection, illegal parts and configurations, cheating, and fist fighting in the pits. He listed the different divisions racing that evening and the cash prizes for each. After opening the floor for last-minute questions, he wished everyone good luck. A few drivers asked where we were from and if we were racing. When Chris told them he would soon be competing at Concord, they walked off without comment.

A few races into the evening, Concord's PR manager burst into the VIP suite to inform everyone of breaking news. Former NFL running back and murder suspect O.J. Simpson was holding a gun to his head inside a Ford Bronco that was being chased down by police officers on Interstate 405 in LA. For a moment, I forgot about the blaring stock cars buzzing around below and remembered my father telling me about the 1976 Black Athletes Hall of Fame ceremonies in New York City, where Simpson congratulated my father and driver Benny Scott for their induction. He had offered to help in any way he could. For years, my father has kept a photo of himself with O.J. and Benny hanging on his wall. During the months after the infamous Bronco chase, my father's friends would condemn him for celebrating the alleged murderer. "Regardless of the outcome of the trial, the picture stays on the wall," my father would say. O.J.'s willingness to help meant that much to my father.

I called my dad the next day to give him a recap on the weekend's events. He had some good news: Ron Whitney of R&W told him our new engine was performing well on the dyno and that it would be completed in five days. Now we had to figure out how to get it down to Concord. Since we couldn't afford the high cost—and risk—of shipping it or paying someone with a trailer to pick it up for us, I decided to rent a cube truck near my house in Centreville and pick the engine up myself. I had barely gotten off the plane from Charlotte and was now looking at a three-hour drive to and from southeastern Pennsylvania for the pick-up, as well as a six-hour drive from Centreville to Concord for the drop-off. A couple days later, I stopped at a hardware store to buy a hundred feet of nylon rope, which I needed to firmly secure the 700-lb. piece of machinery. The floor space of the cube truck was about five times the space needed, but it was the only vehicle I could find on such short notice. I hoped that we could secure the engine in a way that would prevent it from sliding around the back of the truck. Even the slightest impact could damage our soon-to-be most prized possession.

I drove past the horse stables, Amish dairy farms, and bed and breakfasts of southeastern Pennsylvania's countryside before pulling up to R&W's unmarked building. "You couldn't find anything smaller than that?" said Ron Whitney when I waved hello. I backed the truck toward the receiving door of his garage. The roof of the truck barely cleared the eaves. We positioned the engine over the truck's rear axle and used the nylon rope to tie all four sides of the engine stand to the inner walls of the cargo space. When we were done, the rope job looked like a giant spider web. Ron told me he'd had several conversations with Nick Smith to make sure the engine would fit properly in the chassis. Ron typically measured a car's engine compartment himself before starting a project, but we were so strapped for time that Nick had to give him the information over the phone. Ron wished me luck and within an hour I was on my way back to Centreville. When I got home, I held my breath and opened the rear door of the truck. The giant spider web hadn't moved an inch. The next day, I drove through a constant downpour and bumper-to-bumper traffic in Durham on my way down to Concord. As soon as I arrived at the speedway grounds and parked, a rainbow appeared in the western sky. I hoped it was a sign that our engine had made the long journey intact.

About a half-dozen people greeted me when I emerged from the truck. The small crowd wanted to sneak a peek at the engine that was driven down all the way from Pennsylvania. Judging from the informed questions and comments, I suspected Nick had spread the word. I opened the rear door to see that the engine hadn't budged. Nick brought in his engine hoist from next door and jumped into the rear of the truck. He sliced up the giant spider web, hooked the engine up to the hoist, lifted it off the truck floor, and sat it next to the No. 21. "That engine better run as good as it looks," remarked Jody Starnes's father in his thick-as-molasses drawl.

Once the crowd dispersed, Nick delivered a long but informative monologue about what odds and ends we needed in order to complete the car. Nick also offered to start working on the No. 21 in his spare time. I was skeptical at first because this would require unlocking the gray wooden doors between our adjacent shops. I thought of the Big 10 weekend, the freeloaders using Nick's equipment, Chris and the pretty white girls, and the spectacle that was Hollywood. I thought of how much easier it would be for a rival to steal or harm our equipment when we weren't around. Still, Nick's offer meant we would be racing that much sooner. I agreed. I had already planned on spending the next couple of days in Charlotte to pick up parts, which meant I could keep a close eye on the new open-door policy.

"You brothers do what you say and say what you do," said the bellhop when I checked in at the Hilton and told him about the engine. "Those rednecks are going to be sick." The girls at the counter asked if Chris had made his move down south yet. I told them two more weeks. One girl said she had told everyone in her neighborhood and her church that an African-American driver was coming to town.

The next morning, Nick and I met to draft a list of all the items we needed to finish the car and he directed me to local parts stores. "Go to BSR on Route 29 and buy a clutch pack, a light-weight bellhousing for a reverse mount starter, and a reverse mount starter, a Tilton, if you can," said Nick. "After BSR, go to Butler Built Equipment and order a dry sump oil tank and filter. If Butler has any questions, tell him to call me. But before you go there, stop at WRC on Victory Lane behind the Charlotte Motor Speedway and buy an aluminum radiator and an electric fan. I have the specific sizes on the sheet." The parts would cost over $6,000—$6,000 that I didn't have.

"Do all these places accept MasterCard?" I half-joked with Nick before heading out on my parts mission.

The BSR staff was friendly, but excruciatingly probing. A heavyset man behind the counter asked, "What car are you building? Do you live in the area? Do you work for a team? Where's your car? Are you the driver?" When I handed the heavyset man my MasterCard that had AOPA (Aircraft Owners and Pilots Association) inscribed on its face, more inquiries ensued: "Are you a pilot? Do you own an airplane? How long have you been an AOPA member? What kind of pilot's license do you have?" I ended up going back to BSR on numerous occasions, and every time I reached the counter the heavyset man asked me the same things over and over: "Where you from? You don't sound like you're from around here. Are you the driver? How do you know about all this? Have you ever done this before? How did you find us?" By the second or third trip, the requisite grilling became frustrating. Like my recent experience at Sy Earnhardt's shop, where A.J. Sanders interrogated me, it was as if the heavyset man at BSR was masking his deeper reluctance to help in these superficial, monotonous questions. I wondered, Does this guy hope that I'll get so tired with all of the questions that I'll just take my business elsewhere? Or, does he take me for a forgetful, stock-car racing naïf? Not only were the "Twenty Questions" encounters—as my father and I often referred to them—at BSR emasculating, they sometimes prevented me from getting last-minute parts to Nick in time for practices and races.

After BSR, I picked up the requested parts from Butler Built and WRC and headed back to Nick's shop. We unloaded everything from the trunk of the rental car and lined the items along the cinderblock wall of the garage. First, Nick was going to configure the gearbox, clutch, flywheel, and bellhousing to fit the engine. Then, he would align this assembly with the driveshaft. Once he got underway, he ran into some problems piecing the flywheel, bellhousing, and starter together. I went to BSR, a half-hour away, three more times that day to pick up various combinations of parts to try and make the setup work, but we were unsuccessful. The next day we tried bolting the bellhousing onto the rear of the engine, over the flywheel, and then connected the starter. Nick lifted the re-jiggered assembly with the hoist and lowered it into the car. It took some time and maneuvering, but we eventually got it situated on the engine mounts. The bottom of the bellhousing cleared the ground by only two inches, which meant the slightest bounce on the racetrack could lead to costly damage. To fix this, Nick rolled out a cutting torch and trimmed almost two and a half inches off the bottom of the bellhousing. Sparks danced around the shop floor as the torch's blue flame cut through the steel like a knife through butter.

The No. 21 was almost ready for competition. A handful of odds and ends still needed to be dealt with, though, including electrical wiring, oil lines, exhaust configuration, chassis tuning, and installing the radiator and fan. Nick, who was juggling three or four other customers in addition to us, estimated that he could have the car done in a couple of days. It was now July, and I knew we had to complete the car soon if we had any hopes of racing in '94. When I got back to Virginia, I apprised both my father and

Chris of the remaining work. Chris volunteered to drive down to Concord with Robby Fuller, the nephew of drivers Jeff and Rick Fuller, and some of his other racing buddies from Massachusetts to work on the car. He felt that if he and his old pit crew could finish work on the No. 21 during the daytime on Saturday, he would be able to race that night. Chris's plan sounded ambitious, but I agreed and booked rooms at the Hilton for the forthcoming weekend. Additionally, we had to scrape up $800 for racing tires and fuel. Money was getting tighter and tighter, and if Chris crashed, we would assuredly have to go into debt to keep things running. But it was a risk we had to take if we were to get him up and racing anytime soon.

On Friday afternoon, Chris's friends pulled up to the Hilton in a station wagon overflowing with equipment. The following morning, Chris and his friends went to work on the No. 21. It was impressive watching everyone work together. Wrenches twisted, saws buzzed, drills hummed, and parts changed hands in a steady rhythm. By 2 p.m. the car was nearing completion. Robby estimated that they would be done in four hours; by then, all the No. 21 would need was a quick chassis setup by Nick. Qualifying started around 6 p.m.

The usual hangers-on started to gather in Nick's shop for last-minute help. Tonight's gossip centered on the crew of New Englanders that had descended upon shop No. 10 and the black driver who was scheduled to race that night. Many of the crowd members approached Chris and Robby and flooded them with questions. A woman with bleached hair came over to me and said, "A whole bunch of people up at the track are wantin' to know when the brothers are racin'." Her name was Kathy Miller. Her husband, David Miller, drove in the Street Stock class at Concord. David was working on his gold and black Chevy next door in Nick's shop when he overheard a small hubbub coming from our shop. He asked if he could help out.

"Can you do wiring?" asked Chris.

"Sure," said David. He jumped inside the No. 21 and began working on some wiring for the starter and ignition switches.

David donned a bushy, brownish-red beard, a rebel flag tattoo on his arm, and a trucker cap. He spoke with a deep Carolinian drawl. I found out later that he hailed from Cabarrus County, North Carolina, and had been immersed in stock-car racing since he was a child. During the week, he was a brick mason for a large housing contractor. He and Kathy lived in a small trailer in the woods on Old Sam Black Road, not far from the speedway, and spent all their free time at the track.

The drivers' meeting was now minutes away. Even with David's added help we were still a few hours from having the car completed. Plus, the heat and humidity were taking a toll on everyone. At 5 p.m., Robby Fuller yelled, "We can't get ready for tonight. I'm cleaning up." We packed everything up and headed to the VIP suites to watch the races. On the way, Chris and I stopped at the pit-pass shack to tell Yvonne that we were not going to be racing that evening but we'd be ready soon. "Honey, don't worry about it," said Yvonne. "At least you're getting close. Everyone is waiting for you to get out there, Chris."

Soaking in the electric atmosphere and Southern hospitality from the VIP suites, Chris's friends were giddy about the Concord racing experience. They reveled in all of the latest gossip from Paul Wilson and foreign terms like "slaw," "barbecue," and "sweet tea." Robby reassured him that he was making the right decision by relocating. Robby and the crew members even expressed interest in moving down to Charlotte to find jobs with top teams (a few later ended up finding such jobs). I was inspired by the cultural exchange I was witnessing. Here were young, stock car–loving Northerners bonding with the likes of the Wilsons, the Furrs, and David and Kathy Miller in the heart of racing country. If stock-car racing's popularity continued on its current trajectory, scenes like this one would become more and more common across America. I did wonder, though, when enough corporate and social barriers would fall in order for us to be able to claim our piece of the burgeoning NASCAR pie. Once the races finished for the evening, Robby and I struck up a conversation about the subject at the Beach Club, a disco bar on the premises of the Hilton that extended onto a large deck outside and got raucous on the weekends. Amidst the yuppies, manicured white girls, and volleyball area filled with sand, Robby gushed about Chris's potential and expressed interest in becoming our crew chief. His dilemma, however, was that he was committed to his father's motor-home rental business in Massachusetts. My problem was that I couldn't afford to pay him. Though he never came on board as our crew chief, Robby stayed in touch and always gave me words of encouragement.

Within a week, Chris was finally moved into his place at Summer Lake Apartments. A few days before leaving Massachusetts, Chris phoned me feeling a little jittery. He was going through his farewell routine with friends and family and he was experiencing the typical anxiety that comes with making a big move. A childhood friend who was a trucker drove down Chris's clothes and furniture while Chris followed in his old brown Honda Accord. It took them two hours to unload his belongings. When it was time to say goodbye, the two friends were so broken up they couldn't look each other in the eyes. Chris's friend ran to his truck in tears.

Back in Virginia, I called Nick to let him know Chris was in town for good. "Let's get this No. 21 on the track for a test," said Nick enthusiastically. "Let me know when Chris can come to the speedway. When are you coming back?"

I said I could get to Concord before the next weekend, and that I needed a shopping list of any additional parts. The list wasn't too long—mainly spare tires and fuel—but, factoring in Nick's service charges, I figured we would need to lay out at least another $1,000 in order for Chris to practice and enter his first race. On top of the smaller costs that were piling up, we had larger costs on the horizon. Our shop was still bare, and we would need $20,000 worth of equipment if we had any hopes of performing all car maintenance ourselves. For the time being, we would have to rely on our access to Nick's equipment. We had no truck or trailer, either. Being located on the speedway grounds somewhat alleviated the need for one, as we could put old tires on the No. 21 for the short drive to the pit area. While tedious, this step was necessary, because pebbles and debris could puncture the ultrathin racing tires. We soon found out we were the only team at Concord who had to physically drive our car to the pits without the help of a trailer.

Chris called me shortly after I got off the phone with Nick to tell me about his first day at Plaza Ford. Archie Kindle introduced him to everyone at the dealership, Chris said, from the salesmen out front to the repair shop guys in the back. Just like at the Hilton, many of the African-American employees at Plaza Ford were amazed that he drove stock cars. Chris said he was broadsided with questions all day about his New England accent, racing at Agawam, when he would start at Concord, and so forth. Also, Archie told Chris he would have to get rid of his Honda Accord now that he was a member of the Ford family. Archie said he would give Chris a good deal on a trade-in for a much newer Ford car or truck. When folks at Plaza Ford learned that Chris was going to drive a Chevy at Concord, they didn't take too kindly to it. Archie had to know that the only amenable way to solve the problem was to have the dealership sponsor us in some capacity. In time, we broached the subject with Archie, but a sponsorship never materialized. It was too costly for Plaza Ford. Before Chris and I got off the phone, I told him to prepare for testing on Thursday and Friday, and for racing on Saturday. Chris said he would be at the shop working on the No. 21 every night until then.

When I arrived on Thursday night, Nick and Chris had the car ready to go. They had inspected every bolt, wire, and bracket several times. Nick told me that the Furrs weren't going to charge us for the two hours of practice on Friday morning. It typically cost $200 an hour to test without an ambulance, or $300 an hour with an ambulance. Many Saturday night racers either couldn't afford the extra expense of testing or couldn't have their cars prepared in time. Others who did test sometimes chose to do so without the ambulance, which was risky. Broken bones, excessive bleeding, and head injuries can occur even in practice runs, and the time it took for an ambulance to arrive from a hospital miles away could make a vital difference. On top of which, all drivers and team members had to sign a waiver that released the track's liability for any injuries suffered on the premises. (NASCAR's France family had forced drivers to sign such liability waivers since the stock-car league's inception, spurring an on-again, off-again attempt by drivers to unionize. To date, the all-powerful Frances have quashed any such attempt.) For our practice run, Yvonne Furr scheduled an ambulance and a wrecker.

I stayed at Chris's new apartment that night. It was a way to save money. He hadn't yet unpacked and the only furniture he had was a pair of mattresses on the bedroom floor. The apartment still hadn't been cleaned. I asked Chris if he planned on addressing the sanitary issues with the pretty young thing at Summer Lake's front desk. He wasn't satisfied, he said, but he didn't want to move all his belongings to another unit. As I settled into a worn sleeping bag, ruffling a couple of musty rolled-up towels for pillows, Chris told me he had heard through David Miller that word was spreading about a black driver racing on Saturday night.

"Guys are saying things like, 'Those niggers won't last around here,'" said Chris.

I was anxious about the next day's practice, I couldn't get comfortable on the floor, and now I was worried about good ol' boys running Chris off the track. I barely slept at all that night.

Flip the Switches

Chris and I parked in front of Nick's shop. Inside, Nick was on the phone. Pam told us he was ready to go and that he had organized the necessary tools for the test laps: a stopwatch, a clipboard, an air pressure tank, rags, a floor jack, and jack stands. Pam and I started packing up Nick's station wagon with tools. Nick ended his call and told us he wanted to check all the nuts and bolts on the No. 21 one more time. Chris got into his driver's suit: a faded, black get-up with purple stripes running down the legs. Once Nick finished his inspection, he gave Chris the green light to start the car. Chris pulled the spring-loaded pin from behind the seventeen-inch-diameter steering, placed the steering wheel on the dashboard, climbed through the window feet first, and slid into the seat. With the flip of the battery and ignition switches, the engine compartment worked up an even-keeled hum; and when Chris pushed the rubber-coated start button, the No. 21 belted out a ravenous roar. Chris shifted into first gear and eased out of shop No. 10.

Nick and Pam hopped in their wagon and tailed Chris by about forty feet toward the tunnel. Since Nick's car was packed to the gills with tools and support equipment, Chris said I could drive his car up to the pit area. I closed the shop door, grabbed Chris's helmet, jumped in the Honda, and fell in behind Nick and Pam. Chris slowly maneuvered across the gravel portion of the access road and turned onto the asphalt path that connected the shop complex to the tunnel entrance. The three-car caravan climbed the slight slope inside the tunnel and emerged near turn two of the track. Chris parked on pit road and shut off the engine. The No. 21's roar faded like a passing clap of thunder. Chris removed the steering wheel again, hopped up onto the windowsill, and swung his legs onto the ground. I helped Pam unload the tools from the wagon and line them up against the pit wall. Nick inspected the No. 21 from nose to tail one last time.

By now it was late morning. The humidity was already stifling. The ambulance paramedic and wrecker driver, a portly gentleman named Big Ed, made their way over to the pit area. Smoking a short tobacco pipe, Big Ed waddled around the No. 21 and embarked on the Twenty Questions routine, asking if Chris had ever raced before, if my father and I had any experience running a stock-car team, how we accumulated the money for our operation, and so on. We later learned that Big Ed was one of Concord's gossip kings, meddling any rider in his wrecker for inside information.

Nick took Chris around the track in his wagon about thirty times, pointing out visual reference points along the walls, asphalt, and light posts. He showed him where to use brakes and where to hammer the gas. I could see Nick in the car talking a mile a minute, using his hands to coach Chris through one of the trickiest short tracks in America. Instead of being a true oval with equidistant straightaways and uniform turns, Concord had a sweeping 180-degree turn between turns one and two; a slight right turn coming out of turn two that led into a crooked dogleg turn; and a slight, awkward left off of the second straightaway into turns three and four. Adding to Concord's treacherousness were the thick concrete walls that lined every inch of the course. Where some tracks had guardrails that are a little softer on impact, Concord's unforgiving perimeter punished its colliders, causing severe damage with even the gentlest bump or scrape. It was important for even an experienced driver like Chris to familiarize himself with the nuances of a new track. Some courses are proper ovals. Some, like Michigan International Speedway and the newer California Speedway, are D-shaped. Concord's odd shape, like Daytona, Talladega, and Pocono, is defined as tri-oval, meaning roughly half the course resembles an oval while the other half resembles a triangle. Nick's tutorial of Concord's contours would allow Chris to anticipate the awkward rises, descents, and turns.

Pam tested the stopwatch and secured a timing record sheet on the clipboard. Nick and Chris pulled back into the pit area in the wagon, and, without further ado, Chris hopped back into the No. 21 for a practice run. Nick helped him secure the five-point safety belt system. (A racecar seat belt system has a belt over each shoulder, one on each side of the waist, and one at the crotch, all of which join together below the stomach. Should a driver need to exit quickly in case of fire or other hazardous conditions, a lever releases all of the belts.) Chris put on his helmet and fire-proof gloves while Nick attached the window net. Once Chris was all secure, Nick gave him limits on rpm. Nick wanted Chris to go slow at first, in case there were any loose components they may have missed during inspections. Racecars don't have speedometers, so a driver has to gauge speed using his experience and instinct. A Late Model Stock car at Concord could reach speeds of 110 mph, sometimes higher when descending from the banked, 20-plus-degree turns leading into the straightaways. Chris once again flipped the switches, punched the starter, and the Lumina belted out another earth-shaking roar. He eased off of pit road onto the track, and steered the No. 21 in a shallow "S" pattern, a routine technique that created friction and heat on the tires to get them sticky for a better grip on the asphalt.

Chris had completed about four laps when Nick gestured for him to come in for another inspection. Chris said he didn't feel anything out of the ordinary, so Nick gave him a higher rpm limit for the next run. He also said that Chris's lines on the track were almost perfect. (Lines, also referred to as grooves, are the particular routes and angles a driver takes on a course. The best lines are the quickest ones around the track.) Chris blasted out of the pits and hit the track much more aggressively this time around. Using hand signals, Nick told him to pick up a little more speed. Since we couldn't afford a two-way radio, Nick used hand gestures to give basic commands. Pam wrote down times and comments for each lap. Chris had completed about thirty laps when Nick motioned for him to come in again. Chris said he was feeling comfortable. Nick told Chris to go as fast as he wanted now, and to smoke the rear tires a little and accelerate through turn two and the dogleg. As he crossed the finish line on the front straightaway, the engine screamed even louder. The second time across, Pam shouted that he was only four-tenths of a second slower than the previous week's fastest qualifying time. During the third go-round, however, something went wrong.

Chris cut the engine entering turn four. After a little squeaking from the brakes and a fading patter from the tires, the car went silent. Nick, Pam, and I ran over. I could hear Big Ed start his wrecker. Not having radios, we didn't know what was wrong. My first thought was a serious engine problem, which would have financially wiped us out for the year. Nick got to the car first. Chris told him the oil pressure light had come on, so he killed the engine immediately. Running an engine without oil pressure can ruin it almost instantaneously. This was a $17,000 engine that took four weeks to build, and we had no backup.

Nick and I unpinned the hood and noticed that the oil pump belt was shredded to pieces. It had slipped off its pulley and needed to be replaced. Big Ed towed the No. 21 to Nick's shop. We propped the car up on jack stands and saw that the pulley system was slightly out of line, which, at high speeds, can cause the rubber oil pump belt to fall off. Wally Bell, who had just pulled up his immaculate dual-wheel pickup next door, popped his head into our shop to find out what happened. Wally knew where to buy a better belt and pulley system and made a quick phone call to have the parts delivered. He was friendly with many parts suppliers in the area and would get a fair price. The belt was only thirty dollars, the two pulleys were about a hundred dollars. I pulled out my blue vinyl checkbook and thought, We've already invested $50,000 in our Concord operation and our first race is tomorrow. What's another $130?

Around four o'clock on Saturday evening, the usual steady stream of trailers was approaching Nick's shop for last-minute work. David Miller, the bushy-bearded fellow who pitched in to help Chris and his friends work on the car the previous week, suggested we try to get the car to the pits since the lines were already growing long. The night before, David pledged to Chris that he would help us out for our first race and beyond, if we wanted. He and his wife Kathy respected our nerve and ambition. He had some tools he would make available for us, and his wife Kathy knew how to take lap times. I was all for it.

Chris still had to put on his uniform and buy a pit pass, so he asked me to drive the No. 21 up to the pits. David warned me that the pits would be extremely busy and told me to find a temporary place to park until he arrived to guide me. Some drivers purchased assigned slot locations for the year; the rest were first come, first served. As I climbed through the driver's side window, it dawned on me that this was the first time I had actually sat inside of our car. I'd driven stock cars before, I'd been in Formula racers, I'd flown airplanes, and still, I couldn't help but feel a little giddy about flipping the switches on the mean, school bus–yellow racing machine. It was the first car I had helped assemble from beginning to end. I felt a little pain in my left hip, because the seat was at least three inches misaligned with the floor. I was surprised Chris hadn't brought this to anyone's attention. I also noticed the lack of visibility outside the car, but this was normal. A seat is typically mounted low to the floor, and various mechanisms and safety devices block most of the peripheral vision. I couldn't even see the top of the hood.

David, Kathy, and Chris motioned for me to start the car. Sweat flowed from every pore of my body. The temperature outside was over 90 degrees, and it was probably another 10–15 degrees hotter inside the car, which didn't even have the engine turned on yet. Out on the track, the drivers would face excruciatingly high temperatures on a day like today, all the while wearing a helmet and a heavy, fireproof suit. I flipped the switches, put the car in first gear, and crept out of the shop. I saw about a hundred people in line for pit passes and dozens of trailers waiting to get through the tunnel. In the rearview mirror, through the blurry rear plastic window, I could just make out David and Kathy getting into their pickup. Even though many of my views were blocked by equipment, I could still make out the crowds of people turning their heads to watch the black stranger steering the shiny No. 21 toward the tunnel.

When there was a break in the trailer line, I eased through to solidify a spot. Ours was the only stock car in line that wasn't mounted on some sort of trailer. The woman checking pit passes got flustered when she saw me behind the wheel. She signaled for me to stop, but I couldn't, because I had already built up enough momentum to clear the steep hill in the tunnel and keep the car in first. The tunnel was cavernous, and the blaring growl from the exhaust system ricocheted off the cement walls. I had about twelve inches of clearance on either side. When I reached the top of the slope, I could see the swarm of cars, trailers, and people buzzing around the pit area. Like David had predicted, I didn't see a single parking spot open. As I maneuvered along pit road, keeping an eye out for a parking area, I tried not to fixate on the cold stares shooting at me from all directions. After easing around the pits for what felt like an eternity, David and Kathy finally caught up. David jumped out of his pickup and signaled me to stop. Shouting over the noise, he told me he could make a spot, and asked a team to move over one space so we could squeeze in. It was a bold request, considering this was our first night of racing. I figured some of the good ol' boys at Concord were waiting for any excuse to start trouble with us. Yet, David stepped to these good ol' boys unflinchingly. Already a fixture at Concord, David was risking his reputation—and personal safety, perhaps—in order to ensure that we would get the same opportunity as everyone else. David's courage was infectious, and in the years to come it would help sustain our effort through trying times.

Dripping sweat, I climbed out of the No. 21. David jacked up the car and started doing routine checks. Several people came over to observe, but not one said a word or offered assistance. Chris emerged from the tunnel in his driver's uniform and mirrored sunglasses. Just as he had shrugged off the racial epithets at Agawam, Chris proudly sauntered toward our plot and paid the icy glares no mind. He took the No. 21 out for a dozen practice laps alongside at least fifteen other cars and pulled back into our plot with just enough time to make the 5 p.m. drivers' meeting. I stayed with David to watch over the car. We were so close to race time that the last thing I wanted was for some troublemaker to sabotage our $50,000 investment.

Chris returned to our plot just before the track's technical inspection. Officials scrutinized weight, safety items, body shape, dimensions, tires, and engine parts. Following a race, inspectors would reexamine the top five cars to make sure no one cheated after the initial check. There were a lot of cheaters at Concord, drivers trying to win any way they knew how. One popular cheating method was soaking tires in a softening agent that made them more pliable and sticky. Some cheaters took very fine drill bits and pierced barely traceable holes into the side of the manifold to get more air to the engine. (The manifold sits beneath the carburetor and has air ducts leading to a cylinder that mixes fuel and flicker from the spark plugs to create explosiveness.) There was even an engine builder in Tennessee who sold illegal manifolds, ones that he dipped in an acid-like chemical that made them porous. Other cheaters sprayed ether, the same chemical people use in the winter to start their cars, on the air duct before a qualifying run to get a little engine boost. There were those who added weights to their cars for the pre-race weigh-in to clear the class's restriction, only to remove the weights before racing so their car would be lighter than the field's. The weigh-in cheaters who placed in the top five almost always got caught at the post-race inspection because they didn't have enough time to re-insert the weights. Advanced cheaters manipulated hard-to-reach internal parts. For example, a team could ask an engine builder to lighten the crankshaft so it spun around faster and created more horsepower. Such tactics were very hard to identify, which was why at most short tracks, for a fee of $250–$1,500, one could request a thorough check of a suspicious competitor's car. Track officials would go the lengths of tearing the engine apart and sending any suspect components to a specialist at a lab.

When it was our turn for inspection, the officials looked at the No. 21 extra hard. "Did you guys rob a bank?" cracked Big Bird, a seven-foot tall official with a nose like a beak. Big Bird wore oversized sunglasses that looked like safety goggles. He spoke loudly and fiddled with a small, soggy cigar between his lips. Like a bouncer at a bar, Big Bird was a menacing specimen who kept order by intimidation. A second official was unhappy with a bracket under the car and didn't like the fire extinguisher setup. He wanted to disqualify us, but David talked him out of it. "You boys better have this stuff fixed if you come back next week," the second official said.

"That ol' boy was making up stuff to discourage you guys," David said as we walked back to our parking area.

Chris had one practice session of twenty laps before qualifying began. He blasted through the first three laps, but during the fourth he started to slow down, and by the fifth he coasted to a complete stop. David ran over to the wall and shouted, "What happened?" Once the wrecker towed Chris and the No. 21 back to the pits, David removed the hood and saw that the oil pump belt was once again shredded to pieces. A.J. Sanders, the skinny-framed driver/mechanic Chris and I had met at Sy Earnhardt's engine shop a few weeks back, noticed David working on the engine compartment and asked, "What's giving you trouble?" He glanced at the pulleys and saw that they still weren't aligned properly. He said he could fix the problem if we had an extra belt, which we did. Sanders darted out of sight and returned five minutes later with a box of washers and three wrenches. He dove into the engine compartment, removed one pulley, placed three small washers on the pulley shaft, and worked the new belt onto both pulleys. He eyeballed the alignment of the belt, tightened two bolts, and told us confidently that the belt would never come off again. While I hadn't forgotten about Sanders's ambivalence toward us earlier in the summer, his work looked sound and his gesture seemed genuine. Plus, qualifying was just about to start.

Qualifying consisted of two laps. The better time of the two laps counted toward the driver's position at the starting line. It was a little different up North. There, drivers of the same class divided into smaller groups and participated in heat races. NASCAR used the two-lap format, however, so it was beneficial for Chris and our team to adjust to the big boys' qualifying format. Chris's first lap was solid enough to qualify him for tenth out of twenty-five cars. Kathy, who had been wandering around the pits, told us that other drivers were amazed at Chris's performance. They inundated her with questions about him.

It was dark by the time track announcer Doug Smith called the Late Model Stock class over the loudspeakers. Concord's lights beamed down on the eight-thousand-plus in the grandstands. As Chris and other Late Model drivers headed out of the pits toward the starting line, David jumped on top of a friend's trailer so he could have a bird's eye view of the race. Kathy disappeared somewhere in the pits, while Nick and Pam also found a spot on top of a trailer. I chose to watch from the grandstands near turn one. I was anxious, and I couldn't bear the Twenty Questions routine in the VIP suites. Chris was experienced, so I wasn't too worried about his performance. I was more concerned about the oil pump or some loony adversary looking to run the No. 21 into the concrete walls.

The green flag dropped and the collective bellowing from the cars ignited the crowd. The No. 21's school–bus yellow paint job looked even meaner under the lights. As usual, the field was stacked bumper-to-bumper early. Chris shot into eighth place after the second lap, and by the twelfth lap he had worked his way up to seventh. Fans around me screamed for their favorite drivers. Around the twentieth lap, the flagman in the crow's nest waved the yellow caution flag after a five-car wreck in the rear of the field. Several cars came into the pits for mechanical attention. So far, the No. 21 was unblemished. After six or seven laps under caution, the race started again. As the top five cars started to break away from the pack, Chris caught up to the sixth-place car. After three laps of nose-to-nose battling, Chris moved into sixth. Moments later, Chris slid into fifth. Finally, we're here, I thought to myself. Visions of the NASCAR Busch Grand National Series and big speedways like Charlotte, Daytona, and Richmond dashed through my mind. Another caution came, and the field tightened up once again. The race restarted, and just as the first three cars managed to distance themselves from the rest of the field, I noticed a green Chevy Lumina with No. 5 on its side gaining ground on Chris. According to the leaderboard, No. 5 was at least one lap down and out of contention. The green

Lumina started nudging Chris's back bumper, and then sidled toward No. 21's left rear wheel in an attempt to abruptly pass. After about five laps of constant brushing, the green No. 5 knifed into Chris's left side, pushing him into the wall of turn one. As the No. 21 spun out, I saw that the entire right side was crushed.

My heart fluttered. As I swallowed, I felt like I was forcing the entire $50,000 lump sum down my throat in one agonizing gulp. Thankfully, Chris was OK, as evidenced by his jumping out of the car, violently throwing his helmet through the window, and walking to the pits in disgust. Once the yellow caution was signaled, the wrecker came out and hooked the crane to the No. 21. Since the race still had fifteen laps to go, I had to exit the grandstands, walk around the outside of the track, and head up to the pits through the tunnel. During the long fifteen-minute walk, worst-case scenarios filled my thoughts. When I reached our plot in the pits, David was recounting a shouting match he'd just had with the reckless driver. "He did it on purpose," David informed the group. "He said, 'I'll never let a nigger beat me in any race.'" Nick sent word to the track officials to take the No. 21 to shop No. 10. David and Kathy threw the tools in the back of their pickup. Chris and I jumped in the truck bed for the ride through the tunnel to the race shop complex. Big Ed backed up the wrecker and eased the crumpled Lumina into Nick's shop. When it hit the floor, the No. 21 rattled like a bucket of bolts. Kathy Miller started to cry. We assessed $3,000 worth of repairs and at least a week's worth of labor to get her ready again.

While the damage could have been much worse considering the impact of the crash, I had no clue how I was going to come up with $3,000 within the next five days. Tired and deflated, I phoned my father as soon as I got home for his advice on how to proceed. He had some hopeful news. He had recently attended a banquet in Baltimore for a fraternity he belonged to—an organization with a handful of very wealthy African-Americans—and had a promising discussion with a top-ranking General Motors executive about sponsorship. They'd set up a meeting in the suburbs of Detroit on August 19, 1994, and I was invited to attend. There was one condition, though: The GM exec would help us only if we kept his identity and any conversations with him a secret. Apparently, "black," "motorsports," and "sponsorship" were a potentially volatile concoction in the halls of the mega car company. In the better interest of keeping his job, he would need to gradually warm his associates up to the concept. While I scoffed at the apparent shame this lone soldier had to contend with at his company, my father and I figured secret support is better than no support. The recent collision at Concord stressed the need for a firm financial backbone. For all we knew, someone might try to wreck Chris every time we raced. Meanwhile, the down payment I had accumulated for a single-family home was just about gone.

A few days later, I called Yvonne Furr to tell her we were sitting out the following weekend's race. That way, we had some extra time to get our finances in order and didn't need to rush repairs.

"Honey, don't worry," she reassured me. "Henry Lee and I suspended that ol' boy who wrecked Chris—for the rest of the season."

7

Almost Sponsored

We nicknamed him Deep Throat. Like former FBI deputy director W. Mark Felt, who tipped off *Washington Post* reporters Bob Woodward and Carl Bernstein to the Watergate scandal, our inside source at General Motors would be risking his job and reputation in the interest of a greater good. My father and I had no idea what to expect at our meeting in Detroit, but we were excited about a potential relationship with the automotive conglomerate.

Of the Big Three American automakers (Ford and Chrysler being the other two), GM had the deepest, most successful history in NASCAR. When the checkered flag dropped at NASCAR's inaugural Cup race—then called Strictly Stock Division—at the old Charlotte Speedway in 1949, cars by Buick, Cadillac, and Oldsmobile shot off the starting line. Later that year, Robert "Red" Byron cruised to the first Cup series championship in an Olds. In 1957, legendary driver and driving school founder Buck Baker became the first back-to-back Cup champion in a Chevrolet, a GM brand named after early 20th century racecar driver and innovator Louis Chevrolet. Joe Weatherly, the '62 and '63 champ, drove to victory lane in a Pontiac, another GM-owned company. Though the rest of the '60s were relatively slow for GM, Cale Yarborough's trifecta of championships from '76 to '78 spawned a run of dominance that would span over three decades, with drivers like Darrell Waltrip, Jeff Gordon, and Jimmie Johnson all going down in NASCAR's history books alongside the name Chevrolet.

There is no bigger name attached to GM's racing résumé than

Dale Earnhardt, however. GM's hot streak in stock-car racing also coincided with the rise of motorsports as a marketing tool, and when Dale Earnhardt emerged as the biggest thing to hit NASCAR since Richard Petty, the auto empire hopped along for the ride. Beginning in 1988, GM Goodwrench Service Plus became the primary sponsor of Dale Earnhardt's No. 3 car, with the parts and service imprint's logo gilding the hood and sides. To a NASCAR fan, Earnhardt's No. 3 GM Goodwrench car became as emblematic of the sport as Michael Jordan's No. 23 jersey in basketball. Every die-cast model car, key chain, ball cap, and T-shirt sold out of Earnhardt's souvenir trailer—an idea he introduced to the sport in 1985—gave the GM Goodwrench brand that much more cachet and recognizability for the NASCAR fan base. In return, GM Goodwrench devoted money, parts, R&D, and marketing expertise to Earnhardt's effort. My father and I felt that if we could get a visionary bigwig at GM to buy into our mission, we would have a mainline to virtually all of the resources we needed to push our effort up through the NASCAR ranks.

Plus, it seemed like the timing couldn't have been better. The fresh-faced Jeff Gordon had just rocked the NASCAR world by winning the Brickyard 400, the first major NASCAR race at Indianapolis Motor Speedway, on August 6, 1994, while Earnhardt was racing to tie Petty's record of seven Cup championships. The sport and its GM-backed stars were shining bright. If we could join forces with GM, we felt the sky was the limit for Chris Woods and Miller Racing.

My father and I landed in Detroit within forty-five minutes of each other. Deep Throat, clad in a crisp white dress shirt and tie, met us at the passenger pickup in a black Cadillac sedan. He told us he had tickets to a Detroit Lions preseason football game in nearby Pontiac. Another GM executive, who was indirectly involved with a few GM motorsports activities, would be joining us, he said. Deep Throat drove us through Oakland County, an affluent suburb of Detroit, to pick up the other GM exec. He was glued to his cell phone the entire drive. Heading north on Wood-ward Avenue in Bloomfield Hills, we gazed at the Old World–style mansions, manicured lawns, and lakefront views. Many of the homes had double oak doors and tall panes of glass that revealed baby grand pianos and expensive sculptures. Deep Throat told us a number of GM higher-ups lived in the area, along with a smat-tering of K-Mart, Ford, and Chrysler executives and a few professional athletes. After pulling out of the driveway of the second GM exec, we headed to the football game.

Over the cheers of NFL fans, my father reiterated his decades-long dream of integrating both the sport and business of car racing, while I talked about our pilot NASCAR program at Con-cord. "There aren't black folks around this environment," said the second GM exec of our NASCAR aspirations. "You're dealing with good ol' boys. It's dangerous." Still, he was impressed with our moxie and assured us he would try to help. But, like Deep Throat, he stressed that he didn't want his name or our conversa-tions to surface in the public in any way. My father and I nicknamed our second GM insider Silent Sam.

Before dropping us off at our hotel, Deep Throat assured us that he was going to do everything in his power to get General Motors behind Miller Racing. He told us to give him two months to find out which folks at GM held the keys to the motorsports sponsorship money, and he would start buttering them up. As we waited for our flights to depart the next morning, my father and I agreed to invest another $30,000 in the team. That amount would allow us to finish out the 1994 season. We hoped GM would come through for us the following season.

To broaden our options for potential sponsorships, I once again leafed through my National Association for Minority Auto Dealers (NAMAD) directory and placed a cold call to Robert Hill, the president of NAMAD and owner of a Ford dealership in Southfield, Michigan. When I got him on the phone, I described the Miller Racing effort and pitched a marketing plan that would involve minority auto dealers nationwide. He was intrigued and referred me to Sam Johnson, who owned a large Ford dealership network in Charlotte. Hill also wanted to meet in Southfield within the next two weeks. Since I had planned on going back to Charlotte for the upcoming weekend's race, my father offered to fly back to Michigan to meet with Hill. While we were tempted to have my father pay Deep Throat a visit, we realized that telling him we were meeting with a heated corporate rival might upset him, enough to delay his inside work for us. My father and I heard stories about strict GM practices that directly stemmed from the sheer revulsion for competitors. For example, if a visitor pulled into the parking lot of a GM corporate office in a non-GM car, he or she would be asked to park up the street. On the ride back to the premises, the rogue car owner would hear a lecture about why GM vehicles are the best in the business. This no-competitor's-car-in-these-parts policy even applied to the driveway of a GM employee's house. In the coming years, my father and I would avoid such snafus by renting a vehicle made by the brand we were visiting.

I headed back down to Concord for the next race. My back simply couldn't bear sleeping on Chris's living room floor one more night, so I treated myself to the Hilton. When I told the bellhop how Chris's first race had unfolded, he shook his head in disgust. "I told you, bro, those Ku Klux Klanners on wheels are going to kill you," he said. "But keep on keepin' on, bro." Making my way to the elevator, I thought more about what the bellhop had said. I envisioned what Wendell Scott must have gone through when he was racing in the South during the Civil Rights era. According to one story retold by his son Franklin in the article "The Lost Trophy" on legendsofnascar.com, after Wendell broke Jack Smith's track record in Savannah in 1962, Smith approached Wendell in the pit area and told him he would drive through Wendell's car. Sure enough, Smith wrecked Wendell later that season in Winston-Salem. "My daddy had had it with him," Franklin remembers in "The Lost Trophy." "On the pace lap he pulled up beside Daddy and started pointing his finger at him. We didn't know it but Daddy had his gun with him and he pulled it out and pointed the gun back." When Wendell beat out Smith and Buck Baker at Jacksonville the following year, Smith, according to a 1983 profile of Wendell in *Grand National Illustrated* magazine, said to Baker, "Come on, Buck, let the nigger have it," regarding Baker's unwillingness to give up the trophy Wendell had rightfully won. Over three decades later, the bellhop was conveying the same fears that previous generations of African-Americans had to confront in order to fight for basic freedoms. Like Wendell, Chris Woods was about to face deeply rooted prejudice that would put his life in danger. I also wondered what it would take for this bellhop to come out to Concord and support our effort. Part of our sponsorship pitch was that we would attract some new fans to NASCAR. But would these new fans feel confident enough to sit in the grandstands of a place like Concord and shrug off the stares, the epithets, the Twenty Questions routine? Would they buy the T-shirts, keychains, and ball caps bearing the No. 21? I had survived racial hostilities at speedways in New Jersey, New York, Massachusetts, and now North Carolina, but could Chris, even in the winner's circle, convince others to do the same? And to what extent were corporate America, GM, and Silent Sam going to cultivate—or decimate—the efforts to develop this fan base?

As more questions danced around my head, the phone rang in my hotel room. It was my father, calling from a phone booth in a thunderstorm. He told me Robert Hill was going to work on a proposal for a motorsports program with Miller Racing as its centerpiece and present it to his Ford colleagues at NAMAD. Hill was also going to contact a good friend of his, Mel Farr, who operated a $500-million dealership empire in Michigan. Locals knew Mel Farr's face quite well from his wacky TV ads, in which he flew around the screen in a red cape and claimed he had the best deals in town. Some African-Americans thought the commercials were shameless and pandering, but the silliness put forth a non-threatening image. Like the image or not, he flew that ridiculous caricature straight to the bank. Farr was also chummy with Edsel Ford II, the grandson of Henry Ford. Hill wanted to present his plans to Edsel Ford II, too. Some solid sponsorship opportunities were starting to percolate. I was pumped.

That Friday evening I headed over to Concord to see how the No. 21 was coming along for Saturday's race. It was hot and humid and the usual cast of characters were gathered outside Nick's shop: magnolia queens in short shorts smoking cigarettes; the same good ol' boys staring hard at Chris and me as if they had forgotten who we were. Our shop floor now had a light yellow mist over it, indicating where Chris and David painted the new body panels. In my conversations with Chris over the past two weeks, he had told me how David was dedicating all of his spare time to working on our car and how Nick's contributions were quickly diminishing. I now had aspirations of hiring David as our full-time chief mechanic, which would cost another $20,000 to $25,000 a year. If we did net any sponsorship money for '95, hiring David was a top priority.

On Saturday night, Chris not only made it through an entire race without a crash, he finished tenth out of thirty cars.

The following Saturday, my father and Ron Whitney drove down together from Pennsylvania. I met them in the Hilton lobby, where the bellhop hesitated a little when he saw Ron, who is white. He pulled my father aside and said, "You brothers racin' tonight? You got nerve." One of the African-American girls at the counter slipped us a stack of free breakfast tickets.

"You guys are in the know around here!" exclaimed Ron.

We dropped our gear in the rooms and headed over to the speedway. I had arranged for us to meet with Skip Pope, the instructor from the chassis-setup course who had expressed interest in working for us, early Saturday morning. Nick was dividing his time among a half-dozen other paying customers, not to mention all of the freeloaders, and I began to worry that small yet vital details would start falling through the cracks. David and Chris had noticed that the engine's power plant was not being maximized due to the current chassis's geometry, which meant precious horsepower was wasting away. Plus, variables like temperature and humidity could diminish the car's performance if they were not addressed on a daily basis. Skip said he could put the No. 21 through a specialized regimen of chassis setups and evaluations throughout the week. This more focused and methodical approach would streamline the preparation process and avoid having to scramble at the last minute. At any level of auto racing, such attention to detail separates the winners from the losers.

Yvonne lit up like a Christmas tree when she saw us approach the pit-pass shack. She gave each of us a big hug and slipped us VIP tickets. At the shop, Chris and David were talking about the evening's race. The gray door between our shop and Nick's was open, so we popped in to say hello. Nick spoke curtly and barely made eye contact with me. When we went back into shop No. 10, Chris told me Nick knew the reason for Skip's visit and didn't take too kindly to the idea that he might be replaced. Skip was a good talker, Nick told Chris, but he couldn't set up a racecar. Chris had defended Nick to me and showed a similar reluctance to bring in outside help. I sensed that Chris was only doing so out of his new-found camaraderie with Nick. It was hard to blame Chris for showing such loyalty. Between his job at the dealership and the numerous hours he spent working on the No. 21, Chris didn't have much time to socialize and meet new friends. The two guys were bonding over their shared passion for racing, and Chris didn't want to betray that bond. I had to explain to Chris that we couldn't let friendships deter us from achieving the highest possible level of success.

A few minutes later, we heard the gravelly patter of Skip pulling up in his spankin' new 'Vette. Skip was upbeat and introduced himself to everyone. He started his inspection by weighing the car and asked Chris to get in the driver's seat. Visibly pouting, Chris dawdled his way over to the Lumina and took his sweet time getting in to the driver's seat. Once he was inside, Chris pretended to be asleep and didn't respond to Skip's questions about the front suspension. Midway through the inspection, Nick slammed shut the gray wooden door between our shops. I could hear him fumbling for the lock on the other side. Skip came across several nuts and bolts that were undone. Apparently, the instant he found out Skip was coming for an assessment, Nick had stopped his current setup in disgust. David quietly sat in a lawn chair with his cap cocked back and tried to learn what he could amongst all the puerile antics.

Around 4 p.m., it was time to go up to the speedway for practice. Teams were starting to fill up the pits. The grandstands were already about half-full. After Ron made a few adjustments to the engine, Chris flipped the switches and barreled off toward the tunnel. David jumped in his pickup with the tools and support equipment, and Skip followed in his 'Vette. Paul Wilson greeted Ron, my father, and me at the VIP suites and fed us the latest gossip. We could see Chris getting ready to enter the speedway at turn one for his practice laps. Skip was on top of someone's trailer holding a stopwatch, his eyes glued on the No. 21. During his fifth practice lap, Chris brushed the back wall extremely hard. A cloud of particulates burst into the air. "What happened?" yelled Paul. The damage was bad enough that Big Ed was summoned to bring out the wrecker.

When Ron, my father, and I got to the shop, the No. 21 was

bleeding radiator fluid. The front clip, the tubular structure that houses the engine and supports the front suspension, had been twisted and crushed. If the impact had been a little harder, the engine could have been totaled. The engine would have had to come out, the front body panels dismantled, and the entire chassis refitted and re-aligned. The bottom line was $5,000 worth of damage and at least forty hours of labor to repair the No. 21. The mishap stemmed from Chris and Nick's childish reaction to the Skip Pope news. They had become so obsessed with the possibility of an outsider joining the mechanical team that they lost focus on the quality of their own work. Chris bore a look of pure shame and apologized to my father and me once we assessed the damage. Nick, who had stepped into our shop, cigarette hanging out of his mouth, left without saying much. Skip told me to call him and darted off in his 'Vette, frustrated with the day's outcome. We were all frustrated. It was already mid-September, there were only five races left in the season, and because of the crash we would now miss at least one race, perhaps more.

I decided to ask someone down at Concord to keep a closer eye on Chris and the car. He had the entire Fuller family watching over him and mentoring him at Agawam, but down at Concord, he was alone. My father and I were devoting more time and attention to sponsorship and trying to minimize our trips down to Concord. My father placed a call to his longtime friend Bobby Merritt to see if he could help out. Bobby was from Shelby, North Carolina, and grew up idolizing Wendell Scott. In the '70s, he traveled all over the country with my father in support of BARA and Tommy Thompson. By trade, Bobby wasn't a driver, a mechanic, or a promoter, but he had given a ton of moral support to my father and other African-Americans in racing over the years. He was a fiery, pro-black, down-for-the-cause type of guy, and we figured some of his experience, dedication, and character might rub off on Chris. Bobby was now a cameraman for a television network in New York City, but he frequently traveled back down to North Carolina to watch NASCAR races and work on his vintage Ford Mustang that he kept at a garage in Shelby. He agreed to mentor Chris for the rest of the season, which ended around Thanksgiving. In the ensuing weeks, Bobby called us regularly with updates. Sometimes he called me from his cell phone in the wee hours of the morning, when he was on assignment in the back alleys of New York City filming stories about murders and drug busts. One time, he phoned from a crime scene to tell me about a conflict at the speedway involving both David and Chris. Apparently, David had gotten into fisticuffs with three guys in the pits after he heard them calling Chris a nigger. David was so incensed, he had to be escorted out by two deputies. Meanwhile, Chris shrugged off the remarks like they weren't directed at him, just as he had at Agawam. In a way, I was proud of both guys. I didn't advocate violence as a response to prejudice in the pits, but David's retaliation made a statement: He wasn't going to tolerate intolerance, period. David was usually mild-mannered, and his rash reaction set the precedent that Miller Racing wasn't going to cower in the face of bigoted chiding. And while Bobby was a little puzzled at Chris's lackadaisical response to the remarks, we agreed that Chris was better off avoiding all side skirmishes. Having Bobby around proved big dividends. Chris got through another five or six races that season without major incident, placing in the top ten consistently.

The fall also brought some chilling news. October saw the exit of NAMAD from our sponsorship plans. Robert Hill told my father that when he presented the Miller Racing proposal to a roomful of his colleagues, they recoiled in disapproval. "Why would we sponsor a racecar to drive around in circles down in North Carolina?" folks asked. "How would this program benefit their dealerships in Michigan, Ohio, or Indiana? It's ludicrous." Many of them didn't want to do anything that would upset Ford

Motor Company, who played big brother when it came to financial support and expanding dealership territories. "Call Sam Johnson in Charlotte," Hill said to my father before hanging up. "You're on your own." When my father and I met with Sam Johnson, he wasn't much help either. He admired our effort but did not see any business potential.

My father and I weren't the only ones feeling alone. As the holidays approached, I worried more about Chris's solitude. His few friends were people related to the racetrack, and once the season at Concord ended, he lost touch with them. Bobby made fewer trips down South now that the NASCAR season had ended. Other than the mild flirtation he had going on with the property manager, he didn't socialize with anyone at his apartment complex. He had the Fullers up in Massachusetts, but the trip North was too expensive. Archie Kindle made multiple attempts to bring Chris into his community, a predominantly African-American enclave about an hour away in Greensboro. He repeatedly offered to rent Chris one of his condos in the area at a discount, he invited Chris to church and cookouts, and he suggested a local barbershop where guys Chris's age hung out. But Chris always declined. By now, it was pretty clear to me that Chris felt more comfortable socializing with white people. Back in Massachusetts, the Fullers, his closest thing to a family, were white. The community was mostly white and all of his acquaintances at Agawam were white. Because whites dominated racing and Chris's upbringing, they also dominated his social circle. Chris would spend both Thanksgiving and Christmas working on the Lumina in shop No. 10, alone.

Toward the end of '94, I moved from Virginia to Novi, Michigan. With our first season at Concord now in the books, I wanted to devote my full attention to finding sponsorship. Being closer to Detroit would allow me to put a full-court press on my contacts at the Big Three automakers. (My years in Michigan brought me something better than any sponsorship, too. In Novi, I met my wife.) By now, I had a clearer sense of how much money it took to compete in our class at Concord for an entire year. We needed a backup car and engine, which totaled $50,000. We couldn't short-change the need for a trailer anymore, as the short drive from the shop to the pits was adding unnecessary wear and tear to the car. Race tires added up to $15,000, and we wanted a reserve of at least $20,000 for crash damage and spare parts. In total, we calculated an annual budget of $150,000. We had accomplished a lot with just a little in the '94 season, and one check could put us on the road toward much bigger things.

In December, Deep Throat called. He had handed the Miller Racing portfolio to a manager at GM Service Parts Operations (GMSPO). GMSPO manufactured and sold automotive parts to retailers for the GM Parts and ACDelco brands, and ran the GM Goodwrench Service Plus division, which operated in more than 11,000 GM dealerships nationwide. GM Goodwrench Service Plus also sponsored legendary driver Dale Earnhardt, who in October clinched his record-tying seventh Cup series championship at—where else—the ACDelco 500 at North Carolina Speedway. In addition to backing Earnhardt's team Richard Childress Racing and others, GMSPO allotted millions to title sponsorships of national racing events, billboards, print advertisements, and TV spots. Deep Throat told us to expect a call by the first of the year. About a week before Christmas, Frank X. Gaughen, manager of sports marketing for GMSPO, called. We set up a meeting for early January.

Over the holidays, my father and I put our heads together to create a marketing plan for GMSPO. In the old days of stock-car racing, a sponsorship plan more or less entailed slapping a few decals of company logos on a car. If the decals appeared on national television, the sponsorship was a success. Beginning in the '80s, as NASCAR grew more popular, sponsors worked closely with race teams to develop strategic marketing and promotional campaigns that targeted the stock-car fan base. By the '90s, most major sponsors had in-house marketing divisions devoted specifically to auto racing. The increased attention to demographics and revenue meant that we would need to present a plan detailing what types of consumers our team would attract and the impact our racing program would have on incremental sales. Every company had different marketing objectives, a different budget, a different culture, a different philosophy, so the key would be coming up with ideas specifically for GMSPO. We researched the clientele of aftermarket-parts retailers like the National Automotive Parts Association (NAPA) and Western Auto. We looked closely at Pep Boys in the Philadelphia area, where early on a Saturday morning dozens of black folks would line up at the door to take advantage of whatever parts sale they had read about in the circulars of local papers. As soon as the parts manager opened the door, they would run in and buy spark plugs, belts, and batteries. Some folks would work on their cars right in the parking lot. Our idea was to hold promotional events at aftermarket retailers in Harlem, South Central LA, and Detroit. At the events, we would showcase a GMSPO-branded car, introduce Chris Woods, and hand out informational leaflets, coupons, and Miller Racing–GMSPO souvenirs. We felt that these black consumers, who were already dedicated to buying auto parts and fixing their cars themselves, would become loyal to ACDelco parts if they knew the company was supporting a black driver. We would also take the show car on the road to both automotive and African-American conventions across the country, spreading the word that GMSPO and a black race team had struck a historic alliance. The potential for marketing, advertising, and publicity was limitless.

On the gray, snowy morning of January 7, 1995 my father and I met in the main lobby of the GM Building. The premises were gigantic and swarmed with employees scurrying through a maze of reception areas, escalators, and revolving doors. We passed a showroom of display cars near the lobby and took an escalator up to a glass-paneled skywalk one story above street level that connected to the adjacent New Center One Building. The entrance to the New Center One side had a grand atrium with clothing stores and restaurants. At the reception area, an African-American woman sat behind a semi-circular desk that had a telephone, sign-in list, and visitor ID tags. The woman introduced herself as Betty and asked us to sign in. Frank would be about twenty minutes, she said. The tables were littered with GM leaflets and trade magazines. Within minutes, the reception phone rang and Betty directed us to Gaughen's office. As we stepped inside Gaughen's office, my eyes widened at his collection of memorabilia. He had GM Goodwrench posters, car models, and coffee mugs—most of it featuring Dale Earnhardt's No. 3—scattered all over the walls and surfaces, and autograph cards of other drivers stacked on the table behind his desk.

From the beginning, the meeting was positive. Gaughen talked about Chevy's Motorsports Technology Group (MTG), a group of GM engineers who developed engine technology for various forms of auto racing (MTG was later renamed GM Motorsports.) A lot of the R&D took place at MTG's Tech Center in Warren, Michigan. MTG also compiled extensive feedback from race teams, sending out hundreds of copies of a new part and later inquiring about how the new part performed. Hendrick Motorsports in Charlotte was the largest recipient of parts and secret R&D projects from MTG, which helped the NASCAR heavyweight stay competitive. My father segued the conversation to our Concord program, Chris Woods, and some of the marketing ideas we had come up with. He showed an old black-and-white photo of Chris standing alongside the Fuller brothers at the track. Gaughen asked thoughtful questions about how we envisioned implementing our ideas, and our preparation for the meeting helped answer all of them. By the end of our discussion, Gaughen said that he wanted to sponsor Miller Racing. I had to keep from jumping out of my seat.

Before we wrapped up, Don Taylor, the NASCAR manager for MTG, walked in and apologized for being late. Don told us his group could not provide sponsorship money, but, if we gave Gaughen a list of parts we needed, he could arrange to ship them to our engine builder, free of charge.

We all shook hands and left Gaughen's office. On the way out, Gaughen asked if we knew the African-American GM employee who handed him the Miller Racing profile in November. In unison, my father and I answered, "We're not sure." We told him we had mailed copies of our profile to several GM Motorsports people over the last two years and weren't sure where they ended up.

"OK," said Gaughen. "I'll get back to you in thirty days."

When my father and I walked outside, a black GM luxury car pulled up to the curb. Deep Throat motioned for us to hurry in. At the wheel in a sharp suit, he put his cell phone on his lap mid-conversation and asked, "How did it go? You didn't mention my name, did you?"

A few days earlier, my father had told Deep Throat about our sit-down with Gaughen. He agreed to meet us immediately afterward. Before we got a chance to say much about the meeting with Gaughen, he said he was taking us to meet Bill Brooks, GM's Vice President of Community Relations. As it started to snow again, Deep Throat swiftly maneuvered through a web of lots and access roads on GM's grounds. We parked and ran through a series of halls and elevators. I had no sense of where we were.

Brooks, an African-American executive, didn't have much time to meet with us. Deep Throat gave him a quick synopsis of Miller Racing, and Brooks told us to call him if we needed anything.

Within five minutes, we were tearing through the halls to our next destination.

Deep Throat walked as fast as he spoke. As we flew by glass walls, security cameras, and a partitioned security guard station near the elevators, he told us we were going to meet some middle managers. It then dawned on me that we were on the famous fourteenth floor of the GM Building, where the CEO and top brass sat. We met a few middle managers in a section called Cobo Hall, where, over a gourmet lunch, Larry King addressed about 500 employees. I didn't have much time to take in what King was saying. Deep Throat whispered a few introductions and whisked us back through the hallways, all the way to his car. He dropped off my father at his rental car, took me to my car, said a terse goodbye, and disappeared into the network of lots.

My father and I were ecstatic. The GM Goodwrench Service Plus and ACDelco brands were steeped in a tradition of winning. The very idea of their logos adorning our No. 21 gave me goosebumps. Don Taylor's offer for parts was a huge bonus, too. Certain GM components would not be compatible with our custom engine, but we could still save thousands with the parts that did fit. We didn't know how much GMSPO was going to muster for us in dollars, but we guessed it would be substantial. To our knowledge, all GM teams had formidable, first-class deals. If things proceeded along this promising trajectory, Miller Racing could graduate to NASCAR's Busch Grand National series, the division second only to Winston Cup, within two years.

We wanted to keep our optimism in check, though, as we still didn't know the particulars of the deal. My father and I agreed to keep the GMSPO possibility to ourselves. While it was hard not to break the news to our crew at Concord, we figured it would be even harder on everyone if the opportunity fell by the wayside. One person my father did tell in confidence was Joe Gerber, the motorsports promoter up at Agawam who had tipped us off to

Chris a few years prior. "Oh my God," he marveled. "You guys are going to start a riot down there with a black kid driving a Goodwrench car."

With the '95 season at Concord beginning in late March, my father and I started addressing some immediate needs for the team. First, we wanted to build a second car. If the primary car got severely damaged, we could race the backup and avoid missing valuable track time. Initially, we were going to order a chassis through Butler Built in Concord. But Nick assured us he could build a better chassis and have it completed in time for the season. The chassis would cost $15,000. The fiasco with Skip Pope was still fresh in our minds, and Nick never apologized for his actions. Still, with Nick's shop adjacent to ours, David and Chris could closely monitor his progress. Time was of the essence.

We mailed Nick a $3,000 deposit to get started. It took at least two months to construct a chassis from scratch, so we figured we'd have the backup just in time for the start of the season. We also needed $3,000 for a new 1995 Chevy Monte Carlo body, which would replace the Lumina exterior. The Monte Carlo was the latest racing body released by Chevrolet that met the specs of our class at Concord. Meanwhile, in the Pennsylvania country-side, R&W Engines was evaluating the 1994 engine, dissecting its inner-workings like a medical examiner investigates a corpse. The Whitneys experimented with various combinations of components and new engine parts to help boost horsepower. My father hand-delivered the GM Performance catalog to R&W and told them GM was offering us engine parts for the '95 season. Ron and Ron Jr. started asking practical questions to which we didn't yet have the answers: "How many parts can we order? How long does the shipping take? Are all the parts readily available?" Generally, most race teams placed parts orders in the month of January in order to conduct offseason R&D, and a lot of specialty items sold out quickly. It was important that we heard back from GMSPO as soon as possible to iron out the particulars of both the sponsorship and the parts deals.

When the first week of February rolled around, I put in a call to Frank Gaughen and got an automated, "Mailbox is full" message. I waited two hours, called again, and got the same message. The next morning I called again: "Mailbox is full." A week later I called and got a message saying he would be out of the office for three days.

In the meantime, Ron Whitney needed $5,000 in specialty parts to complete the new and improved engine. "I got this one," my father told me over the phone. He headed down the Pennsylvania Turnpike to drop off a check for the full amount to Ron. Expenses were piling up at the shop in Concord, too. Chris and David desperately needed certain parts and tools to prepare the new Monte Carlo for the season opener. I held my breath as I watched my fax machine slowly spit out the list of parts from Chris. I picked up the curled paper from the floor and rubbed my temples when I saw that the equipment totaled $4,000. I called my father and said, "I got this one." I started worrying about all the money we were shelling out. I was already thinking about selling the second car Nick was constructing if we ended up strapped for cash.

While we played the waiting game for GMSPO, *Stock Car Racing* magazine published a column about the need for a Jackie Robinson in the sport. In the article, writer Andy Fusco asked, ". . . wouldn't racing be better off if there was a greater variety of people filling more and more seats in the stands, and more and more spaces in the pits?" He acknowledged the inroads made by Wendell Scott and Willy T. Ribbs, but argued that NASCAR nation at large wouldn't warm up to a driver of color until he or she reached the winner's circle consistently, adding, ". . . fans, regardless of their ethnicity, want to support a winner." He also mentioned the popularity of female IndyCar driver Lyn St. James, who would not have been allowed to participate at the majority of tracks in America well into the '80s since women used to be barred from the pits. My father and I were elated that the subject was getting attention in NASCAR circles, especially with GM Goodwrench Plus and Miller Racing partnership on the horizon. Bobby Merritt was so appreciative he wrote a letter to Mr. Fusco, to which the journalist responded:

> Dear Bob:
> Thank you for your letter of February 20, 1995. I've received a lot of feedback from that column. The most interesting pair of reactions came on February 17 when a friend called to say I was "brave" to write such a column. I didn't know what he meant, but found out two days later when a guy who I thought was a buddy of mine said I was a "nigger lover" for even writing something like that. I've seen the enemy and it is us.
> Sincerely,
> Andrew S. Fusco

Fusco's sentiment in his letter was in part referring to a September 13, 1994 article in the weekly racing bible *National Speed Sport News*, in which longtime columnist and TV analyst Chris Economaki used the phrase, "African-American in the woodpile." Even though Economaki's column had nothing directly to do with skin color and sports (he used the phrase to describe a situation involving an open-wheel driver's father), the underlying history of his comment—and the ease with which he used those words— spoke volumes. Economaki was perhaps the most connected, powerful, and decorated journalist in motorsports. He had been writing about auto racing for decades and covered the Daytona 500 and the Indianapolis 500 as a TV commentator. He was dubbed "The Dean of American Motorsports" by many of his colleagues. And here he was, dropping a slight variation of the phrase "nigger in the woodpile," an expression used to described slaves hiding from authorities along the Underground Railroad in mounds of firewood in the mid-1800s. It was a reminder of how prejudice still simmered in the ethos of American motorsports.

Both Economaki's and Fusco's articles brought the subject of racism in motorsports to the national consciousness, which, in the long run, could only help our cause. The very prospect of people in the racing community imagining a Jackie Robinson of NASCAR or discussing why Economaki's comment was hurtful meant the minority's role within the sport would inevitably go through some sort of re-examining. I viewed any dialogue regarding the subject as a set of double doors. One door opening toward the history of those who had braved racing's prejudice for decades, and another door looking toward a not-so-distant future of equal opportunities.

The articles made me work that much harder. Until the call from Frank Gaughen came, I resigned myself to spending whatever it took to keep the team afloat for the '95 season. I sent a copy of Fusco's letter to Chris Woods, Herb Jones, R&W Engines, and other key people who believed in our effort. By now, we had also decided to filter news of the GMSPO sponsorship possibility to R&W and the crew at Concord. Chris was so delighted he ran out and bought a metallic green Chevy pickup. Archie Kindle of Plaza Ford fumed at the sight of Chris's purchase of a Chevy and summoned Chris to his office to explain. Chris leaked to Archie that a joint venture between GM Goodwrench Service Plus and Miller Racing was in the works. The news traveled quickly around Plaza Ford and beyond. Within a couple of days, Chris called my father from Plaza Ford in a panic, telling him that the switchboard at the dealership was jammed because local radio stations, newspapers, and racers were trying to reach Chris to ask him about the sponsorship rumor. My father advised Chris to tell people that Miller Racing was in talks with GMSPO, but nothing was official. Chris later told me a story about how two good ol' boys who worked in the body shop at Plaza had drawn a cartoon portraying Chris as Dale Earnhardt's secret, illegitimate African-American child. I figured the media maelstrom and silly cartoon were harbingers of the shock and envy that would rattle the masses when we unveiled a GM Goodwrench Service Plus No. 21 at Concord. Meanwhile, Archie blew a gasket when he found out about the disruptions to his business.

Frank Gaughen finally did call in late February, but the conversation was brief. He was upbeat and enthusiastic, and assured me that he would have the details of the sponsorship worked out soon. He asked me to send him a list of three locations in the Charlotte area where we could do public relations appearances with Chris and the car. My father and I put together a letter that included our choices for the three show-car locations as well as a list of necessary equipment: the show car itself, a truck, and a trailer, as well as GM Goodwrench–branded clothing and paraphernalia.

With open practice now only days away, we had to start making some tough financial decisions. R&W agreed to defer all engine development costs, which were reaching the $25,000 mark, until the end of the season. Chris offered to pay for all crash damage and tires until he was flat broke. Once Nick completed our second chassis, another $15,000 would be entered on the ledger. Our volunteer help at Concord required only that we pay for their pit passes and food, which, while the smallest expense on the books, still could add up to $3,000 by season's end. My father negotiated a race-fuel sponsorship with Sunoco thanks to Jeff Fuller, who was about to embark on a major sponsorship deal with the oil company for his NASCAR Busch Series effort. Jeff put my father in touch with the right people. Sunoco would supply our team with ten fifty-five-gallon drums of race fuel and several cases of racing oil, a $3,000 value. In exchange, we agreed to place two Sunoco decals on the car and a patch on Chris's driving uniform.

Another dilemma we faced was deciding what color to paint the body of the Monte Carlo. While I was enamored with the school-bus yellow of the Lumina, painting the new car black with a silver border and red pinstripe on the bottom would match the color scheme of Dale Earnhardt's GM Goodwrench Service Plus No. 3 car. Chris asked Plaza Ford's service manager Bob Reed if he could use the paint booth in the body shop to paint the panels himself. Bob agreed, but told Chris, "Don't let Archie Kindle find out you're painting Chevy body parts in his Ford dealership." Chris dismantled the Monte Carlo body, packed the pieces in the bed of his truck, and snuck them in and out of the rear of Plaza Ford every day for about a week until the paint job was done. Chris also picked up some slick No. 21 decals outlined with red stripes to put on the doors, roof, headlight, and taillight areas. The day the new R&W engine arrived, Chris and David carefully mounted it into the car. With the first race of the season only days away, the new No. 21 was coming together nicely.

Chris reported that his practice runs were successful and that the Monte Carlo needed only minor adjustments for the following week's race, the first of the season. Instead of spending money on airfare and accommodations, my father and I chose to buy two-way radios, a $2,000 purchase, for the new season. Most Late Model teams at Concord had radios, which allowed the crew to coordinate pit stops with the driver and make faster adjustments.

Without any guarantee of money from GMSPO, we were now at the precipice of having our entire '95 season go sour with one swift, calamitous crash. At the same time, if we put the brakes on racing, Chris would lose the momentum he had built up from last season, not to mention an opportunity to pick up points in the standings earlier in the season. Perhaps, more importantly, we would risk crushing the spirits of our faithful Concord crew—an overworked, underpaid group that was spending thirty to forty hours a week trying to get the No. 21 into the winner's circle. I especially worried about Chris not having racing in his life. That first lonely winter in North Carolina was rough on him, being away from his home, the Fullers, and his other friends. The prospect of following in Dale Earnhardt's footsteps had rejuvenated his spirit.

A week later, Chris raced in the opening day of the season. After an agonizing night of waiting for the phone to ring, Chris called at midnight to tell me the car was intact and that he had placed in the top ten.

At my father's house in Pennsylvania, the team's mailbox was starting to pile up with letters. HBO was interested in doing a piece on the team on one of its new sports shows. Another show called *Pit Stop* on the Nashville Network was interested in interviewing the team. My father and I copied all of the requests and sent them to Frank Gaughen. With word of a black driver in a Goodwrench Service Plus car spreading so quickly in racing circles, my father and I knew the sooner we could confirm the sponsorship the better we would be able to ride the wave of publicity. GMSPO was not responding to any of our correspondence, though. When Bobby Merritt learned about how long we had been waiting for the money, he seethed, saying, "Nothing's changed, man, for blacks. You saw the Andy Fusco letter. No one wants to be a nigger lover, man. If Wendell was alive, he'd be disappointed."

My father and I mustered enough money to take a trip to Concord for a Saturday night race at the end of March. Luckily, we were able to get a room at the Hilton for a discount. When we walked into the lobby, I recognized an African-American gentleman in a tailor-made suit who walked right past us through the doors. I turned around and shouted, "Excuse me, didn't you graduate from Morehouse College?"

The man stopped in his tracks and walked back toward us, smiling. Hubert Humphrey was now an executive for First Union Bank at the company's Charlotte headquarters. We told him why we were down in Charlotte and he invited us up to a private suite on the penthouse floor where some Morehouse alumni were holding a small party. He gave us his key and told us to go up to the penthouse. He would be right back with more wine and cheese.

The alums in the room made us feel right at home. Within minutes, we had the well-heeled doctors, lawyers, and businessmen huddled around us as we explained our program down in Concord. "You guys are challenging the good ol' boy establishment!" someone exclaimed. "Man, two renegades! I know those backwoods country boys are pissed off!"

When Hubert emerged with more cheese and expensive champagne, he asked what all the excitement was about. "First Union sponsors the NASCAR Winston Cup North Wilkesboro race!" he shouted when we filled him in. "NASCAR is the hottest sport in America, brothers." A prominent physician began describing his experience in the Speedway Club at the Charlotte Motor Speedway. "The speedway has gone upscale, but it's still not a place for African-Americans," he said.

At the end of the fete, the Morehouse grads handed us business cards and offered to help any way they could. Two Nations Bank executives wanted a proposal as soon as possible. In his deep, commanding voice, Hubert boomed, "First Union is going to get Miller Racing, fellas."

I called Hubert Humphrey as soon as I got back to Michigan. Before I could say a word, he told me that he had already set up a meeting with Lenny Springs, Vice President of Community Relations at First Union. He briefed me on Springs's background and talked about his access to the CEO and other top-ranking executives. "Lenny Springs is a tree-shaker," he assured me.

Within a couple of days, my father and I rendezvoused at the Charlotte airport for the First Union meeting. For this trip, however, we would not be staying at the Hilton. We planned a one-day turnaround to save on hotel expenses. We even agreed to eat as much as we could on the airplane to cut costs. When we pulled into the parking lot of the restaurant where we were supposed to meet Hubert, my father and I both noted how upscale it looked. We pooled our cash to realize that we had only a few dollars between us. We had been charging up a storm to prepare for the '95 season—not to mention the debt we were still paying off from the '94 season—and our credit cards were maxed out. Sitting there in the rental car, I had a sad, helpless feeling. I thought to myself, Why are we doing this to ourselves? Where is this road of hustling, hoping, and spending leading us? Is Bobby Merritt right? Maybe nothing has changed. Maybe this wall of racist history that we're constantly trying to overcome is just too high. If so, why was I spending my own hard-earned money on stock-car racing? Maybe this *was* a suicide mission. If we quit now, my father could re-focus on his consulting business, I could get out of debt in a few months and start re-saving toward a down payment on a home. Besides, being a commercial pilot isn't such a bad life for a young African-American male. Why *am* I doing this to myself?

Why? Because so many people before me had paved the way for us to get even this far. Because Charlie Wiggins had fended off the KKK to start the Gold and Glory Sweepstakes, and ten years after its demise, Wiggins worked as a janitor at the Indianapolis Motor Speedway because it was the only job the venue offered to African-Americans. Because my father and my Uncle Dexter worked day and night in the garage to transform the junked 1955 Chevrolet station wagon into the drag-racing marvel that was Mr. Diplomat. Because Wendell Scott and Bruce Driver never received their fair moments of triumph in the winner's circle. Because Sol Walker wore his Afro and black leather jacket to dragstrips with pride. Because Tom and Crystal Rice sat apart from each other in the grandstands at Old Dominion. Because the White family relied on heaps of rusty spark plugs and torn metal in order to race. Because Chris Woods had relocated all the way from Massachusetts to be a part of Miller Racing and was now spending all of his extra money on racing tires. Because David Miller was now putting in fifty volunteer hours a week to keep the No. 21 in top form. And because of Deep Throat, who was doing risky reconnaissance for us at GM and was expecting to hear news soon about our pending sponsorship. As a family, as an operation, and as a team, we had come too far to abandon our dream now. Sure, we were holding on by the thinnest of strings, but we were on the brink of opening doors to African-Americans in racing that had never been open before. And besides, what was I going to do without racing in my life? It was in my blood.

We adjusted our ties, grabbed the proposal, and headed into the restaurant, hoping Hubert reached for the bill first.

8

Chasing the Check

The restaurant was bustling with bank executives. Amidst the chatter of investments and golf games, Hubert described the internal politics of First Union and primed us for Lenny Springs, who had aspirations of becoming an official at the NAACP. After lunch, we headed over to the First Union building. My father and I had a little more bounce in our step because Hubert had picked up the tab for lunch.

Overall, Springs was intrigued. He wanted to host an invitation-only reception in the First Union lobby, where bank executives and community leaders could meet the team and see the car. My father, Chris, and I would all make speeches, he said, and the function would come out of his budget. He wanted to hold it by the end of May, then pitch a sponsorship arrangement for 1996 to First Union's marketing executives. Hubert chimed in to say they would invite two hundred to three hundred people. Springs also handed us a folder with information about an African-American youth science club that toured stock-car race shops in Charlotte and studied racecar design. He suggested that we contact the club. Its president, like Lenny, was a member of a professional group called 100 Black Men.

The next day, my father faxed me a letter that had arrived in the team's PO Box. It was from Johnny C. Lineburger, a stock-car driver at Concord who was also a production coordinator for the TV show *This Week in Motorsports*. He had watched us race the previous season, and after hearing all of the GM Goodwrench buzz, he wanted to do a story on our team. While we were thrilled with the widespread exposure a TV story would garner, we wanted to stall Lineburger's offer until we had full confirmation from GM. If, for whatever reason, the GM Goodwrench sponsorship fell through, the last thing we wanted from a publicity standpoint was to generate a lot of hype for naught. We felt extra pressure to foster an image of accomplishment rather than failure. We had too many naysayers—from the doubters in the black community who thought we were crazy to the racist good ol' boys at Concord—who were lined up waiting to say, "I told you they couldn't do it," those who already saw us as a farce and a novelty in a world where we did not belong. We were fighting for a legitimacy in auto racing that had never been achieved, and appearing on Lineburger's show at this premature stage risked not only setting back our own effort but tainting the future of enterprising black race teams. Failure in the public eye was a precedent we were trying to fend off, but in the years to come it would plague a handful of black celebrities who started stock-car teams. Most recently, Willy T. Ribbs had been racing in the CART series as the top driver for the Bill Cosby–backed Raynor-Cosby Racing team. Ribbs qualified for the Indianapolis 500 in 1991 and raced competitively for a few seasons but, without corporate support, Raynor-Cosby had to let him go in 1994. In 1997, former NFL running back Joe Washington and NBA legend Julius Erving took a crack at launching a Busch Grand National Series team; the effort fizzled after only two seasons. In 1999, former Olympians Jackie Joyner-Kersee and her husband Bob Kersee formed Joyner-Kersee Racing, a joint partnership with Roehrig Motorsports. JKR raced once in 2000 and would end up folding due to a lack of funding. Such celebrity efforts debuted to moderate fanfare and publicity but, sadly, their inability to sustain would raise the fundamental question we were trying to eradicate: Do minorities belong in NASCAR?

Meanwhile, down at Concord, Chris continued placing in the

top ten. Nick Smith was demanding more money for the second car he was building, but during an April trip to Concord my father and I didn't see much progress on it. We had already given him $10,000 for parts and labor, but the car was only 15 percent complete. When we questioned Nick about his marginal progress, he gave us a long-winded technical dissertation that amounted to a pile of excuses. My father and I agreed that something was wrong and pumped Chris for information. Chris later told us that Nick was in dire financial straits. He was six months behind in his rent for the shop, which drew a threat of eviction from the Furrs, and he and Pam were seriously behind on their mobile home payments. We were the only customers who paid Nick regularly, Chris said. Chris also told us that when Nick got wind of my father and me coming to town, he would clamp body parts on the chassis to conceal the fact that he had barely worked on the car. In the end, Nick was not upholding his end of the bargain and was using us to pay his debts. My father and I scolded Chris for not warning us earlier. Chris said he didn't want to upset Nick, that he had to see him and deal with him every day. I was furious with Nick's dishonesty, but I was even more disappointed with Chris's failure to inform us sooner. Chris's loyalty to Nick threatened the growth of the team and came at the expense of our extremely tight financial situation.

My father and I drafted a letter to Nick reprimanding him for his actions and demanding that the second car be completed by a set date. Chris told us that Nick was livid when he received it, and Nick instantly turned his back on us at the speedway. David took over as crew chief and upped his volunteer contributions to seven days a week. He and Kathy later reported to us that Nick was telling everyone we were arrogant "wine and cheese niggers" and that we didn't pay our bills. We ended up selling the unfinished second car to another driver at Concord.

My next call to Frank Gaughen was once again routed to voicemail. My father called Deep Throat and told him Miller Racing was on life support. Deep Throat was outraged that we still hadn't heard anything and said he would lean on a friend in the accounting department for information. A few days later, Deep Throat called my father back. "You guys are going to get $25,000," he said.

Near the end of April, I finally reached Frank Gaughen. He told me that GMSPO had indeed budgeted $25,000 for us. He said we needed to send him an invoice for the full amount on letterhead that included the language "for marketing and sales activities." I accepted the offer and asked where the team could get uniforms, GM paraphernalia, and decals for the car. Gaughen directed me to Champion Sports Group in Charlotte, which handled GMSPO's promotional materials. Before he hung up, he told me to plaster the "Goodwrench Service Plus" decals all over the car and make it look just like Dale Earnhardt's No. 3 car.

We needed $150,000 to win, but we viewed the $25,000 as the beginning of what we hoped was a long-term relationship with GMSPO. We figured once GMSPO saw the impact an African-American driver would have on its business we'd be able to leverage a more substantial budget. Besides, my father and I were now masters at stretching money. We would find creative ways to make the $25,000 work for the rest of the '95 season.

The following Saturday I flew down to Charlotte and drove directly to Champion Sports Group. It was already starting to feel like summer outside. A blonde magnolia queen greeted me in the reception area, which had a few Goodwrench and ACDelco illustrations hanging on the walls. The receptionist introduced herself as Wendy Wegner. I told her my name and that we were a race team sponsored by GMSPO. She blurted out, "David!" and pointed me down the hallway toward the office of David Allen, the owner. Seated at a wooden desk, Allen asked what he could do for me. I told him that Miller Racing was being sponsored by

GMSPO and that I needed to order uniforms and Goodwrench decals. "Didn't Frank Gaughen tell you about us?" I asked.

Without answering, he picked up the telephone and dialed Frank Gaughen's number from memory. To no surprise, he got Gaughen's voicemail. "Are you the driver?" he asked. Before I could answer, he jumped out of his seat and muttered to no one in particular, "Earnhardt's gonna love this." He escorted me back toward the reception area, told me he would have to wait for Frank Gaughen's instructions before giving me any merchandise, and showed me the door. I was in and out of Champion so quickly that the air inside the rental car was still cool.

The moment I returned to Michigan I called Frank Gaughen to find out what went wrong. Gaughen said there was a miscommunication and assured me that everything would be ready for my next trip to Charlotte, which was the following weekend.

That Friday, my father and I met in Charlotte. It was a big race weekend for Winston Cup teams, so we expected Champion to be a ghost town. No one was at the front desk, but as we peeked down the hallway we saw a woman walking toward us. Her name was Marta Leonard. Marta greeted us warmly and walked us back to a small warehouse in the rear of the building that housed all the racing merchandise you could think of: GM Goodwrench crew shirts, shoes, pants, umbrellas, gloves, hats, patches, and even doormats. She gave us two complete uniforms for every crew member, several oxford shirts, cashmere sweaters, hats, decals, and a couple of umbrellas for good measure. We filled the trunk of the rental car and put the rest of the gear in the back seat. Chris was giddy about our score. He began wearing his GM Goodwrench apparel every day, even at Plaza Ford, which of course made Archie Kindle grimace.

I was cautiously excited about our new Goodwrench gear. It was now May and we still didn't have the check for $25,000 in our hands. In the meantime, Chris was faring well in the black

No. 21 Monte Carlo. Toward the end of May, he led all rookies in points and managed a few top-five finishes. The chassis setup was not perfect, due in large part to the departure of Nick Smith. We were riding on the strength of R&W's explosive powerplant and Chris's steadily improving driving.

My father and I returned to Charlotte on Memorial Day weekend, one of NASCAR's biggest weekends of the year. Fans, corporate executives, and the sports media flocked to the 100,000-plus-capacity Charlotte Motor Speedway for two annual races: the Busch-series 300 and the Coca-Cola 600. We jam-packed our itinerary. On Friday, we scheduled an auto signage specialist to apply the GM Goodwrench Service Plus decals to the Monte Carlo. With the hordes of bigwigs and journalists swarming around town, we wanted to have our Goodwrench car ready to show anyone who was interested. On Saturday morning, we arranged for a photographer to take team photos alongside the car. We needed to start creating promotional materials that depicted our operation in full, living color. Chris Woods, David and Kathy Miller, Bobby Merritt, my father, and I would all be in town, as well as our newest crew member, Kenny Barnes, who was chipping in hours of volunteer help at the shop. Kenny was a driver from Pennsylvania who knew Chris from their days of racing at Pocono International Speedway. Kenny had a familiar backstory. He had moved down to the Charlotte area to be around stock-car racing 24-7. He was divorced, lived alone in a one-bedroom apartment with his stray dog, and spent all his time at the track. He had just started a parts-coating business for Cup teams in nearby Cornelius.

Frank Gaughen mentioned that his associate, Dave Fortunato, would be in town for the weekend. Fortunato ordered perform-ance parts for GM race teams out of his office in Detroit. I wanted to track down Fortunato to discuss our parts needs and probe him for inside information regarding our check. Gaughen was evasive about the specifics of Fortunato's trip itinerary. I had to nudge him to tell me that Fortunato was staying at the Courtyard-Marriott, which was across the street from the Hilton. It was pretty mind-boggling how many hoops my father and I were jumping through. Typically, soon after a sponsorship deal is solidified, the sponsor helps arrange tasks like photo shoots and applying signage to the car. But the process at GMSPO had been so drawn out that we had to take a lot of matters into our own hands.

When we got to our shop on Friday, Chris told us he'd gone ahead and purchased a trailer for the car. It was a hasty decision, though, as the $1,500 trailer was made to tow a farm tractor, not a racecar. It didn't have a winch, there were no cabinets for tools or extra race tires, and it was so high off the ground it would take six people and two large wooden planks to push the 2,900-pound stock car onto it. We ended up using that cumbersome contraption for almost two years. We would hook it up to David's twenty-year-old Chevy pickup; store all of the spare tires, tools, and pit equipment in the pickup's bed; and the crew would sit atop the mountain of machinery for the ride to the pits.

A gentleman named Daryl from Classic Sign & Design showed up to adorn the car with our Goodwrench decals. When he was finished, I took a long, proud look at the newly minted Goodwrench No. 21. The car looked like a force to be reckoned with.

Back at the Hilton, I started calling Dave Fortunato's hotel room. I was hoping to arrange a meeting at Saturday's Busch-series race. I called him every hour on the hour starting at 8 p.m. By midnight, I was fighting to keep my eyes open, but I figured this was the best time to reach him. We needed GM engine parts, and we needed that check. Plus, I thought we might have an opportunity to meet more GMSPO employees at the race. At 1 a.m., I finally got an answer. Fortunato sounded so peppy—and I was so sleepy—that I almost wasn't sure what time it was. He told me he would leave three VIP suite tickets for us at the front desk of his hotel and that we could find him in the suite right before race time. I hung up the phone and passed out with my clothes on.

The next morning, I arrived at shop No. 10 just before 8 a.m. for the photo shoot. It was an overcast, slightly misty morning. When the rest of the crew showed up, we passed out GM Goodwrench shirts and hats. Chris looked sharp in his black driver's suit. The photographer, Dustin Peck, pulled up in his van right on time. He was tall, had long hair tied back in a ponytail, and had a hippieish look about him. Dustin and I outlined all of the setups and combinations of crew members for the shoot. When I expressed concern about the weather, Dustin replied, "Overcast days are the best for photography, especially for African-Americans."

I laughed.

"No, I'm serious," he said. "African-Americans can black out in a developed photo on a sunny day. This is perfect."

Dustin set us up on turn three in the pit area. He unfolded his six-foot tripod and an aluminum ladder. It took almost thirty minutes to position the car properly. Then, Dustin started snapping away. We went through endless angles and poses: kneeling, looking forward, looking up, face to face, shaking hands, with hats, without hats, in front of the No. 21, next to the No. 21. The three-hour shoot was exhausting, and it cost us the equivalent of eight sets of racing tires. But in the end, I was happy. I felt like we had just captured a small bit of history on film.

After lunch at Bojangles Fried Chicken, where some customers glared at our GM Goodwrench oxford shirts, my father, Chris, and I picked up the VIP tickets from the Marriott-Courtyard and drove over to Charlotte Motor Speedway. We wiggled our way through the throngs of racing fans decked out in colorful hats and T-shirts of their favorite drivers, all the way up to the VIP area. We flashed our passes and entered the GMPSO suite, which was astir with about sixty people. The suites were impressive. The cushy, climate-controlled accommodations sat six stories above the majestic 1.5-mile quad oval, with panoramic views of the sweeping grandstands, bustling pit area, and lush North Carolina countryside. We were the only African-Americans in the GMSPO suite and drew stares from the corporate gentlemen in polo shirts and women in their best dresses. The first person I recognized was Wendy Wegner from Champion. Holding a piece of pecan pie in one hand, she gave me a half-smile and pointed out Dave Fortunato with her free hand. He was sitting on a tall stool, gazing out at the speedway with a two-way radio on the counter in front of him. As we worked our way across the suite, more people started to notice us. David Allen, the unhelpful owner of Champion, flashed an uninspired smile. Marta Leonard gave us a warm hello and asked if there was anything she could do for us. A man in his fifties wearing white cotton khakis and a pink Ralph Lauren shirt cut through the crowd to introduce himself to my father. He was Gar Smith, a GMSPO General Sales Manager. Gar spoke optimistically about what he had heard of our effort and said he was 100 percent behind us.

Dave Fortunato was thirty-something, clean-cut, and had a neat mane of curly hair. As the radio on the counter chattered away, my father and I gave Fortunato a brief synopsis of our racing background. Intermittently picking up the two-way to give orders to GMSPO employees on the speedway grounds, Fortunato listened to our story and asked Chris how he got into racing, how far he wanted to take his career, and where he worked during the day. We always took a deep breath when the question about Chris's job surfaced with a General Motors employee. When Chris told him he worked at a Ford dealership, Fortunato said, "We won't talk about that too loud. Maybe we can talk to a Chevrolet dealer here in Charlotte." When Fortunato asked how things were going at Concord, I dove into the list of engine parts we needed for the season. Knowing that big GM teams received truckloads of parts every year, I arbitrarily picked the number twelve as the amount we needed of each part: twelve cylinder blocks, twelve cylinder heads, twelve sets of valves, twelve sets of harmonic balancers, twelve sets of valve covers, twelve intake manifolds, twelve sets of gaskets, twelve crankshafts, twelve cam shafts, twelve sets of wire harnesses, and so forth. "I can take care of that for you," Fortunato said casually. "I would be concerned if you ordered fifty of everything."

My father and Chris each smiled about as wide as the North Carolina skyline in front of us. We were so used to struggling to buy every nut and bolt that Fortunato's nonchalant response to my request of $100,000 worth of parts made us feel like we had won the lottery.

When I told Fortunato about the morning's photo shoot, he said, "I wish I had known that. GMSPO uses a photo studio in High Point called Norling Studios to photograph all our teams and drivers. Champion Sports Group organizes the sessions, and Norling designs autograph cards, posters, brochures, point-of-sale materials, and other stuff." Norling was located within a 200,000-square foot furniture-catalog publishing studio in High Point, North Carolina, the state's furniture manufacturing capital, Fortunato explained. Race teams rolled their cars in through a door large enough to accommodate a full tractor-trailer, and the studio provided helpful amenities like lighting equipment and backdrops. "No one told you about all this?" he exclaimed. "We could have saved you some significant dollars on the photo work."

Chris nudged me and pointed out Tom Blocker of Hendrick Automotive Group in the next suite, which was separated by a wall of glass. It was hard to believe that nearly a year had passed since Chris and I nervously strolled the lavish, oil-painting-lined hallway to Blocker's office at the Hendrick headquarters, Chris eyeing every step of the chic receptionist's enticing gait. Blocker was enjoying the pre-race festivities from the Chevrolet suite. I asked Fortunato if he ever interacted with the Chevy people. "We do some things with them in motorsports, but that's a different world," he said. Apparently, because GM had so many divisions operating in so many different areas, each sub-entity seemed to have its own isolated culture and bureaucracy.

Once the green flag dropped, the collective snarl of unbridled horsepower pulled all eyes in the suite toward the race. My father, Chris, and I cheered for our buddy Jeff Fuller in the Sunoco car. At the first caution flag, we wrapped up our conversation with Fortunato and began making our way to the door. Before we got far, he yelled, "Just one second, guys. Let me introduce you to Ernie Callard, our GMSPO performance parts specialist." Ernie said hello and gave me his business card, which showed that his office was in Flint, Michigan. "I'm on your side," said Ernie. "Give Dave your order. He'll put it in the computer system, and I'll get the parts to your front door."

Now that the race tempo had slowed because of the caution flag, a lot of folks in the suite turned their attention to our conversation with Ernie Callard. We said so long to Ernie and made our exit. As soon as we stepped outside I realized I had forgotten to ask Dave one crucial question.

"You're kidding!" he said when I told him about the waiting game for our check. "You should have received the money over two months ago." He told me to call him or Frank Gaughen in the next week. He also told me to submit our parts list as soon as possible, because it would take two to three weeks to deliver the order.

Overall, the weekend was a success. The 1 a.m. phone call to Dave Fortunato led to a few more contacts at GM and another parts offer with some substance. R&W could improve the performance of the engine by experimenting with various combinations of the duplicate parts. Also, despite not having the money from GMSPO yet, I was excited that our Monte Carlo was now flaunting the Goodwrench logo. The car looked as sharp and professional as any other at Concord. The following weekend would be a big test, though. It was the first time we would be racing at Concord with a semi-sponsored car, and emotions would be running high. Most teams at the small track didn't have a sponsored vehicle, let alone an African-American one bearing the same color scheme and brand as a NASCAR legend. Gossip about the alleged sponsorship had been circulating for weeks, but I imagined many at Concord would not believe the hype until they saw the car with their own eyes. Icy looks, boos, fistfights, a scrupulous car inspection, a lethal bump into the concrete walls—every disconcerting scenario flashed through my mind in that week leading up to the next race. Every member of our team, most importantly Chris, would have to remain focused on racing and nothing else. We were still in such a dire financial state that any lapse in preparations or altercation out on the track could send Chris and the No. 21 into the walls, and our '95 season into an irrevocable tailspin.

My father and I scraped together whatever money we had for the return trip to Charlotte. When we got to Concord, the usual Saturday night crowd was lingering around Nick's shop. David, Kenny, and a few other volunteers were going through the final chassis setup. When it was time to load the car onto the trailer for practice, we opened the fourteen-foot doors and David, Kenny, Chris, and I pushed the black No. 21 past a crowd of spectators onto the clumsy farm trailer. Jody Starnes grimaced as he watched us. He wasn't the only one. Magnolia queens puffing on cigarettes consoled their visibly shaken boyfriends, ushering them back into Nick's shop so they could worry about their own cars. The distraught good ol' boys couldn't stomach the fact that we had a GM sponsorship. We secured the car to the trailer, hooked it up to David's pickup, and packed up the necessary equipment in the cab. David had to drive slowly since he didn't know how the new trailer would respond to the weight of the car. The turtle's pace allowed for every onlooker to ogle the Goodwrench No. 21.

"How ya doin', honey?" Yvonne Furr asked us through the window of the pit-pass shack before motioning us inside. She gave us each a big hug. "It looks like you guys got that sponsor!"

Yvonne and my father talked up a storm. Yvonne could count money, bark orders on the speedway radio, tear off pit passes, and carry a conversation all at the same time.

A competitor with grease on his face asked me through the small hole in the glass window, "Is dat Goodwrinch sponsire-ship from D'troit or a locile deelership?"

"GM headquarters in Detroit," I answered. The greasy inquirer ran over to his friends and told them the news. A father of a racer asked if we wanted to buy a box of peaches. I told him we were from out of town and couldn't take peaches back on the airplane. "Geez," he said. "I thought y'all was from around these parts. You must fly down here every Saturday."

We flashed our pit passes to the deputy at the entrance to the tunnel and walked up the incline to the pits. Engines were revving up with ear-splitting pulsations. David, Kenny, and Chris, who was already in his black GM Goodwrench driver's suit, had the car off the trailer. Kathy told us that people in the pits were asking her how Chris Woods had gotten a Goodwrench deal. Kenny overheard two good ol' boys at the urinals saying, "How did those niggers get Goodwrench on their fuckin' car? That's a fuckin' disgrace."

"This place will never be the same," Kenny said with a laugh.

"If anybody gets in my face, I'll go to jail," said David.

One driver came over and asked Chris how he had managed to get the deal. "It was a lot of work, I'm here to tell you," Chris replied. The young driver circled the car, admiring the logos and paint job.

"Earnhardt, no, no. I'm gonna start calling you Burn-hardt

from now on," said the young driver. "Good luck tonight, buddy."

As the crew pushed the black No. 21 into the technical inspection area, a hush fell over everyone in the immediate area. The only person who spoke was Big Bird, who yelled, "Hey, Chris, you're movin' up in this world fast!"

"You need to hinge the rear trunk lid," said the technical inspector. "Git it done by next week or I'll have to disqualify ya' next time. Move on, you're holdin' up the line."

Relieved that the No. 21 passed inspection, the crew pushed the Chevy back to our plot. Competitors passed by, gazing and whispering, as the crew put the finishing touches on the No. 21. The country music stopped blaring over the loudspeakers and the single-car qualifying sessions got under way. Chris put on his helmet, hopped in through the window, and flipped the switches. The roar of the engine sounded as glorious as ever. Chris exploded off the line when it was his turn for qualifying. By now, darkness had set in at Concord, and the black and red No. 21 looked even more menacing under the lights. Chris solidified the eighth slot. Once the race started, Chris steadily maintained his position and occasionally reached fifth place in the thirty-car field. In the middle of the race, Chris tapped the rear bumper of a slower competitor, a common occurrence at any level of stock-car racing. When the caution flag was waved near the midway point of the race and most cars in the field entered the pits for service, a crew member of the car Chris had tapped ran over to him shaking his fist and screaming, "Come out of the car, nigger!" Chris reached out of the window and tried to grab the threatening good ol' boy, who kicked the car and scuffed the decals. David and Kenny quickly entered the fray and chased the heckler away. We later complained about the incident to the Furrs, who witnessed the entire incident from their private VIP suite. They suspended the rabble-rouser for a month.

Chris finished the night in eighth place. Typically, once the awards ceremony ended, a handful of fans and crew family members visited the pit area. On this Saturday night, at least fifty fans lined up for Chris's autograph. With Chris standing there in his black GM Goodwrench uniform surrounded by excited fans, it was hard not to conjure an image of a certain NASCAR legend.

"Is Dale Earnhardt black, Momma?" one youngster wondered.

"Shh," she replied.

Once the crowd thinned out, the exhausted crew pushed the car up the crude wooden planks onto the farm trailer and headed back to the shop, where we had a discussion about dealing with racial flare-ups.

"We're gonna have to watch our backs," said David. "I think some cats are gonna deliberately wreck us down the road. And we better make sure this shop is locked up tight. Chris, you need to get a spotlight over this door."

My father and I told Chris he would have to try his hardest to avoid altercations. As David foreshadowed, the envy and hate of our rivals was likely to grow over the coming weeks—especially if Chris continued to race well—and retaliating could give our detractors just the fodder they needed to expel us from Concord. Thus far, Chris had managed to avoid such conflicts by maintaining that same aloof cool he had shown at Agawam, but tonight's race indicated that even he had a breaking point.

It was almost 1 a.m. when we left the speedway. I had to fight to keep my eyes open on the drive back to the Hilton. Overall, my father and I were relieved with the results of Chris's first race in the Goodwrench 21. Not only did the car—and Chris—come back in one piece, some of the Concord faithful had expressed interest and encouragement once they found out a black driver was behind the Earnhardt No. 3 clone. If Chris continued to have success out on the track, the crowds approaching us after the race would only get bigger.

Within a couple days of returning home to Virginia, Tom Cotter phoned to invite Chris and me to lunch. Cotter and Todd Moore hadn't met Chris yet, and now that word of our Goodwrench car was spreading, they wanted a full update. The four of us met at Chris's Pit Board Grill, another local stock-car hangout; it was the kind of place where team executives lured personnel from rival teams over to their side and competitive secrets leaked. Cotter sized Chris up quickly, asking about his ambitions in stock-car racing and how he anticipated dealing with the impending contentiousness from envious competitors. I told Cotter about the recent altercation in the pits and the crowd of people awaiting Chris's autograph, to which he responded, "You guys are blazing trails. Your team has a lot of courage. You guys are going places; just be patient, don't get frustrated. I know the racial incidents alone can wear you down." Tom then said something I heard him say more than once: "You guys are doing all the right things, but you may only benefit the next African-American team, not yourselves. Pioneers shake the trees and break the barriers down, but get ostracized for making change. The next guy walks in clean after everyone has learned the lesson you taught." While I wasn't sure any black driver or team would be entering NASCAR cleanly anytime soon, I did understand the weight of Cotter's message. Sure, there was a real chance that we wouldn't make it to NASCAR as we had hoped. Perhaps the obstacles of the current NASCAR landscape would prove too difficult to overcome in my lifetime, maybe beyond. But I firmly believed that with determination and courage on our side, and a little help from some powerful places, we could change things in the sport *now*.

"I think we'll make it," Chris said in the parking lot after lunch. "I think we'll make it."

A few weeks later, Chris was invited to be a guest on a call-in radio show on WLXN AM 1450 in Lexington. Just before they went on the air, the host told Chris he wanted to downplay Chris's skin color and Miller Racing. "I won't tell the listeners that you're African-American," said the host. "I'll just tell them you're from Massachusetts." Chris agreed. The interviewer posed run-of-the-mill questions: "How do you set your car up? How did you get a sponsor like Goodwrench? How much does it cost to race at Concord?" Goodwrench was mentioned nearly forty times on the show, Sunoco Race Fuels was mentioned ten times. Miller Racing, zero.

The incident ruined a golden PR opportunity for Miller Racing, and Chris's compliance with the interviewer posed a problem. Chris was now the face of our effort, and if we were going to promote him as the Jackie Robinson of NASCAR, he would need to embrace his skin color with some level of pride. Granted, the interviewer put Chris in an awkward position, but it was yet another instance of Chris all too easily ignoring his own blackness. Just as he had at Agawam, Chris continued to show a naiveté at Concord when folks treated him like an outsider, like the time when Chris was handing out cold drinks to random passersby in the pits. Walking out of the restroom, my father heard one passerby say to another, "That nigger thinks we like him," before tossing the unopened can in the trash. When my father told Chris about the episode, he replied, sheepishly, "Well, they usually stop by and talk to me about the No. 21." When my father probed Chris a little more about how well he knew the two guys, Chris admitted that he didn't even know their names and that they had stopped by to talk about the car only once. Such an instinct to placate those who wanted to keep Miller Racing on the margins of NASCAR—especially at this critical stage, when we were gaining some momentum toward both sponsorship and media coverage—was a concern, as it told our doubters Chris was vulnerable. On the track, Chris was performing extremely well, consistently placing in the top five throughout the month of June. But off the track, Chris's conciliatory actions showed his vulnerability.

The racing season was reaching its midway point, and my

father and I were flat broke. I made another round of calls to Dave Fortunato and Frank Gaughen to no avail. My father called Deep Throat, who was livid when he found out my father and I had been waiting nearly six months for our check. "Len, I've been here for decades, and GM doesn't do business this way," he said to my father. He was going to make some calls to GM insiders to find out what he could. Meanwhile, I made a follow-up call to Hubert Humphrey at First Union Bank.

"Sorry, man," he said. "I talked to Lenny Springs a few days ago. It looks like your project has come to a complete stop. Lenny is focusing all his time on his campaign to run for national president of the NAACP. I'll have to find another avenue at the bank to make things happen for Miller Racing. Let me know the next time you guys are in town." I felt sick.

Three days later I received a call from Bill Brooks, Vice President of Community Relations for GM. Brooks, one of the most distinguished African-Americans at GM, said he would talk to Bill Lovejoy, general manager of GMSPO, and tell him we needed the $25,000 as soon as possible. Half an hour later I received a call from Rodney O'Neil, Lovejoy's number two. O'Neil, who was African-American, ran GMSPO's warehousing network. He promised to rectify the situation and asked me to come to his house in the suburbs of Detroit the next evening.

I almost shredded the skin on my knuckles knocking on Rodney O'Neil's mahogany double front doors before noticing the intercom system. "Who is it?" a man's voice asked. I identified myself. "Hold on, man," the voice replied. I waited on the front porch for several minutes, in awe of the GM exec's large, rustic home. It was just like the majestic ones we had driven past on the way to the Lions game with Deep Throat and Silent Sam. One half of the towering double doors opened, and O'Neil invited me in. He led me through the tall hallways of his home without saying a word. When we got to the kitchen, he finally spoke.

"You have five minutes. I'm on the way out to dinner with my family."

He whipped out a leather-bound Franklin Planner and a Mont Blanc pen to take notes. I zipped through the story of our offer from Frank Gaughen, the meeting with Dave Fortunato, and the ongoing waiting game. O'Neil told me he would get the $25,000 in motion for us. Like Deep Throat, he wanted to keep his and Bill Lovejoy's involvement in the process a secret. As he walked me back to the front door, he told me he hated stock-car racing and would be more interested in us if we were into golf, like him. He was occasionally forced to attend stock-car events for corporate reasons. At the doorstep, he smashed his index finger into my chest repeatedly, saying, "You'll be a hero messing around with those stock-car boys. But just remember, most heroes are dead!"

The check finally arrived in July. We used the $25,000 to pay off most of our debts and purchase crucial parts for the car. The money was gone in five days.

Now, we had to figure out how we were going to make it through the rest of the season.

"Wendell! Wendell! Wendell!"

There was an air of change in NASCAR during the summer of '95. Just shy of his twenty-fourth birthday, Jeff Gordon took first place in the Cup standings after his win at the Slick 50 300 in New Hampshire. Gordon would hold on to the top spot for the remaining fifteen races of the season, edging out legend Dale Earnhardt by thirty-four points for his first Cup championship. With Gordon's star on the rise and Earnhardt well into his forties, just hitting the downward slope of his career, NASCAR and its corporate cohorts saw an opportunity to expand the sport's audience. Earlier in the year, track impresario and founder of Speedway Motorsports, Inc. Bruton Smith got the go-ahead from NASCAR president Bill France Jr. to build a $75-million super-speedway in the Dallas-Fort Worth area that would hold nearly 160,000 spectators. It was the first in a string of new speedways that would pop up in other major markets like Southern California, Las Vegas, and Kansas City. These new mega-venues would be state-of-the-art facilities that catered to families and a more upscale clientele. They would have more women's restrooms, more concession areas, more parking, and more luxury boxes. With expansion at the forefront of NASCAR's business agenda, I thought our opportunity to cash in was right around the corner.

Despite our financial straitjacket, my father and I started looking ahead to the '96 season and beyond. That way, if an adequate sponsorship did materialize we wouldn't miss a beat. First, we looked into building our own self-standing racing facility. The racing industry was growing rapidly in and around Charlotte, and the top race-shop constructors had one-year waiting lists. Tom Cotter recommended we contact Tim Hepler of Hepler Building in Statesville, who quoted me $75,000 for a basic 50-by-100-foot structure. It would cost another $75,000 to endow the facility with all of the necessary race-shop equipment and machinery. Plus, the plot of land would run us another $150,000. Second, we set our sights on entering Chris in the NASCAR Slim Jim All Pro Series, a semi-pro tour that made stops across the Southeast, including a handful of Busch Grand National races. These goals brought our ideal budget for the forthcoming couple of years to about a half million dollars.

Since NASCAR sponsorship budgets were usually determined by late summer or early autumn, I called Dave Fortunato to broach the subject of another GMSPO deal for the '96 season. We set up a meeting with Frank Gaughen to discuss plans for the upcoming year.

At the GMSPO reception area, the African-American receptionist named Betty gave me a warm smile. By now she recognized my name and face, and decided to make small talk.

"Are you a GM supplier?" she asked?

"In a way," I replied. "My father and I are pushing an African-American NASCAR effort. GM Goodwrench Service Plus is on our Late Model Stock car."

"It's about time!" she exclaimed, her eyes tearing with joy. "There are a lot of African-American GM employees, including myself, that would go to the stock-car races if an African-American driver were behind the wheel. Most of us are not interested in watching a bunch of rednecks race cars. Do you know Rodney O'Neil? Have you met Bill Lovejoy yet?" I didn't have the heart to tell her about my dealing with Rodney O'Neil, but I asked for her home number and address so I could keep her posted on the team.

Fortunato started the meeting without Frank Gaughen. He told me he had already placed our parts order and that it was set to be delivered to Ron Whitney. Then, he pulled a white envelope out of a desk drawer.

"Do you know a Dr. Anderson from Asheville, North Carolina?" he asked.

He was the eye doctor my father and I had met the previous year. I told Fortunato we had met with him and that he was only interested in driving.

"Listen to this letter he sent me," said Fortunato. "I don't know how he got my name. I've never heard of the guy."

Dr. Anderson's letter outlined how he could do a better job reaching African-Americans through motorsports than Miller Racing. He asked GMSPO to drop us and continue with him. Fortunato crumpled up the letter and chucked it in the trash, saying, "We're doing this deal with you guys for a reason. That guy has a lot of nerve."

He sure did. My father and I had approached Dr. Anderson with the idea of forging an alliance. One year later, he was trying to undercut the sponsorship we had worked so hard to get. Dr. Anderson's ploy spoke to the rarity of our opportunity. He was smart enough to know that a GM sponsorship for a minority team was truly once in a lifetime, but he was also conniving enough to try and steal it. His tack was sad and selfish, and fostered divisiveness within the community of African-American race teams. It wasn't the last time we would experience such a me-first attitude.

Fortunato switched the conversation to ask us about our progress down South. I told him Chris was in the top five in the standings at Concord and had a great chance to win Rookie of the Year. I explained to Fortunato that we could have been farther down in the standings. On a couple of occasions, biased officials docked our team points for tapping a slower competitor's rear bumper, a common occurrence that hardly ever drew a penalty from officials. Yvonne Furr secretly added the points back, though.

I also recalled a recent escapade down at the Anderson Speedway in South Carolina. Despite the top five finishes, Chris had not yet picked up a victory at Concord, which frustrated David Miller, who felt Concord's tricky tri-oval was keeping the team out of the winner's circle. Many teams never mastered it, I told Fortunato. David suggested we try racing down at Anderson Speedway, which had a true oval-shaped course, during an off night at Concord.

"Let's go for it," agreed Chris, who requested that Nick Smith make the trip since he knew how to set up the chassis in accordance with Anderson's specifications. I agreed and left David in charge since my father and I wouldn't be able to make it.

According to David, during qualifying, fans cheered on the GM Goodwrench No. 21 loudly, most likely because it reminded them of Earnhardt's car. No one at Anderson Speedway had ever heard of Chris Woods, and the 3,000-plus crowd had no idea an African-American was driving the replica of the Goodwrench Service Plus No. 3. When the green flag fell, Chris settled into second place behind the leader. There were a couple of wrecks near the halfway mark. The field was tight. After a ten-lap caution, the green flag dropped again. Chris took the lead, and the crowd went crazy. The car behind Chris was banging his rear bumper, trying to rattle him, but Chris hung on for about ten more laps. Finally, the car behind got the best of Chris, spinning him around into a collision. The No. 21 was done for the night.

With the tow truck lights flashing, Chris hopped out of the car and removed his helmet. At first, the crowd cheered. Then people started to yell, "Hey, it's Wendell Scott." Chants started: "Wendell! Wendell! Wendell!" As Chris walked to the pits, the tow truck pulling the No. 21 toward the team's plot, other crews looked on with smirks on their faces. When the race finished, dozens of fans from the grandstands traversed the track and stampeded toward the crew chanting, "Wendell! Wendell!"

"Holy shit! We're dead!" cried Kenny Barnes. "Grab some wrenches out of the toolbox. They're going to kill us."

Bearded, potbellied men in leather jackets, railroad hats, and rebel flag T-shirts drew close to the crew. David held out a ball-peen hammer for protection. Chris stood beside the truck with his hand on a jack stand. The chants grew louder: "Wendell! Wendell!"

When the mob reached the Monte Carlo, a large biker-type gentleman asked Chris, affably, "Where ya' from, Wendell?" These fans weren't looking for trouble. They simply wanted to know more about Chris, as they hadn't seen or heard of a black stock-car driver since the days of Wendell Scott. The fans stood in line to shake Chris's hand and asked when he would be coming back to Anderson.

Fortunato shook his head and asked, "Do you guys feel comfortable down there?"

I said comfort had no bearing on what we were trying to accomplish. We knew what we were up against, and we just had to try our best to deal with the challenges.

Fortunato stood up and said, "Let's take a walk."

He led me out to the atrium, across the glass skywalk, and down an escalator into a carpeted showroom that had about eight new GM models. Behind the display vehicles were half a dozen large photographs of GM's top brass hanging on the walls.

Fortunato pointed out the only African-American face. "See that guy?" he said. "His name is Bill Brooks, VP of Community Relations. I'm going to try to get him involved with this deal."

Back in Fortunato's office, Frank Gaughen was waiting for us. I started right into our plans for a race shop, the Slim Jim All Pro Series, and the Busch Grand National races. I told him we would need a half-million dollars over the next two years to achieve our goals. I also talked about the team's greater plan of entering Chris into NASCAR's top-level Winston Cup series, which I estimated as a $7 million investment over a five-year period. Gaughen's face looked serious, and he excused himself briefly to get a notepad. When he returned he told me they had too many race teams on the books and that budgets were airtight. He could give us another $25,000 for 1996. Fortunato jumped in and said, "It doesn't matter what series you race in. You can race where you want." One engine costs that much, I thought to myself. We needed at least $150,000 to survive at Concord for an entire season. I explained that crash repairs alone had tallied over $15,000, and we were only halfway through the season. (The gravedigger's son, Jody Starnes, initiated many of the wrecks. He didn't take too kindly to the GM Goodwrench–certified car. The conflict between Chris and Jody got so heated that Henry Furr stepped in to mediate.)

After a long minute of silence, Gaughen said, "If we review this 1996 proposal, it will have to go all the way to the top for the big brass to evaluate. It's likely the proposal will get shot down by my boss, Ken Robinson, director of promotions." I talked more about the marketing opportunities for GMSPO and the excitement we had already stirred in only a few months. Gaughen appeared to be taking notes, though the tip of his pencil was barely touching the paper.

"We'll give you some parts, too," said Fortunato.

"Unlimited parts," added Gaughen. "How about that!"

I smiled, but underneath I was frustrated. Even if we ordered a tractor-trailer load of parts we still needed money for all other aspects of our effort. Plus, racing technology changed frequently, which meant a parts inventory could become obsolete in a matter of months.

"Let's talk about this again next month," said Gaughen, excusing himself.

Fortunato pulled out a receipt and said, "I have to pay this $17,000 fuel bill."

"What fuel bill?" I asked.

Fortunato explained that Dale Earnhardt and his team owner Richard Childress had flown one of Childress's private jets from Charlotte to Alaska for an autograph session at a Chevrolet dealership. GMSPO agreed to pick up the tab for jet fuel.

Before leaving, Fortunato gave me VIP credentials for the upcoming GM Goodwrench Dealer 400 Cup series race at Michigan International Speedway. It would be an opportunity to meet Bill Lovejoy and some of the other GM bigwigs in person.

Michigan International Speedway was little more than an hour's drive from the Detroit metro area. On race day, traffic was backed up for miles on the country roads off I-94. At the GMSPO suite, Dave Fortunato was perched on the roof wearing a headset, listening to Dale Earnhardt's crew prepare for the race. Inside, after helping myself to the buffet, I noticed Bill Lovejoy across the room. I had seen pictures of him in *Automotive News* and in a GMSPO publication, and his height made him stick out from the crowd. Lovejoy shook my hand and introduced me to his wife. I whipped out one of our new Miller Racing autograph cards. One side of the card had Chris's signature scrawled atop a photo of him next to the car, the other a team photo and profile. Lovejoy scanned the autograph card and then asked me how old Chris was.

"Twenty-nine," I said.

"How are you doing on the track?" he asked.

I told him we were in the top five in points.

"That's good. Keep me posted," he replied.

As Lovejoy walked away, I noticed half a dozen African-Americans standing in the corner. They were whispering among themselves and peering at me. They were the only African-Americans I had seen at the track so far. Before I got a chance to approach them and introduce myself, David Allen of Champion Sports Group hopped in front of me to say hello. He had noticed that I'd handed Bill Lovejoy an autograph card and wanted to see one for himself. He analyzed the quality of the photo work, offered some constructive criticism, and handed the card back to me before leaving the suite.

The black huddle was now over by the buffet table, still whispering to one another and looking in my direction. Finally, one gentleman broke away from the huddle and walked through the sea of white folks chowing down on Buffalo wings to say hello. His name was Mike Lewis. When I told him I had launched a stock-car effort in Concord, he grew ecstatic. The other curious souls started making their way over to me one by one. Before I knew it, I was in the middle of the huddle answering questions about Miller Racing. The autograph card flew around the huddle. Lewis and his associates were all GMSPO employees, and they couldn't believe we had sponsorship from their employer. One of the guys in the group said he wanted to start moonwalking, but decided to hold it back in front of the white folks. Lewis snatched the card back, reviewed the Genuine GM Parts that were listed, and said, "Look, I'm a zone manager. I have all these parts. I'll be glad to give you some parts. Here's my card. Do you play golf?"

I was just starting to play golf, I told him.

"Call me next week," he said.

Juiced from the giddy response of the six black GMSPO employees, I watched the first half of the race on the roof with Fortunato. Not only was I happy to have another inside contact at GM, it was reassuring to see black folks genuinely excited about an African-American racecar team. It was just the kind of reaction I thought could sweep the nation if we ever had a black driver in a NASCAR race.

Earnhardt's car went out early with engine trouble. I shook Fortunato's hand and left the race early so I could beat the traffic on the way home. Between the face time with Bill Lovejoy and the introduction to Mike Lewis, the day was a success.

I called Lewis the following week and left a message. No response. A week passed, I called again. No response. I called him seven weeks in a row and left messages, each time to no avail. I would never see or speak to Mike Lewis or any of the other members of the black huddle again.

Once fall arrived, my father and I started looking for additional sponsorship help. We needed a commitment beyond the $25,000 promised by GMSPO for '96. A friend of ours tipped us off to a small sports conference that was going to be held at the Harvard Club in Manhattan on September 27. We perked up when we heard James Adamson, CEO of the Flagstar Corporation, would be speaking. Flagstar owned Denny's, El Pollo Loco chicken, and Hardee's, a team sponsor for driver Cale Yarborough's No. 28 car in the '80s and a title sponsor for NASCAR races. The Denny's company was still reeling from the 1993 lawsuit in which black customers in California accused the twenty-four-hour eatery of discrimination; Denny's paid out a $45.7 million settlement. While we weren't looking for that kind of money, a Denny's-Miller Racing alliance could help assuage the restaurant chain's lingering PR mess. Plus, other corporations like Nike and Reebok would be hosting workshops on sports marketing. My father and I tried to attend such workshops at least once a year to learn about the latest approaches in proposal writing, sponsorship presentations, and sports law. In the years to come, when we would incorporate lessons learned from such workshops in our presentations to Fortune 500 companies, we would often hear, "Your presentation was one of the best we've seen dealing with motorsports."

My father and I met at the front doors of the Harvard Club. It was a typical Ivy League setting: dim lighting, old wood furnishings, older white men walking around in gray suits. One of the first people my father and I met was Lisa Delpy, a PhD in the sports management department at George Washington University. She listened to our spiel about seeking NASCAR sponsorships and told us she could help us out with her business contacts. Once lunch was served, James Adamson started his keynote address. We savored the seared fish and listened to Adamson speak about Flagstar's corporate agenda. As soon as the speech ended, my father whispered, "Make your move, make your move." Armed with an autograph card, I scrambled across the floor toward Adamson. I shook his hand and got right to the point: We had a stock-car team with a black driver that could help restore sales in Denny's minority markets. He glanced at the autograph card and said, excitedly, "I can do something with this. We just stopped our Hardee's NASCAR sponsorship to cut costs. Here's my card. Call me in the office next week. Can I have this GM Goodwrench card?"

Any hopes for a Flagstar partnership quickly fizzled. When the day arrived to call Adamson, his secretary told me he was in a meeting and she could take a message. Two days passed with no call back. I called again. His secretary took down my name again and said he had received the first message. Another day went by. I called again. This time, the secretary had a message waiting for me.

"Oh, Mr. Adamson wants you to call Ms. Ray Hood-Phillips," she said. "She runs our diversity program at Denny's."

I called Ms. Ray Hood-Phillips, who had already talked to Adamson and had a general sense for what we were seeking with Denny's. Before I could say much, Ms. Hood-Phillips told me that Flagstar Corporation was not into auto racing, and that she didn't have a large enough budget to support a race team. I explained that Miller Racing was not the typical stock-car team and that Denny's stood to benefit from a sponsorship, but she didn't pay me much mind.

"If you can come up with a program that gets black kids off drugs for $5,000, I'll read your proposal."

This was a scenario I would confront multiple times in my journey for financial support, too: getting routed to a company's diversity group. These mini-divisions could only afford to dole out one-time handouts of a few thousand dollars, nowhere near the amount it took to run a NASCAR program. The pass-off to a minority division was an easy way out for a corporate honcho. If the Rainbow/PUSH or the NAACP or the Urban League ever came knocking, he could say he helped out.

Within a week, I met with Frank Gaughen again to see if he had made any progress squeezing more money out of the higher-ups at GM. I didn't expect favorable news, but with October on the horizon we needed to set up our financial backbone for the 1996 season as soon as possible. Otherwise, we would have to consider pulling the plug.

Gaughen was his usual jovial self, but didn't have much to report. "We have your proposal for 1996, and I know we can do at least $25,000," he said. "Things are getting tight around here. Everything in the area of racing is under review."

He then told me the GMSPO advertising staff was interested in doing an ad with Chris Woods in a magazine.

"Which magazine?" I asked.

"*Stock Car Racing*? *Racer*?" He said he would try to find out.

I took the crosswalk from the New Center One Building to the main lobby of the GM Building. Near the elevators I ran into Silent Sam, who was wearing a crisp blue business suit and carrying a briefcase. When he noticed me, he pulled me aside.

"What brings you to the GM building, sir?" he asked.

I told him about my meeting with Frank Gaughen and the $25,000.

"Do you have any allies?" he asked. "Have you talked to Bill Brooks? Roy Roberts?"

"Yes," I said.

"What are they doing for you?"

"Nothing, yet."

"I'll try to help you. I have the Miller Racing autograph card in my desk. I look at it every day."

I frowned at the idea that the card was *in* his desk and not displayed *on* his desk.

As we chatted, a white woman handed him some papers. "I'll see you upstairs in the meeting," she said. Once she walked out of hearing range, Silent Sam told me the woman had been in a GM meeting where a stock-car legend told a group of white GM employees that GM was messing up in racing because there were too many niggers running it. To my knowledge the hateful comment was inaccurate, as I hadn't heard of many black folks holding high-ranking positions in the GM Racing department.

"That's why I don't want to have anything to do with that hillbilly sport," said Silent Sam. "Keep me posted."

He took the next elevator and vanished. I drove back to my apartment with a headache. Before it wore off, Chris called to tell me that a camera crew had shown up at shop No. 10 to take pictures of him posing next to the car. I asked who they were.

"Some outfit called D'Arcy Masius Benton & Bowles, Inc., or DMB & B for short," he said.

They had dressed him up in a satin, baseball-style GM Goodwrench jacket and told him it was for a magazine advertisement. They didn't want him in a driver's uniform, Chris said. One member of the camera crew said, "Ken Robinson loves this deal. He thinks it's funny." I had never heard of Ken Robinson; I later found out he was director of promotions for GMSPO, and Frank Gaughen's boss. After the shoot, two of the gentlemen took Chris to a restaurant and "wined and dined" him. The two men laughed it up the entire dinner, as they apparently could not get over the idea of Chris being billed as an African-American version of Dale Earnhardt.

I called my father, who was as surprised as I was. We never

signed a personal services contract, which typically includes language regarding a team's print advertisements, with GMSPO. Nor had anyone told us about the nature of the ad or its intentions. The next day, I tracked down account manager Michael Byrne at DMB & B and asked about the camera crew. He told me GMSPO was planning to put ads in the African-American magazines *Black Enterprise*, *Ebony*, and *Jet*. GMSPO wanted the ads to look upscale, he said. They had one idea for an ad showing Chris walking down a city street in a tuxedo bearing a GM Goodwrench logo.

"We want to get something in the December issue of *Black Enterprise*," said Byrne.

My father and I were disgusted. We contacted our attorney, Leon Tucker, who drafted a letter to GMSPO demanding that GMPSO cease and desist any ads. It became clear that GMSPO had gone around our backs to portray Chris in an advertisement that did not mention Miller Racing. Ken Robinson seemed to view Chris as a black caricature of Dale Earnhardt, and wanted to play on this motif for an ad in black magazines. Our cease-and-desist letter did not reach the right hands at GMSPO in time. The ad ran in the December 1995 issue of *Black Enterprise*.

To compound our growing discontent, GMSPO failed to acknowledge our on-the-track achievements at Concord. I sent a letter informing GMSPO that Chris finished fourth in overall points in Late Model Stock and that he would be receiving Rookie of the Year honors at the year-end awards banquet in November. I mentioned that our entire team would be in attendance and invited a representative from GMSPO to join in the celebration. No one from GMSPO responded. No commendation letter, no congratulations phone call. The night of the banquet, a local TV reporter asked Chris what fans should expect for 1996, and if GM Goodwrench would be on the car. Chris didn't know what to say. None of us did.

In the search for more sponsorship possibilities Chris suggested we call his friend Rick Raducha. Back during Chris's days in Massachusetts, Rick, who was a paraplegic confined to a wheelchair, used to travel with Chris and the Fullers to races at Riverhead Speedway on Long Island. They would leave the coast of Connecticut by ferry and cross the Long Island Sound with the racecar, equipment, and crew loaded onto the boat. As Chris pushed Rick's wheelchair around the boat, the two discussed racing and ended up forging a bond. Rick was now president of Driver Connection, a small motorsports marketing firm in Connecticut. Chris told me Rick had a few corporate connections in New England.

"Chris is an easy sell," Rick said when I called him and told him we were looking for more avenues toward sponsorship. "He has a personality and driving talent that any sponsor would want." I told Rick about the bigotry at Concord, the rough patch we were hitting with GMSPO, and the dead ends I had experienced with other companies. I thought that he, being a white male, might be taken more seriously than I was.

"Can you give me $1,000 for phone bills, postage, and supplies?" asked Rick. I told him we could get him money in a week. Rick said he would drive his modified van to visit corporations with headquarters in New England, including Subway, Friendly's Ice Cream, and Polaroid. He asked if I had any sponsorship leads outside of GMSPO.

"How about Shell Oil?" I said.

"Do you have a name?"

"Jim Malloy is the motorsports manager. He's African-American. I mailed our entire racing portfolio with Chris's photos, then called him in Texas."

"What did he tell you?"

"'What do you want me to do?' That ended the conversation."

Rick was speechless.

"Remember what I told you," I said.

Rick developed a proposal for Shell Oil anyway, along with sponsorship pitches for several other companies. He sent letters, he made phone calls. Over the course of the next twelve months Rick got turned down so much that he started sounding defeated over the phone. Soon enough, Rick gave up.

As the year drew to a close, my father and I worried that Chris would once again spend the holidays by himself. Thankfully, he had Thanksgiving dinner with Nick and Pam at their trailer park, which was up the road from Concord. Since he had exhausted his vacation days for the year, Chris ended up working at Plaza Ford right up until Christmas. He didn't want to visit my father or me for Christmas since we lived so far away, and he declined Archie Kindle's repeated invitations to social gatherings. Just like the previous year, Chris spent Christmas alone in shop No. 10, working on the No. 21.

The New Year brought mounting frustration with GMSPO. Charlie Reichard, owner of Camcraft in Easton, Maryland, worked closely with R&W. When Ron Whitney told him about Miller Racing, Charlie volunteered to spread word of our effort around his stomping ground. Charlie was one of the best camshaft developers on the East Coast. Charlie talked up our team to many of his clients and colleagues between Washington, DC, and Maryland's eastern shore. Pretty soon, GM dealers in the area were asking him if Miller Racing would be willing to make a promotional appearance with the GM Goodwrench No. 21. One dealership in Easton wanted to introduce Chris to customers and have him sign autographs. We were so broke that we didn't have the money to tow the car from Concord to Maryland and pay for accommodations. We asked the dealership in Easton to write GMSPO a letter requesting a promotional appearance by Miller Racing and the Goodwrench No. 21. The letter was mailed, but no one ever replied. The Miller Motorsports Show, an annual expo held in Fort Washington, Pennsylvania, wanted us to appear. They also wrote a letter to GMSPO. Same result.

To add insult to injury, a long floating rumor about a rule change at Concord became an expensive reality. For the 1996 season, Henry and Yvonne Furr changed the chassis specifications for Late Model Stock. The new requirements conformed more closely to NASCAR regulations. We had two choices: We could either purchase a new Late Model Stock chassis for $25,000, or we could enter Chris in the faster Late Model Sportsman division, which allowed for our current chassis setup. If we did move up to Late Model Sportsman, however, we would need R&W to develop a higher performance engine, which would also cost around $25,000. The season started in March, and since it took a minimum of six weeks to develop either a chassis or engine, we had to act fast. My father and I decided to move the team up to Sportsman. The new Sportsman engine would need to operate at 500 hp, a big step up from our 325-hp Late Model Stock engine. With R&W in our corner, we knew our investment would be sound. Plus, based on his performance the previous season we felt Chris was ready for Concord's premier class. If anything, it was one step closer to the big leagues. Of course, even if GMSPO came through with the $25,000 it would take an additional $125,000 to operate a Sportsman level car at Concord for thirty races between March and November, and we still had debt left over from '95. To save money, we would have to start the season without a backup engine. If that engine exploded, we were finished.

In the meantime, *Late Model Digest*, a popular local newspaper, ran a one-page profile about the team. The article, published in the February 14, 1996 edition, included a close-up photo of Chris Woods and an action shot of the Goodwrench racer. The writer, Mike Payne, talked about the racial epithets spouted about us on the radio scanners and around the pits. It was refreshing that *Late Model Digest* wanted to tell the real story, instead of circumventing the truth, like that interviewer on WLXN AM 1450 in Lexington. We hoped that more media outlets would not only cover our story, but also dig deeper into the history of African-Americans in stock-car racing. Except for the occasional small article like Payne's or Fusco's, or a passing mention on TV or radio of Wendell Scott as a pioneer, the media shied away from delving into the harsh, racist realities of stock-car racing. In the years to come, an increasing number of articles and TV pieces would scratch the surface on the subject, but the full story of hatred, denial, and triumph in spite of impossible obstacles was never told.

I dropped off a few copies of the *Late Model Digest* article to Frank Gaughen. He leafed through the packet with a smile, then put it in a drawer. During the visit I told him Miller Racing needed an agreement with GMSPO that prevented print ads from popping up in magazines without our consent. Sheepishly, Gaughen replied, "Well, our advertising department did the ad. I'm not sure how that is done. I'm just involved with giving you guys the twenty-five!"

To make matters with GMSPO worse, Dave Fortunato transferred to another post, a job that was completely removed from motorsports. He had been the one GMSPO employee who delivered on engine parts orders. Hal Mathews, Fortunato's successor, accepted our ongoing parts orders, but often gave us a story about our requests getting lost in the computer system.

Without necessary parts and sufficient money, we told the team there was a real chance we may not be able to race at the start of the upcoming season, if at all. The state of limbo led to a frustration that spread throughout the team. David Miller would call my father every night to find out if there were any updates from GMSPO.

"Doesn't GM Goodwrench know what they have here?" he would say.

It was time to talk to a decision-maker. I called Frank Gaughen's boss, Ken Robinson, to set up a meeting.

Ken Robinson had a corner office on the same floor as Frank Gaughen in the New Center One Building. The day of my meeting with Robinson, I got there a half-hour early. The pleasant African-American receptionist named Betty greeted me and whispered, "Are you making progress? I can't wait until you guys make it!"

I took a seat and scanned the smorgasbord of GM's internal magazines on the table. In the back of my mind, I knew the meeting with Ken Robinson might get heated. The day before, Frank Gaughen had called me from the airport in LA, distraught that I had a meeting with his boss. He wanted to know why I was going over his head. I told him I wanted to confront Robinson about the *Black Enterprise* ad and GMSPO's long-term plans for Miller Racing. "Okay, okay," he muttered.

Ken Robinson was a clean-cut white man with round eyeglasses and a confident air about him. He shook my hand in the reception area and said, "I'm glad you came early! Follow me to my office." We sat down at a round table, where he dumped a stack of papers. It didn't take me long to notice our five-year, $7-million Winston Cup proposal on top of the pile. The stack of papers amounted to all of the correspondence that Miller Racing had sent to GMSPO over the past year.

Robinson leaned back in his chair with his arms crossed. I started the conversation by asking him why GMSPO proceeded with the *Black Enterprise* ad without drawing up a personal services contract for us.

"We don't have any contracts with our race teams," he responded.

"You don't have one with Dale Earnhardt?"

He backtracked, confessing that GMSPO had an agreement with Earnhardt and Richard Childress Racing, adding defensively, "I thought the ad would help you guys."

The ad made Chris look more like a baseball player than a racecar driver, I told him, and any young black man could have posed for it. Plus, there was no mention of Miller Racing or the No. 21.

You could almost see the steam blowing out of the arrogant white man's ears, his arms now resting on the stack of papers. I proceeded to ask the $7-million question: What specific, long-term objectives did GMSPO have for Miller Racing?

He pointed his finger at the stack of papers and said, "You guys submitted a five-year, multi-million-dollar plan. We just want to help you. We're not sponsoring you up through the ranks of NASCAR."

"We submitted a five-year business plan, not a mandate," I told him calmly. "It illustrates where Miller Racing is going."

I started to talk with a little more urgency. "We have the GM Goodwrench Service Plus logo all over the racecar, but the $25,000 you're now giving us covers only a fraction of our costs. The money arrives months late, and some parts we order never show up. Meanwhile, the 'N' word is being shouted at us on scanners and in our faces. We need to be taken seriously."

Robinson made it clear that he didn't have any more money to offer Miller Racing. Still, he wanted GM Goodwrench Service's logo on the entire car for $25,000.

"If GM Goodwrench is on the entire car," I responded, "we don't have any space to allow for additional sponsors."

"I want the entire car for $25,000," he said.

"I think we have a major problem here," I said. "What do you suggest we do?"

I was not going to take the $25,000. I was prepared to walk and look for another sponsor or temporarily close our doors on the season.

Pauses started to grow between our exchanges, and we talked in circles. I said that placing the ad in *Black Enterprise* magazine was exploitation.

"I don't want to exploit him," Robinson replied. "I'll pull the ads." Then he asked if I had talked to anyone at Chevrolet.

"I have not had the opportunity to talk to John Middlebrook, General Manager of Chevrolet," I answered.

"Why do you always want to shoot for the top?" he asked. Because, I replied, that's where all key decisions are made.

Then Robinson asked, "Do you know Roy Roberts, who runs GMC Truck? He's an African-American."

I knew Roy Roberts, but I guessed that he wasn't going to be an internal asset for us. He had recently won a discrimination battle against Bloomfield Hills Country Club in order to gain membership. Most of GM's white executives, including CEO Jack Smith, had resigned from the club until Roberts was accepted. While I was happy with the outcome, I imagined that Roberts would not want to rattle any more cages with the higher-ups at GM.

By now, Robinson was standing by his telephone with his back turned to me, wondering aloud how he could find more sponsorship dollars for Miller Racing. "I can't promise you anything, but I'm going to call Duane Miller of ACDelco sales to see what he can do." While we waited for Duane Miller to stop by the office, Robinson lectured me on the ACDelco brand. He told me it was a "do-it-yourselfers" brand, and that most of ACDelco's parts and spark plugs were purchased by people who work on their own cars with their own tools. He said African-Americans didn't fit this category. I told him that he was wrong, that parts stores in urban areas drew plenty of "do-it-yourselfer" African-Americans, guys who would line up at the door before a store's opening just to get the parts they needed. In fact, many African-Americans in lower-income areas worked on their cars out of economic necessity, I told him. I had witnessed such scenes at Pep Boys and other retailers in Philadelphia, Trenton, and South Central LA.

"I disagree," said Robinson. "Do you know Mike Lewis?" he added abruptly.

"Yes," I said. "I met him at the GM Goodwrench race at Michigan International Speedway." There was that assumption again: All black people know each other.

"Well, Mike says that where he comes from, blacks drive Cadillacs and get service; they don't work on their own cars."

I thought of the motivational speaker "Spark Plug Head," who was sponsored by ACDelco. The character, portrayed by African-American Anthony B. Thomas, visited urban, predominantly minority, schools to talk to kids about discipline and hard work. Spark Plug Head had a pockmarked face and popped around on his feet mimicking a spark plug, all the while wearing an ACDelco shirt. Someone at ACDelco must have thought these young African-Americans might grow up to be "do-it-yourselfers."

Duane Miller arrived. He was tall and spoke like a straight shooter. Robinson gave him a synopsis of Miller Racing and the financial conundrum in front of us.

"How much do you need?" asked Miller.

"Two hundred fifty thousand," I said.

"Can I get some advertising on the West Coast?"

"Sure."

"I can get the $250,000," he said before making his way out of Robinson's office. "Give me a few days."

"Don't get your hopes up," said Robinson. "Duane talks a good game, but I don't know if he can get that much."

Robinson walked over to his door and yelled, "Come in here, Frank!" Frank Gaughen walked in with a white notepad and a beet-red face. The meeting had lasted ninety minutes so far. Robinson filled in Gaughen on what Duane Miller at ACDelco was trying to do for us. Gaughen listened and took notes.

After a while, Duane Miller burst back in and said, "I can do $75,000, that's all."

Robinson told Gaughen to work with us and to get the

ACDelco sales people in Charlotte involved with the team. He shook my hand and said, "I hope this helps."

"We're doing a little better," I said. Whew, I thought. Even with an additional $75,000 I knew the new Sportsman engine and higher operating costs were going to keep us in the red through 1996. Still, the higher financial commitment gave me hope that our standing with GM would continue to improve over time.

The season started in two weeks, and we weren't even close to being ready. Chris was cautiously optimistic about our move to Sportsman. When he found out about the ACDelco brand taking over as our main sponsor he asked, "What type of red, white, and blue scheme should we paint the car?" Without time to wait for an official word from GMSPO, we mimicked the paint scheme of NASCAR driver Kenny Schrader's ACDelco Craftsman Truck, which we found on his autograph card. In the wee hours of the night, Chris towed the Monte Carlo to Plaza Ford and secretly used the painting facility to convert the No. 21 from its intimidating black-red design to a cheerful red, white, and blue. I called Champion Sports Group to have them prepare a batch of new ACDelco uniforms and accessories. Of course, David Allen's team knew nothing about us changing over to ACDelco and had to call Frank Gaughen to confirm the order. Meanwhile, in southeastern Pennsylvania, R&W was finishing up our explosive 500-hp Sportsman engine.

While we awaited the check for $75,000 my father and I maxed out credit cards and tapped into personal savings. To date, our collective investment had exceeded $350,000. We still had debt from 1995, and we were two months behind on the rent at Concord. Thankfully, the Furrs worked with us on the back rent, and Ron and his son sold old parts and tools that were lying around their shop to help front the cost of the engine. GMSPO was not delivering performance parts that Ron and his son had ordered. I called Hal Mathews to try and expedite the process, but he sounded dumbfounded as to why the parts weren't arriving. While I had him on the phone, I told Mathews we needed any ACDelco paraphernalia we could get our hands on while we waited on Champion. Mathews said he would ship us shirts and hats from the GMSPO office in Detroit. We opened the package to find out that all the shirts were long-sleeved and made of thick wool. There was no way we could wear them in the hot Carolina summer. I guessed the shirts were from past seasons, and that GMSPO might have thrown them out had they not been sent to us.

The first race came and went, and we were still on the sidelines piecing together the No. 21. Since this was our first year in the Sportsman division, we had a chance to win Rookie of the Year again, but missing races would set us back in the standings. The new engine arrived two days before the second race, which wasn't enough time to get the car fully prepared. The night we finally did roll out the patriotic-looking Monte Carlo, we got the same stares in the pits. The same cast of characters milled about the speedway: Big Bird, Big Ed, the wooden soldier, Nick and Pam Smith, the freeloaders. Hollywood cruised the pits for women while his crew worked on his strip club–sponsored car that had "Leather and Lace" written on the rear quarter panels. Chris showed up to our plot in his new red, white, and blue driver's suit, which finally came from Champion. You could see the splashy get-up from a mile away. Earlier, when No. 21 was raised back at the shop, I noticed a volunteer crew member had written in gold paint beneath the chassis: "Dear Lord, please get Chris out of this car safely if he turns upside down." While I snickered, the Sportsman cars were no joke. If Chris made even a slight mistake on the tricky tri-oval, the thick concrete walls would swallow him and the car alive. A. J. Sanders, who also made the move up to Sportsman, drove so aggressively that he would find himself on an ambulance stretcher at least once a month. His car often ended up in pieces.

The premier Sportsman class raced last, usually starting around 10 p.m. Chris started tenth out of twenty-nine cars. When the green flag dropped, the ground rumbled, and the collective scream of the Sportsman engines virtually drowned out the track announcer's play-by-play. Chris was tapped from behind early, and the car suffered enough right front damage that we had to call it a night. Big Ed towed the No. 21 out through the tunnel and into the shop. Even though it was a short night the first time out, the crew was still in high spirits. We had competed in a Sportsman race, the highest level of competition at Concord. The damage amounted to $1,000.

As we packed up, Ron Whitney Jr., who was in attendance for the big night, noticed that the gray door leading to Nick's shop was open. He peeked inside and raced back, red-faced and smirking. "Hollywood's fucking one of the female infield regulars on the floor behind Lamar Long's Chevy Camaro!" he cried.

"You're joking," said Kenny Barnes, who poked his head in and screamed, "Hey, hey!" with a laugh. The couple quickly put their clothes on and disappeared out the other end of the shop.

10

Shot Callers

Since NASCAR's inception, the France family has run its stock-car empire with a my-way-or-the-highway attitude. The founding owner of NASCAR, Bill France Sr., set that precedent early on. Following World War II, the stock-car scene picked up steam at small tracks across the Southeast. France Sr., then an auto mechanic in Daytona Beach, took in local races and eventually started promoting events. As the crowds grew bigger, he saw dollar signs. France Sr. pulled together drivers, promoters, and local businessmen to form the National Association for Stock Car Auto Racing in 1948. For NASCAR's first order of business, France Sr. made a point of cleaning up the sport, which to date did not have clear-cut rules about competition and still reeked of bootlegging, irreverence, and shoddy venues. He drafted and enforced a steadfast set of bylaws that covered car specifications, behavior in the track and in the pits, and everything in between. France Sr. let it be known that he could change the rules wherever and whenever he saw fit. This meant not only that drivers and teams had to conform to stringent regulations regarding car types and modifications, but automakers had to follow suit any time a significant change in body type or parts restrictions came down from above. When drivers tried to unionize in the '50s in order to fight for higher payouts in the winner's circle, France Sr. quickly quashed the collusion by forcing drivers to sign a form releasing them from the union. If they didn't want to sign, France Sr. would show them the door. In 1957, France Sr. secured a plot of land in his hometown where he would construct his grand racing edifice, the Daytona International Speedway. Two years later, Lee Petty won the first running of the Daytona 500 at France Sr.'s 2.5-mile, high-banked, fan-friendly megatrack. In 1968, France Sr.'s International Speedway Corporation (ISC) broke ground a little more than 50 miles east of Birmingham, Alabama, to resurrect Talladega Superspeedway. Over the next four decades, ISC would either build or acquire controlling interest in the following tracks: Darlington Raceway, Watkins Glen International, Phoenix International Raceway, California Speedway (later renamed Auto Club Speedway), Michigan International Speedway, Richmond International Raceway, Kansas Speedway, Chicagoland Speedway, Homestead-Miami Speedway, Martinsville Speedway, and, for a brief period of time, Rockingham Speedway. With simultaneous control over the schedule, France Sr. dictated where and when major races took place.

One of France Sr.'s last major moves before passing the NASCAR reins over to his son, Bill France Jr., in 1972 was signing R.J. Reynolds Tobacco Company's Winston brand as the title sponsor of the Cup series. The partnership, which lasted just over three decades, helped bring hundreds of millions of dollars into the sport and opened up the floodgates for team and race-title sponsorships. When TV broadcast rights became a sought-after commodity in the '90s, France Jr. took a nod from the other major American sports and helped broker a deal that packaged the rights for two major networks, Fox and NBC, and netted NASCAR a reported $400 million annually. In short, the Frances had a firm grip on the infrastructure of the sport they owned. Any road toward success in NASCAR would need to go through the all-powerful family.

Back in February, I had placed a cold call to France Jr. I wanted to talk to the NASCAR president about our own ambitions and how we could help NASCAR broaden its fan base. His secretary took a message. After I hung up, I stepped out to get a bite to eat.

When I returned home, France Jr. had already called me back and left a voicemail. The next time I phoned France Jr. his secretary patched me through. I introduced myself and launched right into the plight of Miller Racing. I explained our goal of making it to the Cup series within five years and the difficulties I was having fighting through corporate bureaucracy for adequate sponsorship.

"You guys need engines and tires, too!" France Jr. replied jubilantly. "I want to talk more about this. Give me a call after the Daytona 500. I'm looking forward to meeting with you."

Three weeks later, my father and I flew down to Florida to meet with France Jr. We passed palm trees and malls along Route 92 before reaching the NASCAR headquarters in Daytona Beach. The building had a quaint, tropical flare, with plantation shutters on the windows. Before we met France Jr., my father suggested I pick up a NASCAR Slim Jim All Pro Series rulebook while we were in the building. That way, Ron Whitney and his son could start studying up on engine specifications. A receptionist pointed me to the office of Jerry Cook, who headed the All Pro Series. My father went straight to France Jr.'s office.

"You normally have to pay for the rulebooks and provide an All Pro license," he said to me. "But since you're standing in my office, I'll give it to you." Before I could step out of his office, Cook's phone rang. The voice on the other end gave orders for me to go to France Jr.'s office immediately.

France Jr. was sitting at the head of his desk, a long, glass-topped structure that looked like a fancy dining-room table. One end of the desk held a stack of papers almost a foot high. France Jr. was smoking a cigarette and was already engaged in a conversation with my father. I introduced myself and handed France Jr. a packet with a Miller Racing autograph card, the *Late Model Digest* article, our résumés, and other team materials. France Jr. suggested that a NASCAR representative accompany my father and me when we visited potential sponsors. Then, he walked over to a dark wooden entertainment center and inserted a VHS tape. The promotional video highlighted NASCAR's marketing value, its fan loyalty, its adrenaline-fueled action, and its growth. When it was over, France Jr. handed me the tape, telling us to take it with us for our meetings with potential sponsors. He shook our hands, told us NASCAR's doors were open to everyone, and sent us off to Doug Fritz, a marketing manager in a different building a few miles down the road. When we saw Fritz, he was equally encouraging and offered to visit corporations with us.

The next NASCAR power broker we approached was Humpy Wheeler. The long-time track promoter was now chief operating officer and president of Bruton Smith's Speedway Motorsports, Inc (SMI). SMI owned and operated Charlotte Motor Speedway, where Wheeler held the title of president and general manager. I had met briefly with Wheeler, Tom Cotter, and Todd Moore a few months back to discuss how we could improve the miniscule numbers of African-Americans who attended races at Charlotte Motor Speedway. Cotter and Moore also broke down the tough time they were having marketing our plan. A major oil company's motorsports representative told Moore, for example, "Look at the grandstands, Todd. Do you see any blacks? Why would we sponsor a black stock-car team?" I asked Wheeler if he could help set up a practice run for Chris at the speedway. In anticipation of any movement up the NASCAR ranks, I wanted Chris to start acclimating himself with a longer course. Wheeler was open to the idea, but said that he wanted to meet Chris in person. He also suggested that Chris read *Muhammad Ali* by Thomas Hauser. Wheeler, a fan of boxing, wanted Chris to understand Ali's long, hard journey toward becoming a champion.

Wheeler's office was located on the seventh floor of Charlotte Motor Speedway. Chris, my father, and I showed up for our meeting with Wheeler about twenty minutes early, so we killed a little time in the gift shop. My father rummaged through the die-cast model cars to see if Wendell Scott's No. 34 car was still being sold. He couldn't find it. As we browsed, an African-American couple entered the shop. After innocently staring at us for a few minutes, the couple introduced themselves. They were from West Virginia and had stopped by Charlotte on their way home from a church retreat in South Carolina. The husband told us that a white co-worker in the plant where he worked had been boasting about NASCAR and suggested that he and his wife visit the speedway.

"What do you guys do around here?" the husband asked.

My father told them Chris was a driver at Concord.

"Lord, Lord, Lord!" said the husband. His wife's eyes glistened. "Look, brothers, I'm a part-time preacher, and I want to say a prayer for y'all," he said. I looked at my watch; we were due in Wheeler's office in five minutes.

"Let's step outside the gift shop, brothers, and form a circle."

I looked at my watch again, nervous that we might be late for the meeting. Given where we stood with our effort, though, how could I turn down a little divine intervention?

The five of us gathered in a circle and held hands.

"Dear Heavenly Father, please watch over Chris when he is going fast out here at this dangerous track."

The circle started to rock back and forth. The preacher's voice grew louder. I opened one eye to look at a passerby in the lobby and caught my father sneaking a peek. We were going to be late for the meeting. We both kind of shrugged, as we didn't want to ruin the moment. We just swayed along to the invocation of the Holy Spirit. When the husband ended the prayer, he asked Chris how fast folks raced at the speedway.

"190 miles per hour."

"Lord! Lord! Lord!" the husband belted out, shaking his head from side to side.

He and his wife wished us luck and walked out. We darted to

the elevator and headed up to the seventh floor. By the time we introduced ourselves to Wheeler's secretary, we were five minutes late.

Wheeler's office at the speedway made the best offices at General Motors look shabby. Tall, wooden doors opened into plush quarters that featured leather chairs and couches, high-priced art on the walls, and giant windows overlooking the speedway. We reiterated our problems getting sponsorships and told Wheeler about Chris's progress at Concord. Wheeler suggested we invest in a Legends car, a smaller racer designed for amateurs. The Legends car stemmed from an idea Wheeler and his colleagues at Charlotte Motor Speedway had for making auto racing more affordable and accessible to fans who had aspirations of driving. Legends cars typically ran on an engine with 125–150 hp and were outfitted with hip, retro-inspired bodies. Wheeler and company had started a series for Legends cars and other junior racers at Charlotte Motor Speedway called Summer Shootout. He thought Summer Shootout was the best way for Chris to get in track time at Charlotte. Wheeler's suggestion did not make much sense for us, as Chris was too experienced for the recreational series. Chris certainly could have garnered some attention by winning races at Charlotte, but we wanted to devote all of our resources to getting Chris closer to NASCAR. Plus, Wheeler had a vested interest in pulling in more fans for lower profile races. In the end, Wheeler did not provide much assistance in getting us closer to our ultimate goal of the Winston Cup.

The $75,000 ACDelco check arrived ten races into the season. My father and I used some of the money to pay a portion of our $100,000 of debt and poured the rest into the operation at Concord. The money dried up quickly, as Chris was involved in a handful of significant wrecks. On some occasions, the car was so mangled the team could barely get it up the wooden planks and onto the trailer. Under David Miller's leadership in the shop, the crew figured out creative ways to keep the No. 21 on the track. My father and I would sit with David and figure out which new parts we absolutely needed, which bills we needed to pay immediately, and what areas we could temporarily afford to let slide. Despite the aerodynamic nightmare of racing with a damaged front fender, bumper, or hood, Chris managed to consistently place in the top ten of the thirty-car Sportsman fields. With Chris faring so well under such adverse conditions, some of the good ol' boys started to warm up to him and the rest of the team. The season wasn't without some incidence of prejudice, though.

Sunoco Race Fuels continued to supply our fuel, which saved us at least $5,000 for the season. One day, when the team was running low, Jeff Fuller told Chris to visit the Sunoco Busch shop off Route 29 to get gas and several cases of oil. Chris went on a Sunday, when no one was around. He parked his truck and knocked on the steel door. No one answered, so Chris decided to go back home. As he walked back to his car, he noticed two men sitting in an old car across the street. The one behind the wheel was talking on a cell phone. Chris didn't think too much of it at the time. When he made the right turn off Route 601, back toward Summer Lake Apartments, a police car pulled him over. The officer said he received a report that someone of Chris's description had been seen trying to break into the Sunoco shop. Chris said he was a racecar driver and was told to pick up race fuel.

"Are you lying to me, son?" said the officer.

Chris showed him our autograph card. After some coaxing, the officer relented.

"I guess this is you," he said. "Okay, that will be all."

Chris finished second overall points in Sportsman and once again won Rookie of the Year. I sent Frank Gaughen a letter with the good news and included all of the pertinent information regarding the awards banquet. Just like the previous year, my father and I, Chris, David and Kathy Miller, Kenny Barnes, and a few other volunteer crew members attended the awards banquet. Once again, no one from GMSPO attended. No congratulatory phone call, no letter to say, "keep up the hard work." Nothing. Chris and the team were hurt by GM's apathy. The crew worked tirelessly through many late nights, under the tightest of circumstances, to get the No. 21 in competitive condition, and Chris was showing that he could run with the best of them at one of the most prestigious short tracks in America. Yet, no one from our sponsor seemed to care.

After receiving his trophy, Chris did a TV interview and was asked, similar to the previous year, "What is ACDelco planning for you next year, Chris?"

"That's the Millers' department," he replied.

Chris was right. I had been hustling to find a corporate backer, but to no avail. If the team lost hope in our chances of progressing, or at least sustaining, people would eventually start quitting or look to join other teams who had more stability. To compound matters, David told us that Chris was falling in love with a married white woman at Plaza Ford and that he was starting to lose his focus at the shop. I had to act swiftly if we were going to keep our NASCAR dreams alive.

Toward the end of '96, I packed my calendar. In October, NASCAR had opened up a marketing office on Park Avenue in New York. I called and set up a meeting with Maria Formisano, senior manager of corporate sponsorships. I also circled the date for the Society of Automotive Engineers (SAE) Motorsports Conference, held biennially before Thanksgiving in Dearborn, Michigan. I planned on stalking CEOs and other bigwigs from the Big Three automakers. Cotter Communications was not having much success selling our team to its contacts, so I decided to hire another professional marketing firm. After reading through a book of sports agents, I targeted three possible firms: DeAngelo Minton and Associates in Warren, Ohio; Empire Management

Group in Charlotte; and The Gazelle Group in Princeton, New Jersey. "You're tough, Len, you're tough," my father told me over the phone as we discussed my loaded itinerary. "Maybe we'll turn the corner soon."

In a conference room overlooking Park Avenue, Maria Formisano leafed through our portfolio of photographs, autograph cards, and marketing proposals. She sounded intrigued and gave my father two large promotional brochures. Her office, she explained, used the brochures to reel in corporate partners for NASCAR. She had some preliminary ideas on companies that she would try to pair with us and asked us to mail her some additional information on Chris and our long-term goals. Since the office was still in its infancy, it could take a while for her to get back in touch with us, she said. After the meeting, she gave us a brief tour of the new office space. In one corridor, we noticed Bill France Jr. sitting at a desk. He looked at the three of us and nodded. The lifeless gesture almost made it seem as if he didn't recognize us from our meeting back in February. Maria showed us to the elevator and told us to keep her posted.

As requested, I sent her all of the documents. I called a few times to follow up. We didn't hear back from NASCAR's Park Avenue for three years.

In the meantime, I caught a glimpse of France Jr.'s stance on diversifying NASCAR in an October 4, 1997 article in the *Charlotte Observer* entitled "NASCAR's Rise Leaves Diversity in the Dust." The article, by Paige Williams, gave a balanced, abbreviated history of African-Americans in racing and included statements from my father and France Jr., among others. "We don't view that as an issue," says France Jr. of the lack of black drivers and owners in NASCAR. "America is what America is today. Anybody can be anything regardless of your race or your national origin or what have you. Philosophically, there's nothing wrong with that. You can't cast a wand and make everything

happen that somebody wants to happen." It was a puzzling sentiment coming from France Jr. Only months prior, he had heard our
explanation of why, when it came to auto racing and more particularly NASCAR, skin color had very much been preventing
African-Americans from being what they wanted to be. And
France Jr. just sounded so helpless. He was the president of
NASCAR, a sporting organization that he *owned*, but he could not
wave his omnipotent "wand" and change the way his business created opportunities for minorities? Later in the article, France Jr.
defended NASCAR's lack of diversity by bringing up golf as
another mostly white sport. "You don't see many African-Americans as professional golfers. Why is that? They were caddies,
though. Country clubs kept them out as members, but a lot of
them were on golf courses as caddies. I'd think you'd figure out
how to get some rounds in." In an oblique way, he almost sounded
as if he just didn't really care. France Jr.'s lack of sympathy raised
an eyebrow about the NASCAR lord's own outlook on race and
racism. He supported George Wallace in the Alabama governor's
1972 and 1976 bids for president—the same George Wallace who,
on June 11, 1963, stood alongside state troopers on the front steps
of the University of Alabama to prevent two black students, Vivian
Malone and James Hood, from registering for classes. The same
George Wallace who allowed police to use dogs and fire hoses to
fight back civil rights demonstrators in Birmingham. The same
George Wallace who said, "segregation now, segregation
tomorrow, and segregation forever" in his inaugural speech for the
governorship. This is not to say that France Jr. shared the same
views as Wallace, who later apologized for his segregationist ideals,
but France Jr. apparently did not have a problem sweeping them
to the side. Perhaps it's because Wallace helped commission the
construction of roads that led right to France Jr.'s Talladega Superspeedway. In the case of France Jr., his actions—and, when it came
to diversity in NASCAR, lack of actions—spoke louder than

words. I was always amazed that the media and civil rights groups never probed France Jr. about his relationship with Wallace, or delved deeper into NASCAR's loose ties with such segregationist history. Maybe no one wanted to take on France Jr. For, if your job at all related to NASCAR, you risked losing it by tainting the reputation of the man in charge. (As far as African-Americans playing golf is concerned, less than six months before the article was published, Tiger Woods showed the world he figured out how to get some rounds in by winning the Masters.)

My next stop was the SAE Motorsports Conference. On a cold, dreary night in November, I drove to the Hyatt in Dearborn for the opening night. The hotel was located across the freeway from Ford Motor Company's world headquarters. I planted myself in the middle of the enormous lobby and scanned the sea of suits for a prominent motorsports executive I might have seen in *Automotive News*, *Stock Car Racing* magazine, the GM corporate literature, or on television. In preparation for such events, I jotted down key names and took mental snapshots of faces.

I made my way into the large banquet hall, which had several racecars on display. The first person I recognized was GM Motorsports chief Herb Fishel. I remembered his face from GM's internal newsletter, *SPO Partners*. Fishel was one of the ten most powerful men in American motorsports, and he was standing by himself eating Buffalo wings. I made my move and introduced myself. He couldn't shake my hand because both of his were slathered with orange sauce, but he listened to me speak about Miller Racing's current lack of resources.

"Can your group assist our team?" I asked.

With his mouth half-full he said, "You need to come to our chassis seminars for GM NASCAR teams in Charlotte. Do you know Don Taylor? He can set you up."

"I know Don," I replied. "That sounds great. I'll talk to him."

"He'll be here tonight, over at our display," said Fishel.

I wandered over to the GM display. Between an Oldsmobile-powered IndyCar and a Chevrolet off-road race truck, I noticed a large color photo of the entire GM Racing staff. Out of about two-dozen employees, there was one African-American. Over my shoulder, I noticed the same gentleman adjusting the steering wheel on the off-road truck. His name was Harry Turner. He was mild-mannered and listened intently to my story about our dealings with GMSPO. He wasn't aware of our effort, but said, "Here's my card. I'll be here all night. Let's talk some more. I'll have you by my office one day at the Tech Center in Warren."

Next, I noticed Don Taylor, whom I hadn't seen since our initial GM Goodwrench meeting with Frank Gaughen. But before I could get to him, another GM Racing staff member, Dave Hedrich, came up and asked me, with a smile, "What does Miller Racing do?" When I told him ACDelco sponsored us, he looked puzzled. He squinted behind his glasses, locked his hands behind his back, and said, "I never heard of you guys." I pulled out a photo of the team and gestured to give it to him, but he kept his hands clasped behind his back. I told Hedrich I was about to speak to Don Taylor and asked if he wanted to join me. Hedrich didn't move. After a brief pause, he said, "Well, there he is," and just pointed. As I walked toward Taylor, I glanced over my right shoulder to see that Hedrich was tailing me, grinning awkwardly with his hands still clasped behind his back. What's with this guy, I thought.

It took him a few seconds, but Taylor recognized me and said, "Hey! How are you doing?" I told him we had ACDelco on the car now and that Chris Woods was Rookie of the Year. Hedrich stood by and listened.

"Herb Fishel told me to ask you about GM chassis seminars in Charlotte," I said.

Taylor paused, stuttered slightly, and replied, "You guys are not at that level yet. What did Herb say?"

I repeated myself.

"No, Herb is mistaken," Taylor said. He told me he was busy and excused himself. Hedrich vanished, too.

I noticed Harry Turner talking to another African-American gentleman near the GM Racing display. The second man was dressed in a dark business suit and was breaking a slight sweat, as it was starting to get hot in the room. I walked up to them and said hello.

"Claude, meet Lenny Miller of Miller Racing," said Harry, before lowering his voice to a whisper, "He and his father have a black driver sponsored by SPO." Claude Verbal was a plant manager for GMSPO in Lansing and the president of the Society of Automotive Engineers. "These guys are not being taken seriously," Harry said to Claude. "They got this far on their own."

"Working too hard, working too hard," said Claude as he shook my hand. "Here's my card. I know Bill Lovejoy. Herb Fishel and I graduated from the same college in North Carolina. You can't navigate GM by yourself. Harry and I have to help you, otherwise you'll get overwhelmed."

Mission complete, I thought. As I got into my car on the cold, misty evening, I was already thinking about my follow-up calls to Harry Turner and Claude Verbal. In the months that followed, they would follow through on their word.

Next on my to-do list was calling the marketing agencies. I called Empire Management Group first since it was located in Charlotte. I got the president, Gordon Grigg, on the line immediately and set up a meeting. My father, Chris, and I all attended. Grigg was tall, built like a wide receiver, and had various football mementos decorating the conference room. At his long, wooden conference table, he talked about his background in finance and how he assisted professional football players with their investments. Grigg called in his colleague Brandon Gandy, who was heading up Empire's new motorsports division. Gandy said to

Chris, "I've seen you race at Concord." Grigg told us we would have to sign a contract that gave Empire a 15-percent commission of whatever sponsorship money they helped reel in for us. Then, he blurted out somewhat unexpectedly, "The good Lord will take care of the rest. If the Lord wants this to happen, He will let it happen. The Lord has given me all of my success! The Lord will help you guys in racing, too." He went on to quote a few Bible passages from memory. My father and I didn't change our expressions. Chris avoided making eye contact with Grigg. Gandy acted as if he had witnessed the mini-sermon dozens of times. Grigg left the conference room to get the contract, and when he returned he told Chris that he visited Concord often and would come by shop No. 10 soon.

"Just fax the contract back to Empire when you're ready, and the Lord will take care of the rest," Grigg said before seeing us off in the lobby.

"That guy was a Jesus freak," Chris said in the parking lot.

"This is definitely a shot in the dark," said my father.

Several days later, we signed and faxed the contract. I had two follow-up phone conversations with Gandy. After that, we never saw him or Grigg at Concord. We never heard from either of them again.

Back in Michigan, I called DeAngelo Minton and Associates. General partner Frank DeAngelo briefed me on his background working with BF Goodrich and off-road racing. He agreed to meet my father and me at the Cleveland airport.

The flight was just a short hop over Lake Erie. My dad was waiting for me at the arrival gate. We met DeAngelo and his motorsports director, Maddy Bullman, at a table in a waiting area. They were enthusiastic from the start, showing us a sample proposal they had composed for an off-road race team. The document had some of the most compelling graphics I had ever seen. DeAngelo said he had a few contacts they could start pitching right away. We asked if one or both of them could accompany us to any future meetings with GMSPO, thinking the white presence might give us a little bit more cachet. While it sounded ridiculous to be introducing such an idea, we needed to try every method possible of proving we meant business. Thus far, business plans, progress reports, legal letters, third-party appearance requests, newspaper and magazine clippings, videos, and radio show snippets did not compel GMSPO enough to take us seriously. At least DeAngelo and Bullman took us seriously, as they agreed to help us for a 10-percent commission plus travel costs.

The meeting with the third sports agency, The Gazelle Group, was scheduled for December 26 in Princeton, New Jersey. Over the phone I had given Gazelle president Rick Giles my usual speech with all the buzzwords: African-American driver, Jackie Robinson, GM, 150 miles per hour, television, glass ceiling. "I'm very interested," Giles said. "How much sponsorship do you need when you get to the NASCAR Busch level?"

"Two million dollars plus per year," I responded. He didn't flinch at the high number and said we should have lunch at the Tiger Tail on Route 206 on the 26th.

I planned on staying at my parents' home in nearby southeastern Pennsylvania for the Christmas holiday. This meant driving to and from the meeting would be a piece of cake for my father and me, as we simply had to dart across the Delaware River. Sneaking away from our loved ones early the morning after Christmas, not so easy. On one of the days before Christmas, amidst the tree trimming, egg nog, and Nat King Cole, my father pulled me aside to plot how we were going to get out of the house on the 26th without the rest of the family asking too many questions. My mother and others were well aware of how much money we had put into the Concord effort, and any mention of racing, especially around the holidays, was sure to draw exasperation. Like most of our friends, our family considered auto racing a waste of time for African-Americans. Our loved ones saw us as members of the black bourgeoisie. We were expected to eat gourmet lunches, go to the movies and social events on the weekends, shop on Fifth Avenue in New York City, and drive a luxury car. Sweating at Concord Motor Speedway around blue-collar white folks, all the while falling deeper into debt, was unheard of. My father and I sparked each other's motivation just enough to keep moving forward, though. Besides, we didn't want to limit ourselves to a boring, routine middle-class life. Despite the hardships, racing gave us a rush like nothing else.

"Let's worry about it on the morning of the 26th," my father finally decided. "And don't say *anything*."

It was clear and brisk on the morning of the 26th. My father and I estimated it would take us thirty minutes to drive to Princeton. We left at 11:15 so we wouldn't have to rush. My father told my mother that we were going out to look for men's shoes.

"When will you be back?" she asked as we approached the door.

"Two hours," replied my father. My mother shook her head. I wondered, Was she onto us?

We got to the Tiger Tail ten minutes early. The place was crowded with well-heeled Princetonians in cashmere sweaters and penny loafers. Rick Giles recognized us immediately, as we were the only African-Americans in the joint. He outlined his background in sports television and described how his firm sold rotating promotional signs at sporting events nationwide. He had contacts who would be interested in NASCAR, and he was confident that The Gazelle Group could deliver on the $2 million we needed.

"I want to fly down to Concord," he said toward the end of lunch. "I want to meet your driver and learn about your racecar. Then, I'll be ready to go forward."

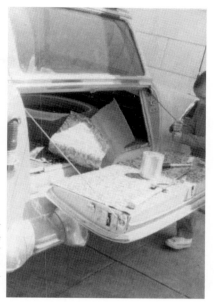

I'm eight years old and already
working on my dad's and uncle
Dexter's NHRA 1955 Chevy
station wagon drag racer, 1969.
SOURCE: LEONARD W. MILLER

Visiting Wendell Scott's NASCAR Grand National team, Trenton Speedway, Trenton, NJ:
(from left) Wendell Lee, childhood friend; me; my dad, Leonard W. Miller, 1969.
DR. WENDELL LEE

Discovering second generation driver Benny Scott (left) in Los Angeles, with my dad (center) and legendary racecar driver and owner Mel Leighton. Leighton owned several winning racecars pre– and post–World War II. And he was the treasurer of the Southern California Timing Association in the '40s and '50s. I'm standing in front of this distinguished group, 1970. ROSE H. MILLER

Relaxing on pit road at the Watkins Glen circuit, Watkins Glen, NY, with my sister, Stephanie (left), 1972. ROSE H. MILLER

My first garage pass pinned on my hat. I'm eager to watch Benny Scott drive a McLaren M-10A in a Formula A race at Watkins Glen, 1972. LEONARD W. MILLER

With childhood friend Eddie Greatti (background), mounting a tire on a Lola Formula Super Vee, 1973. LEONARD W. MILLER

Miller-Woods Racing driver Chris Woods holds the checkered flag at Riverside Park Speedway, Agawam, MA, with his proud parents, 1990. COURTESY LEONARD T. MILLER

Chris Woods (in car) listens to Miller-Woods Racing crew chief David Miller at our home track, Concord Motor Speedway, Concord, NC, 1994. LEONARD W. MILLER

David and Kathy Miller, our allies and friends at the Concord Motor Speedway for eight arduous years.
COURTESY LEONARD T. MILLER

Gentlemen's clubs in Charlotte were a part of the stock-car sponsorship scene at the Concord Motor Speedway during the 1994 season.
LEONARD W. MILLER

Miller Racing Group driver recruit David White at the Summerville Speedway, Summerville, SC, August 21, 1993. RICHARD PRATT PHOTO

African-American driver Tom Rice in car No. 34 at the Old Dominion Speedway, Manassas, VA, with an R&W engine purchased by Miller-Jones Racing, 1993. OLD DOMINION SPEEDWAY

My dad with me at the Concord Motor Speedway with our late-model stock-car, 1995. DUSTIN PECK, KPC PHOTOGRAPHY

I'm ready to go on day one at Skip Barber Driving School, Sebring, FL, 1993.
COURTESY LEONARD T. MILLER

Chris Woods is ready for practice. Concord Motor Speedway, 1995.
LEONARD T. MILLER

A last-minute touch before departing our shop No. 10 at the
Concord Motor Speedway, 1995. LEONARD W. MILLER

Chris Woods takes a victory in the Miller-Woods Racing Legends car, 1995. CONCORD MOTOR SPEEDWAY

My dad (left), me, and driver Chris Woods pose with our much faster Late Model Sportsman for the famous Concord Big 10 Series, 1996. NORLING STUDIOS, HIGHPOINT, NC

The entire team with new driver A.J. Alsup and our NASCAR Slim Jim All Pro car. (Background, from left) Obrie Smith, Chad Talbott, David Miller, and David White. (Foreground, from left) My dad, A.J., and me. ALDERMAN STUDIOS, HIGHPOINT, NC

North Carolina A&T State University homecoming with our UAW-GM show car. (Foreground, from left) Maria Buckles, Leonard W. Miller. (Background, from left) Miller Racing Group drivers, Morty Buckles and Chris Bristol. Greensboro, NC, 1999. NORTH CAROLINA A&T STATE UNIVERSITY

UAW-GM NASCAR exhibit, Lowe's Motor Speedway with our show car. Miller Racing Group driver Morty Buckles is standing behind me, 1998. LEONARD W. MILLER

Miller Racing Group drivers Morty Buckles and Chris Bristol (back turned) engulfed with 25,000 alumni, citizens, and fans at the North Carolina A&T State University homecoming, Greensboro, NC, 1999. NORTH CAROLINA A&T STATE UNIVERSITY

(In background) Chris Bristol and Morty Buckles, with Maria Buckles's assistance, sign more than one thousand autographs at the Lowe's Motor Speedway, Charlotte, NC, inside the UAW-GM exhibit, 1999. LEONARD T. MILLER

Rainbow/PUSH sports director Charles Farrell sits in a NASCAR Winston Cup car at the UAW-GM exhibit at the Lowe's Motor Speedway, Charlotte, NC, 1999. UAW-GM MOTORSPORTS

Miller Racing Group driver Chris Bristol on the tri-oval at the Concord Motorsport Park in the team's limited stock, 1999.
CHAD TALBOTT

Formula driver David Francis, Jr. (left), for CART's African-American Driver Development Program press conference at the Detroit Grand Prix, Belle Isle, MI, 1999.
CHAD TALBOTT

CART's African-American Development Program dais at the Detroit Grand Prix. (From left) Charles Farrell, then–Detroit Mayor Dennis Archer, David Francis Jr., me, and CART CEO Andrew Craig, 1999. CHAD TALBOTT

Miller Racing Group takes delivery of a new NASCAR All Pro car from Townsend Racing Products, Ashland, VA, 2000.
LEONARD T. MILLER

Dr Pepper/Miller Racing Group, unveiling the Miller
Racing Group, Dr Pepper car. Rev. Jesse Jackson;
Jack Kilduff, CEO, Dr Pepper; Texas congress-
woman Sheila Jackson Lee; Leonard W. Miller.
Rainbow Push/Wall Street Project, Midtown
Manhattan, 2001. BEVERLY SWANAGAN, SWANAY PRODUCTION

Miller Racing Group, Chevrolet,
NASCAR Late Model Stock #7
with Franklin Butler behind the
wheel at Old Dominion Speedway, Manassas, VA, 2006.
OLD DOMINION SPEEDWAY

First place, Coastal Plains Speedway,
Jacksonville, NC, July 7, 2001.
Dr Pepper's first corporate win in
history. Morty Buckles, driver, with his
mother, and his wife Maria. Other
gentleman, unknown. CHAD TALBOTT

I'm receiving the "Trailblazer Award" for my contribution to the development of African-American racecar drivers in motorsports (1993–2003) presented by Stan Proctor, president, Quartermasters Drag Racing Team, on February 22, 2003, Colony South Hotel, Clinton, MD. LEONARD W. MILLER

Miller Racing Group, crew member Judee Smith, and crew chief Herman Gantt, 2005. LEONARD W. MILLER

We shook hands with Giles in the parking lot and jumped in my Pontiac. I had it smoking down the back roads of New Jersey. We walked through the door of my parents' house at 1:45 p.m. without the shopping bags of new shoes everyone was expecting.

"Where did you go?" my mother piped up. "We've been sitting here waiting to do something." My father gave a convoluted answer that, to this day, I can't remember. Somehow, no one questioned him. No sooner did my father and I sit down than my mother suggested we pack up the cars and take the family to Princeton. In less than an hour we were back on the country roads of New Jersey, heading toward Princeton. I just hoped we wouldn't run into Rick Giles on the street.

When we got to downtown Princeton, my mother said she wanted to eat lunch at the French restaurant Lahiere's. My father and I had barely digested our cheeseburgers from the Tiger Tail. We ate again, trying not to blow our cover. We had indigestion for two days.

11

A White Driver?

On April 13, 1997, Tiger Woods won the Masters. The feat for the then twenty-one-year-old exemplified a significant change in the sport, which was steeped in privilege, legacy, and exclusion. Country clubs and public courses across the country had strict "no blacks allowed" policies, and up until 1961, the Professional Golfers' Association (PGA) had a Caucasian-only policy that barred African-Americans from playing in PGA Tour events. As a result, black golfers started their own clubs in and around major cities, like Chicago's Windy City Golf Club, which formed around 1915. By the '20s, some of these clubs came together to organize a tournament for African-Americans, called the National, and soon thereafter formed the United Golf Association (UGA), which established additional tournaments across the country. While the National and other UGA events didn't pay out high purses, they, much like the Gold and Glory Sweepstakes, provided an opportunity for African-Americans to improve their talents in the sport they loved.

While he didn't speak about skin color to the media all that much, Woods had to deal with his fair share of prejudice. Born in 1975, Woods showed exceptional talent as a child. To develop that talent, his parents, Earl and Kutilda (Earl is of African, Caucasian, and Native American descent; Kutilda is from Thailand), tried to enter their young golf prodigy at country clubs around their stomping grounds of Southern California, but were turned away by a handful due to age-old segregationist policies. In fact, many country clubs across the US, like Shoal Creek in Alabama and Augusta National—site of the Masters—in Georgia did not integrate membership until the '90s. Still, with uncanny ability and an unshakeable drive, Woods tore through amateur championship tournaments. When he turned pro in 1996, Nike inked Woods to a five-year, $40-million endorsement deal. Nike, seizing the marketing potential of a young, dark-skinned golfing phenom, ran a provocative TV ad in which Tiger uttered the lines: "There are still courses in the United States I am not allowed to play because of the color of my skin. I've heard I'm not ready for you. Are you ready for me?" About 20-million-plus TV viewers were ready. That was the Nielsen number for the telecast of the 1997 Masters, an audience that was more than double the average 9.5 million that were tuning in for the two-day CBS weekend broadcasts from 1977 to 1996. Adding to the drama, the world watched Woods win his first major at a course that had just started accepting members of color. In the years that followed, Woods would become a certifiable celebrity, one of the world's richest (according to a February 2008 *Golf Digest* article, between 1996 and 2007, Woods grossed $769,440,709 in combined prize and endorsement money), most beloved athletes. Not bad for a guy who almost wasn't allowed to play because of his blackness.

Woods's crowning achievement in 1997 embodied all that we were trying to accomplish in motorsports, and then some. Not only did Woods compete and win at the highest levels of a predominantly white sport, he proved that an African-American athlete could change the entire perception and business of a sport.

Meanwhile, as Woods walked off the eighteenth hole at Augusta to put on his green jacket, Miller Racing was on the verge of putting a white driver in its car seat.

Back in January, David Miller reported that Chris was spending more and more time with his girlfriend and less time around Concord. And, according to David, when Chris did appear at shop No. 10, he didn't say much and acted detached. My father and I planned to confront Chris on the matter. We also decided to start testing new drivers. In organized racing, like in other team sports, it's important to have a skilled driver ready to come off the bench; while we still viewed Chris as the quarterback, it was time to start grooming a backup QB. Plus, we figured the news of a test might jumpstart Chris's competitive spirit.

The day we flew down to Concord to have a sit-down with Chris, we also scheduled a meeting with a prospective chassis-setup person. Chris and David were doing an above-average job filling the void left by Nick Smith, but they still had a lot to learn. Getting in constant wrecks only compounded the need for an expert. One Saturday night, a friend and up-and-coming driver at Concord named Robby Faggart introduced us to his chassis guy, Keith Van Houten. Keith was considered one of the best in the area. My father and I planned on picking up Chris for the meeting with Keith, after which we would have our sit-down with Chris.

Keith lived in nearby Mt. Pleasant, where he ran his shop out of a three-car garage in the backyard of his home. He was a smallish man. He wore thick glasses that made his eyes look twice their normal size and talked like a scientist. The day of our meeting, we sat on old race tires on the concrete floor of his garage. The temperature was barely above freezing inside the wood-framed building. I could hear the breeze whistle outside.

"Let me get this woodstove started to get some heat going," said Keith before we began. "It won't take long for this place to warm up."

After stoking a fire, he grabbed a notebook and pen. It appeared as if he had jotted down some notes in preparation for the meeting.

"Chris, you're a good driver, especially being under pressure down here as a black man," he said. "You guys just need better chassis setups."

Chris looked down at the ground. For Chris, the No. 21 was

like a child. He took Keith's criticism to heart. Keith went on to say that he wanted to bring the car to his backyard shop for regular maintenance. He said he was capable of doing all mechanical work on the car, including the engine, and could navigate our trailer through tight areas in his sleep. He had plenty of driving experience, too. A California native, he had raced in NASCAR Winston West and various other Late Model Stock–level series. He, like thousands of others, had moved to the area to make it big as a driver. When it became clear driving would not pay his bills, he started the race shop.

My teeth chattered as Keith talked about his background. The old iron stove still hadn't generated any heat. My father stood up and paced. Chris rubbed his hands up and down his arms. Keith cupped his hands and blew in between sentences.

"How much money is ACDelco giving you guys?" Keith asked.

"I have to speak with forked tongue," answered my father. "We can race all season at Concord, but Lenny and I would have to add tens of thousands of dollars to the pot. The problem is, we're just about broke." Instead of racing an entire season at Concord, my father and I wanted to enter five NASCAR Slim Jim All Pro Series races, which started in June. While racing in five out of the nearly twenty races wouldn't give us a shot at winning the series, it would give us exposure in areas outside of Charlotte. The races took place all over the Southeast, and many of them were televised on local cable stations. My father and I felt confident we could stay within the $75,000 budget from GMSPO. Starting in June would also give my father and me time to pay off some of our debt. Plus, it would allow some time for the check from GMSPO to arrive.

As my toes started to get numb, Keith rushed through some final details. For now, he would cover fees for preparing the car, and eventually he would create a payment plan for us. He wanted us to buy more tools, too, as we were still largely relying on the toolbox Chris had brought with him from Massachusetts. Keith apologized for the frigid conditions and saw us to the door. I could barely feel my legs.

Chris followed my father and me to a greasy spoon on Route 29 in Concord. The heat in the restaurant felt good. Before we ordered, my father got right to the point: He told Chris we wanted to start testing additional drivers in February, and that if Chris was losing interest, as David had reported, we would look to replace him. Chris ordered his food, and said, meekly, "That's okay. I'll be all right." It was not the inspired reaction we hoped to hear. Chris acted lackadaisical throughout the meal and didn't say much.

The next day, we heard that Chris had tried to turn the crew against David, accusing David of ratting him out to us. "There's no way we can survive like this," David exclaimed. "I'm glad you guys are making changes."

While my father started calling his friends to inquire about up-and-coming drivers, I focused my attention on Harry Turner and Claude Verbal.

First, I met with Turner at the enormous General Motors Technical Center in Warren, Michigan. Before I could get through all of my standard proposal materials, Turner was sold. He thought that GM's Pontiac Racing division would be able to provide us with a few parts, a few bodies, and possibly a medium-duty Top Kick truck for towing. He said he would try to clear Pontiac's contributions to our program with his boss, Bill Lovejoy, in the next few days. In the meantime, he told me I should meet with Claude Verbal in Lansing as soon as possible.

I'll never forget the weather on the day of my Claude Verbal meeting. With the wind-chill factor the temperature hovered between 30 and 40 degrees below zero. There was an existing snow cover on the ground, and wicked crosswinds were creating whiteout conditions on I-96 toward Lansing. The parking lot at the GMSPO plant was blanketed in white, and most of the cars were running with no one in them. I decided to leave my car running, too. Bundled up like an Eskimo, I darted through the whistling wind and patches of car exhaust toward the moaning monolith of a factory.

Claude Verbal was behind his desk, talking on the phone. I shed my coat, hat, and gloves, as the heat was blasting throughout the building. As soon as he hung up, Verbal shook my hand and dove into our racing portfolio. He was stunned when he saw the photos of African-Americans racing before World War II. He rolled off a series of questions: "How much money do you need next year? What's the next step? What does GMSPO give you? Have you talked to Rodney O'Neil?" I told him O'Neil had poked his fingers in my chest and said, "You'll be a hero, but most heroes are dead!" Verbal shook his head with a grin and replied, "That's Rodney." He reiterated that he and Harry Turner were going to help us out as soon as they could get to Lovejoy.

It didn't take long. A few days later, Turner called to tell me he had spoken with Gary Claudio, manager of motorsports for the Pontiac GMC division. Claudio could set us up with the necessary equipment.

I met with Claudio at the Pontiac building, which was just outside of Detroit. For this day's meeting, I fought through pouring sleet on my run toward the building. Claudio greeted me in the lobby and led me up an escalator to his office. Before we got into specifics about what Pontiac could give us, he told me his division was looking at another minority-owned team that was just getting off the ground, the one owned by Julius Erving and Joe Washington. Claudio thought the two ex-pros were in way over their heads.

"Do you know Roy Roberts?" Claudio asked. "He's African-American and runs this whole division. I have a meeting with him soon. I'll show him your team information."

Claudio revealed Pontiac's plan to give us three Pontiac Grand Prix racing bodies and an allotment of performance parts, along with decals and T-shirts. As Claudio walked me back down to the lobby, he talked about getting Miller Racing a three-year lease on a medium-duty truck. "A GMC Top Kick will be a long shot," he said. "I can't promise. I'll try, though. Give me a call at the end of the month."

In the meantime, my father had the driver test at Concord all set up. Four drivers were scheduled to participate. Troy Adams and Jesus Vasquez were a couple of go-karters coming from California. Troy's father, Tim, owned the Adams Kart Track in Riverside. When he heard we were looking for drivers he called my father to say that several Latinos and African-Americans, including his son, were racing on his 3/4-mile course. (George Mack, who in 2002 became the second black driver after Willy T. Ribbs to qualify for the Indianapolis 500, cut his teeth at Adams' track.) Like us, Tim and his son had visions of one day making it to NASCAR. Keith suggested we test Ryan Zeck, a Late Model hot shoe at Concord who was also interning for Ford Racing. Ryan was the son of Rudy Zeck, a designer of Bandolero cars. (Bandoleros, like go-karts, are smaller in size and are designed for entry-level racers, with engines running at about 30 hp. Unlike go-karts, which have an open frame, Bandoleros are equipped with a body.) Ryan was also white, which ran counter to the foundation of our marketing proposals. Still, we figured it couldn't hurt to get more drivers out on the course, if only to increase competition. Once the word got out that we were including white drivers, Petey Pistone contacted us and wanted to know if his son Nick could participate. The Pistone family had a racing heritage that traced back to the 1950s, when Tiger Tom Pistone raced in NASCAR's Grand National division. We agreed to put Nick in the car, too. Rick Giles would make the trip down to Concord, as well as a friend of ours, Chad Talbott. Chad was a young,

African-American attorney living in Atlanta. He had always loved auto racing, particularly Formula 1, but didn't have many friends or family who shared his passion. When his godfather, a friend of my father's, told him we were looking for a driver, Chad called my father within the hour and said he'd make the four-hour drive up from Atlanta just to watch.

The 40-degree weather that Saturday afternoon in February felt a lot warmer than Michigan. Except for a few stray employees, the track was a ghost town. Everyone was on time except for Chris, who showed up twenty minutes late accompanied by his girlfriend. Keith, who had worked on the car for nearly a month, took a few laps to make sure it was running smoothly. As Keith hit the straightaways, the roar of the engine ricocheted off the concrete walls. Without decals and paint, the car looked pristine in its new, white fiberglass body. Chad was smiling from ear to ear; he had never seen a stock car up close until now. When Keith brought the car back to the pits, Rick Giles asked to take a look inside. The stock-car experience was new for Giles as well. He fumbled a few seconds for a door handle until he realized the car wasn't equipped with one.

"You have to climb through the window to get in and out," I said, snickering.

"What if you catch on fire?" he asked.

"You climb through the window. Quickly."

I went over some basic ground rules with the four drivers. The plan was for everyone to drive ten laps at a slower pace to get used to the car, and then increase to a comfortable speed for the remaining laps. Jesus Vasquez, who was just sixteen years old, could barely speak English. Nick Pistone's mother looked on in her lush fur coat. Troy's father Tim was standoffish from the beginning, speaking in a very curt manner and only opening up his mouth to make criticisms about the car and the operation. My father and I later wondered if he was speaking out of envy, since

Miller Racing was further along in its NASCAR dream than he was. Or, perhaps he was dismayed at the sight of the white drivers in attendance. Either way, he had hurt his son's chances of taking the seat before his son even got onto the track. My father and I did not want to knowingly add a divisive person to our operation. We wanted team players. Chris wasn't acting like much of a team player, either. He made a point of standing away from the other drivers and spoke only to his girlfriend. He had a feeble, uninspired look on his face. I thought to myself, if this atmosphere doesn't get him motivated to keep his seat, to fight for his spot on the team, then what will?

Chris went first. He was slow and sloppy from the get-go. Next up was Troy Adams, who one-upped Chris immediately, hitting sharp lines on his first few laps. The youngster Jesus Vasquez showed raw talent, too. Nick Pistone looked fast and skilled enough to enter a race that day. Ryan Zeck flexed his experience by running the cleanest lines of all the drivers and notching the best lap times. Keith even took a few laps for kicks and ended up driving faster than Ryan Zeck. My father didn't want Keith to get too comfortable, though, as Keith wasn't in the running for the driver's seat. We needed him to devote his full attention to setting up the car. At the end of the test session everyone was cold, exhausted, and chomping at the bit to find out who was going to fill the seat. My dad and I thanked everyone and said we would think about our options before selecting a driver.

We now had a dilemma on our hands. Nick Pistone and Jesus Vasquez exhibited solid ability, but needed too much training. Troy Adams also showed a lot of promise, and perhaps could have carried us through the All Pro Series, but his father's sour attitude took him out of the running. Sadly, Chris's underwhelming test run and overall apathy came close to sealing his fate. Which brought us to Ryan Zeck, who was, bar none, the best driver we tested. He was experienced, amiable, and gave us the best chance of winning now. If GMSPO co-signed on us adding Ryan, we could put him in the seat for the All Pro Series and, if Chris was indeed finished, look to add a black driver for the '98 season. It would be taking one step backward in order to take two steps forward.

With the All Pro Series beginning in June, my father and I took a few months to mull over the decision. The time period also gave Chris one final attempt to reflect on his standing with the team and perhaps salvage his job. However, over the course of those few months, Ryan Zeck was the one calling on a regular basis to check in and express his enthusiasm about the opportunity. On the flip side, Chris called less and less, and when he did speak he still didn't have much to say. Toward the end of April, I called Harry Turner to explain our predicament. Turner said he had no problem with us putting a white driver in the car, and he arranged a conference call with Don Taylor, Gary Claudio, and Bill Fitzgerald, who had since taken over for Frank Gaughen's position, to clear it with everyone else. Taylor, Claudio, and Fitzgerald acted nonchalant about the whole thing. In the end, the four of us agreed that we should put the best driver in the car, regardless of his skin color. As soon as our check from ACDelco arrived, my father and I would offer the driver's seat to Ryan Zeck.

Claudio also reported that he had solidified a GMC Top Kick for us. The truck was a loaner for one year, renewable annually. He told me I would have to contact GM's mid-Atlantic regional office in Rockville, Maryland, to schedule a pick-up. When I called, a woman with a British accent answered. Her name was Carol Mazzarino, a company car coordinator. Typical of our dealings with GM, she had not been informed about our truck. After a long back and forth, which consisted of me reiterating all of my conversations with Harry Turner and Gary Claudio, Mrs. Mazzarino told me I had to pick up the truck at a dealership in Charlotte.

A few weeks later, my father and I met in the Charlotte airport and drove straight to the dealership. A salesman introduced himself as Maynard Kline. We told him GM had set aside a Top Kick truck for us. He scowled, looked us over from head to toe, and blurted out, "If you're with GM, why are they offering you a truck after the racing season is well underway?"

"That's a long story, Maynard," my father said. "We're treated like an afterthought."

As we walked to the rear lot, Kline gave us the Twenty Questions routine.

"Who are you dealing with at GM to get the truck registered and processed?" he asked.

"Carol Mazzarino," we answered in unison. Kline huffed and shook his head in disbelief. He sighed and pointed in the direction of four white, identical trucks. One of the first things I noticed was that the model did not have a sleeper or lounge compartment, which was an important amenity since the team was going to be traveling long distances for the All Pro Series. I asked Kline who in the area might be able to build an attachment for us.

"I hope you don't need a truck soon," he shot back. "At this time of year it could take up to three months to complete the truck with the lounge configuration you'll need. And it will cost about $20,000."

"Who could do the work the fastest?" asked my father. It was mid-May, and the first series race took place in June.

"Try Touch of Class in Concord. They do good work, and they may be able to finish the truck in six weeks. I'll get you the phone number. Use my name."

Kline took us back to his office and photocopied a small stack of paperwork. One of the papers said the truck's engine was only 180 hp. I worried that the truck may not be able to hack our heavy load. A racecar, tools, spare parts, tires, generator, and a couple of crew members seated in the lounge area added up to 26,000 pounds.

"Oh sure, 180 is plenty," Kline said. He turned his computer screen toward us and cued up a program that calculated whether or not a GM truck model could pull a specified weight. He entered 26,000 pounds for the 180-hp Top Kick and said, "The rig will cruise at 65 miles per hour without a problem."

I thought we needed 275 hp. I asked Kline if GM had stronger trucks in its inventory. He entered some data into the computer and told me nothing was available. Since we didn't have enough time to wait for a special order, which could've taken months, we agreed to take one of the 180-hp Top Kicks. Kline said it would be ready to pick up in a week. Before leaving, he gave us directions to Touch of Class, which was about twenty minutes away.

A husband-and-wife team from New England operated Touch of Class out of a garage on Route 29 in Concord. The friendly couple told us they were backed up with orders and that it would take them at least eight weeks to build the type of lounge and tow hitch platform we desired. As the woman gave us a tour of their shop, my father whispered to me, "We can't start racing until August."

Before we left town we stopped by Concord to check in with David Miller, after which we would visit Keith's shop. David had some troubling news. Keith was acting like a tyrant toward the crew. He worked diligently and meticulously, but didn't listen to anyone else's advice, David said. We assured David we would keep a close eye on Keith. With so much up in the air for the '97 season and beyond, the last thing we needed was division within the team. My father and I guessed that working with such limited resources on a regular basis only compounded the crew's frustrations. I was starting to feel the effects, too. On my recent trips to Concord I was hustling to meetings on little or no sleep, sometimes without food. My dad and I were juggling credit cards, anxiously awaiting the check from ACDelco. From top to bottom, the team had to endure sacrifice and hardship in order to grow.

We made our way down a dead-end road, past a couple of small houses and a double-wide trailer toward Keith's home. Our headlights lit up his tractor-trailer, which looked at least twenty years old and in faded lettering read "Van Houten Racing." As our car crackled up the long gravel driveway, Keith's silhouette emerged from the backyard. He opened the garage door, flicked on the lights, and grabbed his notepad, which contained a long list of updates and needs.

"Okay, we're not behind schedule yet," he said, "but we need to get some things here. I need those tools! We've got to have tools. My tools are getting lost. I like to keep things separate. What about those Pontiac bodies you guys talked about?"

My father told him that GM was slow with these kinds of things, but we would have them soon.

Keith said he could pull together a temporary volunteer crew, adding, "We need to select a driver soon. I have to have a driver I can work with, a driver that I know. I don't want a stranger in the car."

My father looked through Keith's thick glasses and said, "We're leaning toward Ryan Zeck."

"He would be good," replied Keith. "His time at Concord was almost as fast as mine. When are you going to let me know?"

"In a few days."

Keith said he would continue working on the car until he received confirmation on a driver. Neither my father nor I sensed an attitude problem with Keith. But it wouldn't take very long for us to see his dark side.

The ACDelco check came at the end of the month. The day it arrived, I called Ryan Zeck to tell him he was our driver for the All Pro Series.

"I'll meet you anytime, anywhere," he said. "Just let me

know." I told Ryan that we wouldn't be able to start racing until August. We planned to meet down in Charlotte in the coming weeks to finalize the terms of his employment with us.

Then came the hard part. I called Chris to tell him we were going in a different direction. He didn't say much. He told me he understood and hung up the phone, sounding indifferent. Later, though, he called Bobby Merritt to vent. He told Bobby that we were screwing him by putting a white boy in the car. He also made up a story about how we cheated him out of money. Bobby, the militant that he was, called up my father, livid. He felt that we were not only betraying Chris, but as African-Americans we were shunning our inherent obligation to advance people of color. My father explained that it was a temporary solution and that we had every intention of bringing a black driver back on board. Bobby said he never wanted to speak to my father again.

For years my father tried to reconcile with Bobby, leaving voice messages and writing letters. But Bobby stuck to his words.

Sadly, we would never speak to Chris again, either. He cut off all ties with the crew. His departure didn't come as a shock to anyone, as Chris had steadily been distancing himself from the operation for months. The team did feel a collective sorrow, however. For years Chris had given the effort everything he had. He had picked up his life in Massachusetts and moved down south because he believed he could beat the good ol' boys on their turf. At Concord, he accomplished a lot in a short amount of time. And if we'd received adequate financial and moral support from a sponsor, who knows how it would have affected Chris's commitment. How many other black drivers over the years lost interest in racing because they simply didn't have a support system, I wondered. Chris's talent was never a question; with the proper backing he was bound for NASCAR. But his resolve—be it related to the girl he was dating, the instability of the team's finances, or the fundamental hunger to get out on the track and race—had wavered. In our business, a driver who's lost his or her edge is a driver that's unfit to continue.

Chris didn't show his face again at Concord for years. We later heard that he left his job at Plaza Ford and started working at a Hendrick dealership in Charlotte.

When Keith found out from David Miller that we were going with Ryan, he phoned me in a tizzy. He started rambling about a driver he had in mind who was experienced but a little older. Oddly, Keith wouldn't tell me the driver's name. I kept asking, "Who is he, Keith? Who is he?" Keith was trying to coax me into committing to the mystery driver without providing me any details. The conversation went in circles. After some prodding, I got one piece of crucial information out of him.

"How old is the driver?" I asked.

"He's in his mid-thirties."

Had Keith been more forthcoming I might have considered a driver in his or her mid-thirties. Some drivers hit their prime in their thirties. Legends like Richard Petty and Dale Earnhardt raced competitively well into their forties (Petty retired when he was fifty-five); their years of experience behind the wheel and uncanny ability allowed them to outlast the majority of their peers. But Keith's evasiveness made me nervous. I told him that his driver, unless he or she had extraordinary talent, wouldn't be a good long-term fit for us, as we were looking for drivers who could feasibly graduate to Winston Cup over the course of the next five years.

"Jeff Gordon started all this young driver stuff!" he snapped back. "Now everyone wants a driver who's twenty years old. Let me tell you something: I have more experience in racing than you guys! I told you, if you want me to be the crew chief, I have to know the driver!"

"My father and I selected Ryan Zeck," I said firmly.

"Ryan's okay, but his father is hard to get along with," said Keith. "I'll talk to you later."

Two days later, Keith phoned again to complain.

"Ryan Zeck's father is a control freak. If you guys sign up Ryan, I will not speak to his father if he shows up to any of the races. And since we're working out of my shop, Rudy Zeck is not allowed on my property."

He started speaking in non-sequiturs.

"Rudy is not going to let Ryan sign any kind of contract, either," he said. "Let me know what you're going to do, Lenny. We're running out of time. We need a driver soon, or I'm going to quit."

We had a huge problem on our hands. In a couple of days, Ryan, his father, my father, and I were scheduled to meet in Charlotte to sign the contract. My father and I had already given Keith the money he needed to modify the car for the All Pro Series, and the parts from Pontiac had already reached Keith's garage. Plus, quality chassis-setup technicians were hard to come by. Otherwise, we would have dropped Keith from the operation right then and there. Instead, we caved to Keith's strong-arming, as we determined it would be easier (and faster) to find a different driver in time for the All Pro Series.

I was frustrated, my father was frustrated, David Miller was frustrated. "I'm telling you guys straight up, there's gonna be trouble," David told my father and me the day of the meeting in Charlotte. "I'm sick of working with the guy, to tell you the truth."

Ryan Zeck's face turned red when I explained why we could no longer take him on as the driver. Rudy Zeck looked on in disbelief and didn't say much throughout our meeting. I explained that Keith had my father and me in a jam, and that once we got out of it we would consider him as a driver. "I can't believe this is happening," said Ryan. The Zecks were disgusted with Keith's actions, but understood our decision.

Still reeling from the meeting, my father and I picked up David from shop No. 10 and went to Sears to purchase the long list of tools Keith needed to complete the car. As the items crossed the price scanner—a thousand-piece tool set, grinders, drop lights, mechanic's creepers, hoses, air lines, large stacking tool boxes, drills, a generator, sandpaper, hack saws—I wondered if we were being naïve thinking that we still might be able to race that summer. Keith, while skilled at his trade, had manipulated us. As we drove to the airport the next day, my father reflected about how, at Concord, we had bestowed a lot of trust and responsibility to team members that we did not know all that well. These days, David Miller was about the only person down in North Carolina we could trust. My father and I had been operating on the slimmest of budgets, calling the shots remotely from our homes that were hundreds of miles from Concord, and were now working with some crew members who had turned on us. Yet, like a gambler always thinks his next bet will be a winner, we always believed that if we could turn just one more corner we would be that much closer to fulfilling our destiny. Perhaps firing Keith and putting our plans on hold would have been the rational thing to do, but we were caught up in our obsession with racing. Like the drivers who left their wives in the hopes that they could one day make it to Winston Cup, the businessmen and women who relocated to Charlotte to be around NASCAR's hub, the volunteers who put in as many hours at the shop as they did at their full-time jobs, we wanted to race until our dying day.

The next day, as we drove to the airport, we discussed driver options. I thought of A.J. Alsup. We knew his brother Nipper and his father Bill, who drove Formula Super Vees against Benny Scott in the 1970s and raced in the Indianapolis 500 for Roger Penske's team in the 1980s. A.J. had raced Late Model Stock cars at the New River Valley Speedway in Radford, Virginia, and had entered a few All Pro races. When last I heard, he wasn't racing full time.

"Call A.J.," said my father.

Suddenly, it was July. By now, my wife and I had moved down to Charlottesville, Virginia, because of her job. Amid all of the dealings in Concord, I helped packed up our apartment in Novi and we hauled our belongings to a little house we rented off Route 29. I was happy to be closer to Charlotte, which was now a four-and-a-half-hour drive, or short US Air Express flight away.

From Charlottesville, I called the Alsup Racing Team shop. A.J. was delighted when I told him we were interested in entering him in five All Pro races starting in August. "I don't know how you guys picked me, but I'll take it!" he said. For the time being, A.J. was racing a Late Model car at New River Valley but could work the five All Pro races into his schedule. I gave A.J. a complete run-down of what had happened between Keith and Ryan Zeck. A.J. remained upbeat and said he would contact me after he met with Keith down in North Carolina. I told him that if my father and I couldn't make that meeting he should summon David Miller, our trusty watchdog, as a companion.

In the meantime, I set up a meeting at GMSPO's headquarters in Michigan with Bill Fitzgerald, Harry Turner, Gary Claudio, and Frank DeAngelo, and Maddy Bullman. My father and I wanted to present our plan for 1998 as soon as possible. I knew the request might ultimately go unrequited, but we had to try. When I last spoke to Rick Giles at The Gazelle Group, he was coming up empty with his contacts, which meant we might have to milk GMSPO's support for at least one more season.

Bill Fitzgerald was even harder to pin down than his prede-cessor Frank Gaughen. The few times we did speak he tried to talk his way out of a meeting, but he finally caved to my pestering. Fitzgerald said he had to invite a "decision maker" to the meeting. He didn't give me a name. The day of the meeting, my father and I met outside the Northwest Airlines baggage claim at Detroit Metro Airport and headed over to the hotel where DeAngelo and Bullman were staying. They had flip charts, graphs, and two display boards. Before heading out we did a couple run-throughs of the presentation.

As we were picking up our visitor passes at the reception area Harry Turner emerged from a corridor to greet us. We went through introductions and walked upstairs to Fitzgerald's office, where we met the so-called decision maker. The stranger had shaggy hair and a goatee. He made a ten-minute speech praising Rodney O'Neil, gushing about how powerful O'Neil was, how he respected O'Neil a great deal, how O'Neil was a great role model for everyone at GMSPO, and how it took hard work and many years to get to where O'Neil was. He went on to describe how GMSPO gave lots of money to the African-American community through various nonprofit initiatives and that the company's motorsports budget, with millions already earmarked for 1998, was nearly exhausted. I guessed that the decision maker was there to butter us up with the O'Neil praise before GMSPO let us down with some news we didn't want to hear.

The decision maker told DeAngelo to start the presentation. Fitzgerald looked on as if he couldn't wait to get up and walk out of the room. Gary Claudio walked in ten minutes late and apologized to my father and me. The decision maker sat back in his chair with a snide look on his face. Harry Turner jotted down notes on a pad. He appeared to be the only one paying attention. DeAngelo, sensing the apathy, stammered through the presentation. Bullman, my father, and I chimed in at various moments to add our two cents. But it all fell on deaf ears.

"Look, guys, they don't have any money at SPO," Gary Claudio told us on the way out. While I believed budgets were tight, Claudio's statement was a bit of a stretch. When it came to motorsports, GMSPO was pouring money into TV and print ads, billboards, title sponsorships, and dozens of other promotions. Conservatively, I would've estimated that GMSPO was investing over $20 million a year in auto racing. We weren't on Dale Earnhardt's level, so I didn't expect the same level of support. But thus far we had upheld our end of the bargain. We had raced our GM Goodwrench and ACDelco cars up through the ranks at Concord, turning heads in the process. Even those GMSPO employees with a minimal understanding of stock-car racing had to know that we could net more exposure for their brands if we had more money behind us. However, GMSPO was content to keep short-changing us.

DeAngelo and Bullman, disillusioned with the meeting and how ignored they felt, headed back to Ohio frustrated. They never accompanied us to a meeting again.

Toward the end of July, we set up a photo shoot at Alderman Studios in Highpoint. We wanted to have autograph cards and other promotional materials on hand for the All Pro Series. My father and I drove down together from Charlottesville and arranged to pick up A.J. early in the morning at a McDonald's on Route 220 in Rocky Mount. At 7:30 a.m. sharp, he walked out the front door of the McDonald's eating an Egg McMuffin. On the drive to Highpoint we discussed our racing strategies for the All Pro Series. We told A.J. about our problems with Chris Woods, and, of course, discussed how we were going to handle Keith. A.J. said he had experienced similar personalities in racing and that he wasn't going to let Keith's idiosyncrasies distract him.

We waited for David and Keith at the door to the studio. They pulled up in the new GMC Top Kick, which my father and I hadn't seen since Touch of Class had constructed the addition. The new lounge area had a convertible couch, a television, and sophisticated ceiling lights. It looked like a good enough job. As soon as Keith walked off to open the large rear door of the forty-four-foot, two-car hauler, David pulled my father and me aside and said, "Bad news. He's mad again." My father shook his head. "He makes no sense," David added. Brian Bolten of The Gazelle Group also met us at Alderman. Rick Giles had enlisted Bolten to help sell our team to potential sponsors.

The morning air was already hot and humid. Everyone started to sweat through the ACDelco shirts, jackets, and caps that I had just handed around. Keith lowered the electric door of the Top Kick, which revealed the rear of the blue and white Pontiac. The car now bore the No. 02, which was assigned to us through NASCAR's administrative office for the All Pro Series. We guided the car down the ramp and across a grass field toward the studio. A stark contrast from the weather outside, the air-conditioning inside felt like it was going to freeze the sweat on our backs. We pushed the No. 02 into the designated shooting area, which had a gray background and was surrounded by tall lamps. Keith pulled out a red, arrow-shaped decal that he created specifically for the shoot. The sticker resembled the trademark Pontiac logo. When it was time for people to get into position my father asked Keith if he wanted to be in the team picture as the crew chief. He curtly replied, "I don't want to be in the pictures. I'm leaving for a few hours. When do I have to be back?" He said he was going to detach the hauler from the Top Kick and borrow the truck. He didn't say where he was going.

The shoot was like the one we'd done a while back in Concord. The number of poses seemed endless: we knelt, turned, sat, crouched, stood, smiled, looked serious, put our hands on our hips, laughed, and touched shoulders in various places around the Pontiac. After the shoot, I had lunch in one of the break rooms with Brian Bolten. He said he was working on two solid leads from telecommunication companies and had a personal goal of landing us sponsorships within the next three months. I thought he was being overly optimistic, but I wasn't going to argue with him.

From the break room I overhead some yelling. It was Keith. He was lashing out against David and my father about A.J.'s driving ability. He threatened to quit if we didn't find a driver to his liking. David, who had been dealing with Keith face-to-face much more than we had, looked like he might start throwing haymakers. My father tried to keep the peace. He calmly told Keith that we had made our decision and that it was time to pack up for the day. Keith walked out of the studio in a huff and made his way to the Top Kick. He started the engine and, with David on the passenger side and the trailer holding the car and all of our equipment attached, sped off. We ran outside to see which way they were headed, then grabbed A.J. and jumped in our car. I drove as quickly as I could toward I-85, figuring they were going back toward Mt. Pleasant. When we got on the highway, none of us could see the rig. All we could do was head back north toward Virginia. Fortunately, David was with the mutinous Keith.

"I don't know about this deal," said A.J. from the back seat. "If he acts like this at the track it's going to be tough." Keith had already forced one driver out of the picture, and he was on the verge of a second go-round.

As soon as we got back to Charlottesville, my father called David to find out what happened. He said Keith drove like a madman for the first part of the trip as David threatened to kick his ass as soon as they got out of the rig. But as they got closer to home, Keith calmed down and started talking about the adjustments he needed to make on the car. Thankfully, the rig made it safely to Keith's backyard garage.

My father suggested that I attend all of the All Pro races and keep a close eye on Keith. It would be a huge damper on my work schedule to make all five trips, not to mention the budget hit of paying travel costs. But we could no longer leave Keith to his own devices.

In the end, I would make only two of the trips, as Keith's actions ruined the rest of the summer.

Our first race was August 2, 1997 at Greenville-Pickens Speedway in South Carolina. I planned on meeting Keith and his makeshift pit crew at his garage in Mt. Pleasant the Friday night before the race. Keith assured me he would have our tools, spare parts, practice tires, portable shelter, and coolers for food and beverages ready to go when I arrived. The drive down to Greenville would take two-and-a-half hours. David and Kathy would follow the rig in their old Camaro. A.J. Alsup and his brother would meet us Saturday morning at the hotel. Chad Talbott was going to drive up from Atlanta. He wanted to learn more about our operation, as he was interested in drafting more driver contracts for us and representing us if we ever had legal problems. I also called Leroy White in Charleston to see if he and David were interested in attending the race. Leroy said they would make the three-hour-plus drive and help out in the pits. I booked a hotel room for them and told them to meet us there at 8:30 p.m. on Friday.

On Friday afternoon I flew from Charlottesville to Charlotte and drove directly to Keith's. Pulling down Keith's gravel driveway, I saw him cutting his grass on a riding mower. When he saw me he stopped the mower, pulled out his earplugs, and walked over to say hello. He was in an upbeat mood. While Keith finished mowing the lawn, I took a gander at the rig. It looked like Keith had packed nothing thus far. The Pontiac was still sitting in the center bay of his garage and all the tools and parts were laid out across the floor. When he finished cutting the grass, Keith met me in the garage and told me it would take less than two hours to load everything. The crew would get to his place by 5 p.m. In the meantime, he and I could start packing.

Five o'clock came around fast. Keith and I sweated through our clothes in the muggy August air. One by one, Keith's crew members pulled into the driveway and parked their cars under the trees. The crew, a motley but friendly enough lot of good ol' boys, pitched in to help pack. To his credit, Keith was meticulous. He shouted out directions like a point guard, telling us where to find parts in his garage and where to place them in the trailer. I looked at my watch: It was just past 6:30 p.m. The hauler's electric winch pulled the Pontiac up the ramp and into the storage compartment.

The crew members hopped into the lounge area of the truck. I sat in the passenger side. Keith closed and locked the hauler doors, got in the driver's side, and fired up the diesel engine. I looked at my watch again: 7 p.m. Keith cut the engine so he could run inside, get his suitcase, and say goodbye to his wife and kids. As I waited for Keith to come out of the house, I started to feel some jitters. I was sitting in our new truck, with a strange crew and new car in tow. We were on our way to a NASCAR-sanctioned race at a track where I had never been, with a white driver and a topsy-turvy crew chief. I had a few dollars of cash in my pocket. I didn't know if the trip was going to be a success or a total disaster.

We didn't get on the road until 8 p.m. Everyone was hungry, so we stopped at a McDonald's on Route 49 before leaving the Charlotte area. Sitting down with my Quarter Pounder and Coke, I noticed one of the crew members squeezing out dozens of ketchup packs into the empty side of his hamburger's Styrofoam container. He submerged his fries one by one, covering his fingers in ketchup with each dip.

We got back on the road at 9 p.m. As we drove southward on I-85, Keith commented on how nicely the Top Kick was running. He gave me the Twenty Questions routine. He asked how my father and I ended up at Concord, how we earned enough money to travel so much, how we had landed the ACDelco sponsorship, how far we wanted to go in NASCAR. Worried about how the weekend was going to play out, I stared off into the dark stretch of road ahead and gave him short answers. When the truck hit its first slight incline, the speedometer jumped backwards, to under 40 mph. The water temperature gauge shot up three needle-widths toward the overheating icon. Traffic flashed past us in the left lane while Keith had his foot pressed to the floor. I thought back to Maynard Kline trying to convince my father and me with a computer program that the Top Kick could hack the load we needed it to tow. I started to think about future trips through the

Great Smoky Mountains or the Appalachians, where the much steeper mountain roads would cause the truck to overheat. I just shook my head.

As we neared Greenville we hit some bumper-to-bumper traffic that was caused by an accident. It was getting close to midnight, and we saw nothing but a sea of red taillights in front of us. We decided to get off at the next exit and find the hotel using back roads. The roads were dark and windy. Flocks of moths danced off of the windshield like snowflakes—except these snowflakes left a residue of blood and guts on the glass. The roads narrowed at various twists and turns, and I could hear branches and leaves scraping the top and sides of the trailer. Keith had the high beams on and was sitting straight up in his seat, his eyes wide open. We rolled into the parking lot of the hotel close to 1 a.m.

The night manager told us to park at the bowling alley next door. I checked all of the crew members into the hotel with my credit card, passed out room keys, and asked the night manager if Leroy and David White had checked in.

"No sir, don't have a Leroy or David White," he replied.

"Do you have Chad Talbott?"

"Yes. Mr. Talbott checked in at 8 p.m."

I walked out into the parking lot and noticed two dark-skinned bodies reclining all the way back in their car seats. I tapped on the glass a couple of times, but they didn't budge. I tapped the glass a little harder. Still no movement. I rattled the door handle. Leroy jumped up, startled, and rolled down the window once he recognized the tired gentleman on the other side of the window. I asked when he and David had arrived.

"Eight o'clock," he said slowly and hazily. "We didn't know what to do, so we toured the town until it was time to go to sleep." I told him the team was going to meet for breakfast at 8 a.m. Leroy and David checked in, and we all retired for the evening.

The next morning, the hotel was buzzing people in town for the race. Officials were drinking coffee and fraternizing in the lobby. Outside, team members cracked jokes to each other as they loaded up their rigs in the bowling alley parking lot. At eight o'clock, I caught up with Chad and the Whites and we all headed out to a local haunt for breakfast. At the restaurant we saw A.J. eating with his brother Nipper. They had already run into Keith, who told them he would meet us over at the entrance to the track. We scarfed down greasy eggs, bacon, hash browns, and clumps of corned beef hash before making our way over to the speedway.

At the pit-pass shack I made out a check for more than $300 for a stack of passes. Before the ink dried I heard an outburst from a few feet away.

"Fuck you, Keith!"

When I turned around I saw A.J. walking away from Keith in disgust.

"I don't know what happened," Keith told me when I approached him. "I was just telling the kid how I was going to run things today."

A.J. retreated to his brother's trailer, which was parked on pit road.

"Lenny, you have to get rid of that Keith guy," said Nipper. "He's no good!"

"I don't know, man. I don't know if I can do this," added A.J.

Let's just try and get through today, I told him. He took a deep breath, agreed, and said he was ready for practice as soon as the car was ready.

Keith guided his crew through last-minute adjustments on the car. Kathy Miller volunteered to go to the store and buy soda and sandwiches for everyone. I paid a quick visit to Sean Studer, a driver from Concord. He would be racing his Old El Paso–sponsored car. Nick Smith, Studer's chief mechanic, said hello as well. He gave me a bottle of Old El Paso taco sauce and showed me around the Studers' fancy hauler, which came equipped with a cushy lounge that was big enough to host a party. Back at our plot, I saw Jody Starnes, the gravedigger's son, sizing up our car. He didn't say a word to me.

Teams started firing up their engines for practice. The smell of exhaust blanketed the atmosphere. Keith said he would be ready for A.J. in about thirty minutes. I ran over to Nipper's trailer to give A.J. the heads-up. I felt like a divorce lawyer.

When it was time, A.J. emerged from the trailer in his red, white, and blue ACDelco driver's suit. He stood by the No. 02 and chitchatted with the crew. Keith had a driving suit on, too, as he was going to take the first few practice laps to make sure the car was running smoothly.

It was only a few minutes before Keith and A.J. started arguing again. This time, A.J. took off his driver's suit and hurled it in the trailer.

"Forget it, Lenny," he said. "I quit!" He stormed off.

"What did you say to him?" I asked Keith.

He told me A.J. was immature and didn't want him to practice, adding, "Look, he quit. I'm going to have to drive the car, because the crew here is not going to work for A.J. anyhow."

Without hesitating, I said, "If we don't have A.J. as a driver, then we can pack up and go home." I knew Keith was trying to finagle his way into the driver's seat. It wasn't going to happen on my watch.

"This crew will follow me and do what I tell them," said Keith. The next thing I knew the crew was surrounding me with mean looks on their faces. "You are going to have to let me in the car, Lenny," said Keith.

The hot, humid air had everyone on edge, especially David Miller, who snapped. Wielding a wrench in his right arm, he stood between me and the insurgent crew members and yelled, "Someone is driving that car, 'cause I didn't drive all the way down here for nothing. I'll kick A.J.'s ass and then put 'im in the car if I have too. You tell his ass to get down here right now!" Leroy White stood next to David in defense. Chad couldn't believe what he was seeing.

A.J. came back a few minutes later with a look of both exasperation and contrition. He told Keith he would drive, but he just wanted some respect. After about twenty minutes everyone calmed down and started preparing for the practice run.

Keith drove the Pontiac ten laps before returning to the pits. He told A.J. the car was good to go. With sweat pouring down his face, A.J. put on his helmet, climbed through the window, and strapped in.

A.J. maneuvered his way into the stream of cars already up to practice speed on the asphalt oval. I put on one of the new headsets we purchased for the All Pro races and turned on the radio. I adjusted the squelch until I heard A.J. giving feedback to Keith. Keith told A.J. his lines were good, but that he needed to drive closer to the wall coming out of turn two.

"When I drive that line out of turn two, it looks like I'm going to hit the wall!" replied A.J.

"You have to get closer to the wall out of turn two to get more speed," said Keith. The confusion carried over into A.J.'s qualifying laps, which were lackluster. Les Westerfield, head officer of the All Pro Series, came over to our plot to tell us we didn't qualify for the race.

A.J. climbed out of the Pontiac, told Keith and me that he had done the best he could, and walked back over to his brother's trailer. Since our trailer was wedged in between other teams' trailers, we were stuck in the infield for the rest of the night. We watched all the races at Greenville-Pickens that evening, longingly.

Our second All Pro race was on August 9 at Caraway Speedway in Asheboro, North Carolina, which was only about an hour outside of Charlotte. The same cast of characters came along for the ride: Keith and his misfit crew, David and Kathy Miller, A.J. and his brother Nipper, Leroy and David White, and Chad Talbott. Ron Whitney also planned on meeting us down there to check on the engine. When I pulled into Keith's backyard on the morning of the 9th, I noticed that our rig was parked in the exact same place Keith had left it after the last race. Keith hadn't touched the trailer or the car all week. He gave David Miller and me some half-coherent explanation, saying that the Pontiac had been set up properly at Greenville-Pickens and didn't need adjustments. It was bogus. Any halfway decent crew chief makes sure that he or a crew member checks the car thoroughly before every race. Even if a car is idle, parts can loosen, temperature changes can affect the constitution of certain metallic components, liquids may need to be replaced. To make matters worse, a putrid odor permeated the inside of the hauler; it was because Keith never emptied out the coolers. David opened them to see deli meats, mayonnaise, moldy bread, and sour milk floating in three inches of water.

"You didn't do anything this week," I said. "I hope you don't charge us for this." After a nervous snicker, Keith apologized. He dumped the rotten food and prepared the trailer for race day.

At Caraway, a long access road ran alongside old trailer homes and ended at the pit-pass shack. A.J., Nipper, the Whites, and Ron Whitney had gotten to the track early and were waiting for us near the shack. I paid for everyone's passes and Keith drove the truck toward an open spot on the infield. He went into the corner of the hauler, undressed to his T-shirt and boxer shorts, and put on his faded driver's suit for a few practice laps. Keith backed the No. 02 onto pit road and roared onto the speedway. Everything looked smooth until the tenth lap, when white smoke began to billow from the front of the car. Keith pulled back into the pit and parked the car.

"I think the engine is gone!" he said. The crew ripped off the hood and Ron performed an emergency inspection. The tachometer reading indicated that the engine had exceeded its rpm limit. Ron had to take the engine back to Pennsylvania to give me a proper assessment.

A few days later, Ron told me we were facing $10,000 worth of damage. He offered to do $5,000 worth of labor for free, and said that if we could get some parts from GMSPO quickly, he might be able to get us back on track for the next race, which was at Lanier National Speedway in Braselton, Georgia, near Atlanta.

I faxed a parts order to Bill Fitzgerald. No response. For the next few days I left voicemail messages saying we needed the parts immediately if we had any intention of finishing our five-race plan. He never called back. I finally tracked down Fitzgerald's motorsports assistant. After some prodding, the assistant said Fitzgerald had canceled our entire parts order. The assistant also told me that many of our past orders had never reached us because Fitzgerald canceled them. "Bill was going to send you two cases of brake cleaner and that's all," the assistant said.

I called Ron and told him the news: We were done for the '97 season.

A New Hope

1999 could have been the year that changed it all.

In the media, stories about African-American involvement in NASCAR were popping up all over the place. In February, the day before the Daytona 500, the *Orlando Sentinel* ran a small story about David Scott, who at the time was one of only two black crewmen in the Winston Cup series. The article touched on the lack of black fans and team members in NASCAR, and included the following quote from a fan who made his opinion painfully clear:

> "I don't want to have any [racial slur] out here," said Zack Berndgen, thirty-eight, who had a Confederate battle flag hanging from his tent and a makeshift sign requesting women to bare their chests for beer. "We've got affirmative action, desegregation and all that other crap being shoved down our throats, and this is the only place where we can get away from that. NASCAR was born white, and it should stay white."

David Scott's employment with the Penske-Kranefuss Racing team made much bigger headlines that summer. At July's Jiffy Lube 300 at New Hampshire International Raceway, two white crew members, each from opposing teams, mocked Scott with a stunt that involved one of the crew members adorning a white sheet over his head in the style of the Ku Klux Klan. NASCAR's governing body revoked the licenses of the two crew members and president Bill France Jr. reportedly issued a letter of sorrow to Scott. The crew members were also fired by their respective teams. Suddenly, major papers across the country started to take NASCAR to task for the incident and questioned why the sport wasn't making a concerted effort toward inclusion. (In August of 2006, David Scott sued the governing body of NASCAR for race discrimination and breach of contract. David Scott claimed NASCAR executives deceived him and did not fulfill promises of a job following the 1999 racial incident. In June of 2008, NASCAR once again fell under scrutiny when Mauricia Grant, a former NASCAR technical inspector, sued the stock-car organization for $225 million, alleging racial and sexual discrimination, sexual harassment, and wrongful termination. In the lawsuit, she alleged she was referred to as "Nappy Headed Mo" and "Queen Sheba" by co-workers and was frightened by one official who routinely made references to the Ku Klux Klan. Grant and NASCAR reached a confidential settlement six months later.)

In April of '99, two days before the late Wendell Scott was inducted into the International Motorsports Hall of Fame, HBO's *Real Sports With Bryant Gumbel* ran a segment asking the same question. Reported by Derek McGinty, the piece delved into the histories of Wendell Scott and Willy T. Ribbs and probed prominent figures like Jeff Gordon and Richard Petty for answers. Petty used the phrase "colored people," which prompted a slight rebuke by McGinty. In July, *The Atlanta Journal-Constitution* ran a piece about Tuesday Thomas, a black female driver who had her eyes set on NASCAR's Craftsman Truck series. Thomas was the niece of Bobby Norfleet, a Craftsman Truck driver and team owner. (The following year, Norfleet alleged that NASCAR booted him from the Truck Series because of his skin color, the news of which spawned a demonstration outside of NASCAR's Daytona Beach headquarters. Norfleet had failed to qualify for a race in Martinsville, Virginia, and finished thirty-second out of a thirty-three-car field in

Portland, Oregon, before NASCAR officials told him he did not have enough experience to enter a Craftsman Truck series race in Fountain, Colorado. According to its rulebook, NASCAR has the right to prevent any driver from racing if officials deem that the driver is not skilled or experienced enough to race. Editorials defending NASCAR's action ensued.)

Of course, some stories took a different stance, like journalist Herman Hickman's "To Succeed in NASCAR All Involved Pay Dues" column in the September 2 edition of *FasTrack*, a regional stock-car racing paper. Hickman defended the lack of African-Americans in NASCAR by arguing that NASCAR's evolution as a predominantly white sport traces back to white youths immersing themselves in a sport where they were not outmatched physically by black youths. "On a lot of occasions, blacks and minorities are better endowed physically to compete in such team sports as basketball, football and baseball than are most whites," he writes. "A large majority excel and star in these team sports when less talented whites can't even make the team." He goes on: "Thus, many white youngsters often turn to things mechanical and begin tinkering with automotive engines at an early age. Often that interest becomes magnified through the years and the young mechanic becomes interested in building and racing automobiles."

Hickman's proposition reeked of the age-old sports stereotype that black athletes are stronger and more physically adept, while white athletes possess a cerebral advantage. This judgment has historically come up in discussions about the capabilities of African-American quarterbacks in football. For decades, only white players had the opportunity to play the quarterback position, as coaches and team owners did not have faith in the intelligence of black players to master playbooks and read an opposing defense's scheme. Later in the article, Hickman alleged that black drivers and crew members had not put in the requisite time and effort it takes to win at the higher levels of NASCAR. "I haven't been on the racing scene as much as I used to be. But there weren't any blacks or minorities paying their dues when I traveled with the tour regularly," says Hickman of his experience covering Winston Cup. "From what I see on TV there still aren't any or many blacks and minorities down in the trenches (pits) these days." He concludes, "Racing isn't a sport in which you can buy a guy's way to stardom. He needs to pay his dues. Until some begin paying dues they don't really have a gripe."

Hickman wrote as if he was either unaware or ignorant of the African-Americans who worked just as hard as white drivers and crew members in order to make it in racing. To imply that Rajo Jack, Wendell Scott, Malcolm Durham, Benny Scott, and others hadn't "paid their dues" painted a false portrait of African-Americans' small yet honorable place in racing history. More broadly, like the good ol' fan in the *Orlando Sentinel*, Hickman's argument suggested that African-Americans don't belong in the sport.

Still, despite the polarizing nature of Berndgen's and Hickman's comments, the two were engaging in what was becoming a national dialogue about the subject of African-Americans in racing. Because of the David Scott incident and the *Real Sports* story, the general public was just starting to learn about the prejudice that was entrenched in NASCAR. The topic picked up enough traction in the media that Rev. Jesse Jackson decided to formally address it at his Rainbow/PUSH sports conference on July 1 at the Omni Shoreham Hotel in Washington, DC. Charles Farrell, a longtime associate of my father's who was sports director for Rev. Jesse Jackson's Rainbow/PUSH organization, had asked my father if he wanted to function as the motorsports chairman for Rainbow/PUSH. Part of my father's job was sifting through appeals for Rev. Jackson's help from other African-American motorsports efforts. As more and more proposals trickled in and the media buzz swelled, Rev. Jackson wanted to speak publicly about the need for corporate sponsors to help black sports in need of fair, adequate support. The news of Rev. Jackson's involvement was music to my ears. Miller Racing, along with all of the other struggling black drivers and teams across the country, needed a leader who could bring together powerbrokers in the worlds of business, sports, and activism and galvanize a concerted effort to enact change.

Rev. Jackson had given me a little injection of hope when I bumped into him on a flight from Washington to Chicago back in '93. As he walked down the aisle toward the restroom, I slipped him a note written on a piece of scrap paper with a dull pencil that said something to the effect of:

> My name is Lenny Miller Jr. My father and I have a black race team. We're trying to get to the Daytona 500, and we're having problems getting support from corporate America. I wonder if you and your organizations can help us out.

He said hello, softly, positioned his reading glasses, and read my note. We went on to talk about Willy T. Ribbs and how he was having the same difficulty, even with Bill Cosby's support. Rev. Jackson asked if we could attend a sports summit the Rainbow Coalition was hosting at the Operation PUSH headquarters on the south side of Chicago. The event's theme was "Fighting Racism and Sexism in the Sports Industry." Charles Farrell introduced us to a few of his corporate contacts at the convention, the majority of whom brushed us off. "Oh no, guys, I don't want that," said one rep from Reebok. "Reebok is not into auto racing and probably never will be. We deal with basketball, soccer, and other sports." This was a lie, as just weeks before the event I saw the Reebok logo on an open-wheel car on ESPN2. A few weeks later, Jesse Jackson wrote letters to five CEOs of different corporations that we selected for potential auto-racing presentations. Charles Farrell followed up with many phone calls, but we never heard anything back. Still, I was impressed with how vigorously Rev. Jackson and his staff had jumped behind our cause. Fast-forward six years, and the stage was now set for Rev. Jackson to push our agenda into the promised land.

Overall, the year and a half leading up to the Rainbow/PUSH conference was productive for Miller Racing. The time period was not without some hardship, though.

GMSPO pulled out as a sponsor at the end of '97. After two months of leaving unrequited messages to Bill Fitzgerald, I received a letter dated December 16, 1997. Fitzgerald wrote that our performance had been poor during the 1997 season and that our long-term plans didn't fit into GMSPO's motorsports agenda. "We wish you success in the 1998 racing season," he wrote, "but must reduce our activities in order to make more effective utilization of our resources." The news wasn't shocking. Since Fitzgerald took over for Gaughen, it seemed as if GMSPO was looking for any reason to bail on us.

A couple weeks later, Deep Throat called my father. GM's United Automobile Workers of America division (UAW-GM) wanted to offer us sponsorship for the 1998 season. UAW-GM served as the liaison between General Motors and the auto industry's influential union. A man from the UAW-GM office in Royal Oak, Michigan, faxed me a form to fill out. The form asked where we competed, if we had a show car, and if our driver and team members would be available for appearances. I faxed it back the following day. My father then received a call from Fred Gordon in the UAW-GM office. Gordon told my father about the state-of-the-art motorsports exhibits UAW-GM created for big NASCAR races at Charlotte Motor Speedway, Michigan International Speedway, Atlanta Motor Speedway, and other tracks. The exhibits—equipped with laser beams, smoke machines, Motown music, and virtual-reality racecars—were packed into a small village of tents and were designed to highlight the fruitful relationship between one of the nation's most powerful labor unions and the world's largest automaker. UAW-GM also made sure to showcase the car company's commitment to diversity by posting photographs of African-American, Latino, and Asian employees throughout the tent village. During a series of follow-up meetings with Gordon and his crew, UAW-GM expressed interest in sponsoring us on the track and developing a show car program to include as part of the traveling motorsports exhibits.

The UAW-GM prospect landed on the heels of some in-roads I made with Wittnauer International. I had stumbled across an article in *Black Enterprise* magazine about a group of African-American businessmen who had purchased the Swiss watch company for $28 million. I placed a cold call to Wittnauer to inquire about sponsorship. I got through to Phil Schwetz, vice president of marketing. He told me Wittnauer was already in talks with Texaco about partnering up for some type of NASCAR sponsorship. They were highly interested in having African-American involvement, he told me, and asked me to overnight a proposal. A few weeks later, Schwetz invited my father and me to Wittnauer's headquarters in New Rochelle, New York. He told me a Wittnauer-Texaco deal looked promising.

We needed the new sponsorship prospect more than ever. Days before I made the call to Wittnauer, The Gazelle Group gave up trying to sell our marketing plan. Giles told me none of his corporate contacts were biting. We were back to creating leads for ourselves.

The halls of Wittnauer's offices were dotted with glass display cases that showed off the company's artfully crafted watches. The chirpy African-American receptionist told us the whole company was buzzing about the possibility of Wittnauer getting involved with NASCAR. She even said that if Wittnauer sent some employees down to Concord, she would come along for the ride. We met Phil Schwetz in a large conference room that had a long, wooden table in the center with ten chairs around it. He walked in with reams of paper under his arm and a big smile on his face. "The Millers? Phil Schwetz," he said. He whipped out a notebook and fancy fountain pen and said, "Charles will be here in twenty minutes." He was referring to Charles Watkins, who was the African-American chairman of, and a major stockholder in, Wittnauer International. Schwetz pulled out the proposal materials we had overnighted him and started asking us about our long-term goals. Watkins walked in soon after. He was wearing an elegant suit and watches on both wrists. He got right to his agenda.

"Can you guys get a black driver?"

I gulped, as visions of Chris Woods, Ryan Zeck, and A.J. Alsup flashed through my mind. My father told Schwetz and Watkins about the problems we had recruiting and retaining drivers regardless of skin color, and that having some flexibility in the short-term might allow us to develop a stable core of black drivers down the road.

"I don't care if you have to travel to Africa, the Caribbean, or Harlem," responded Watkins. "Get a black driver in that car."

I understood why Watkins was being rigid about this point. Texaco was still reeling from the 1994 class-action discrimination lawsuit filed by black employees who claimed they were denied promotions and advancement opportunities, and the media maelstrom that ensued two years later when two executives were caught on tape using racial epithets to describe minority employees. Even though Texaco settled the suit in November of 1996, agreeing to shell out a total of $176.1 million in cash payments to the plaintiffs, raises for black employees, and a budget for sensitivity and diversity, many consumers were still boycotting the red-and-white star logo. Texaco was already funneling millions into both NASCAR and open-wheel teams. Being the first major company to sponsor a black NASCAR effort through the Winston Cup level would be a small yet significant step in repairing its image. But because of the settlement, the necessary money might have been available in the oil corporation's coffers.

Serendipitously, news of young, talented black drivers started falling into our lap. The first one was Tim Shutt. My father's long-time friend Joe Gerber called to inform us that he had caught wind of Tim from a friend at Indianapolis Raceway Park. Gerber's friend said the twenty-nine-year-old Shutt could run the wheels off a midget racer and had notched a win at Kalamazoo Speedway in Michigan. (Midget racecars are small in stature, weighing around 1,000 pounds, but come equipped with powerful engines and exposed roll bars for safety.) After a series of calls to Indianapolis Raceway Park and Tim's former employers, I found out that Tim was working as a mechanic for a NASCAR truck team based in Mooresville, North Carolina. When I spoke to him, Tim said he was interested in driving for us and would send me a résumé, some photographs of him and the car, and video footage of his races. I was impressed with his background. He started driving go-karts at an early age and had wins at every stage of his driving career. On the tape, I watched him maneuver past competitors around the Kalamazoo oval with ease. Another clip showed him taking the checkered flag at a race in Indianapolis that was broadcast on ESPN. I called my father as soon as I pressed the stop button.

"Let's go to Concord," he said. "We have to meet this kid."

Tim was clean-cut, articulate, and confident. He was adopted as an infant by a white couple and grew up in Gettysburg, Pennsylvania; he didn't know anything about his biological parents. When he was seven, his father bought him a racing go-kart and started taking him out to the track every weekend for practice. We showed Tim the ACDelco car we had wrangled back from

Keith Van Houten, who we dismissed after the incident at Caraway. (To get the car, trailer, and all of our tools and parts back from our volatile ex-crew chief, who refused to release anything until we paid him thousands of dollars we didn't owe, we came up with a ruse. A friend of ours, Obrie Smith, posed as an interested buyer. We told Keith we had to sell the car to Obrie in order to pay the full amount. Keith bought it. My father wrote him a check for the amount of money we did owe, and we left with our racing resources intact.) We had also asked David Miller to start building a car for the Street Stock class at Concord. That way, if we found a black driver with raw talent, we could put him on the track right away. Plus, if we lost any and all funding, my father and I could, at least temporarily, operate a Street Stock effort out of pocket. Tim said he would drive either car and offered to help David prepare the Street Stock model in his spare time. He even volunteered to look into a shift in his job responsibilities so he didn't have to travel as much. My father and I ended the day by taking Tim to the Construction Company for a meal. We told him we would be in touch soon.

However, the possibility of Tim driving for us evaporated almost as quickly as it surfaced. For weeks, David Miller called Tim to schedule a time to start working on the Street Stock car, but Tim never returned his calls. I finally reached Tim at his employer in Mooresville. Cordially, Tim said he was no longer interested in joining our team. He had been offered driving opportunities before, he said, but nothing ever materialized. He worried that my father and I would never land adequate sponsorship.

Hanging up, I felt like I had been sucker-punched in the stomach. Tim had all the makings of a star. On the track, his skill and versatility reminded me of A.J. Foyt, the retired racing icon who won seven IndyCar championships, four Indianapolis 500s, and, in 1972, the Daytona 500. I had no doubt Tim could continue thriving as a mechanic or crew chief for the truck team, but he was squandering away rare driving ability. I understood his decision, however. It was true that my father and I couldn't guarantee long-term stability. I did wonder if someone had gotten in his ear and influenced his decision, as the change of heart was sudden. Had his current, white-owned team asked him to wait out his turn for a driver's seat? Was he shying away from the obstacles faced by predecessors Wendell Scott, Willy T. Ribbs, and others? Or, maybe Tim was just content working hard behind the scenes. His dedication to mechanical work certainly paid off. A few years down the line, he became the only black crew chief in NASCAR's Busch or Winston Cup Series when he earned the title for Mike McLaughlin's No. 20 Pontiac car, which was owned by Joe Gibbs Racing (JGR). "He's one of the best workers I've ever been around," Cup driver Tony Stewart, and then JGR teammate, told *The Atlanta Journal-Constitution* for a March 17, 2001 article entitled, "Shutt's Drive Is Past Skin-Deep." "He'll make sure things are done right even if he has to stay at the shop by himself after everybody else goes home." Tim quietly helped break down doors for future black crew people in NASCAR, for which he deserves high recognition. Still, to this day, I cannot help but wonder what could have been had Tim stuck with driving.

It wasn't long, though, before a newfound colleague told me about Morty Buckles. I met Stuart Lycett, a representative at A-1 Oil and Lubricants in West Palm Beach, Florida, at the Performance Racing Industry Trade Show in Columbus, Ohio. More than 60,000 people flowed through the gates of the Greater Columbus Convention Center for hundreds of exhibits displaying the latest parts, services, and innovations in technology. My father and I stopped by the Sunoco Race Fuels exhibit to say hello to Jim Worth, a Sunoco manager who attended a presentation we had given at Sunoco's Philadelphia headquarters in 1996. Worth perked up when he saw us and asked questions about the progress we were making. I showed him a picture of our team and asked if

Sunoco could continue providing us with fuel for the following season. "Okay, five more drums for 1998," he replied.

Lycett, who had overheard our conversation, walked up to me and asked, "Are you guys looking for African-American drivers? There's an African-American kid named Morty Buckles who races Late Model Stock cars at Lanier National Speedway in Georgia." Morty had a bachelor's degree in mechanical engineering and a fine personality to boot, said Lycett. "Call me next week. I can get you his telephone number. He could go to the top, he just needs better equipment."

My father and I grinned.

"Call that guy next week," my father said.

When I first spoke to him, Morty seemed like a perfect fit. He was in his mid-twenties and had been racing out of the Atlanta area for close to two decades. Morty's grandfather, Sam Buckles, had been a mechanic for a white stock-car team that raced at Daytona in the 1940s, back when part of the course ran right through the beach. Morty's father bought him a go-kart when he was six years old, and by the time he was eight, Morty was racing against other youngsters all over the Southeast. At the end of his go-karting stint, Morty had won 161 of the 252 races he started. As Morty got older and graduated to stock cars, his wife, Maria, not only gave him moral support, she helped him work on his racecar. Both Morty and Maria were engineers. I had never seen an African-American woman in the pits at any racetrack, let alone one working on cars. She wasn't intimidated by the danger or the hypermasculine atmosphere. Neither was Morty's mother, who attended her son's races and cheered from the grandstands. All in all, the Buckles were the most supportive, close-knit African-American racing family my father and I had ever met.

Morty also had a few corporate contacts, including Donivan Hall, a local African-American field manager of automotive products for Texaco. Morty set up an appointment at Hall's office in

Dunwoody, just north of Atlanta. We were still awaiting news on the Wittnauer-Texaco deal, but I figured it couldn't hurt to align ourselves with an insider.

Hall kept a stack of African-American motorsports sponsorship proposals on his desk. He had open-wheel proposals, drag-racing proposals, stock-car proposals, even an offshore power-boat proposal. I told him we were still waiting to hear something definitive from Wittnauer and Texaco about a partnership.

"How much do you need for 1998?" he asked.

"A minimum of $30,000 to run Morty at Lanier." We needed five times that amount, but since Hall wasn't directly involved with motorsports sponsorships, I didn't want to scare him off. Besides, Morty had his own NASCAR Late Model car, which would save us some money up front. The relatively small sum would go to repairs for his exhausted engine, tires, and eventual crash damage. I figured Hall might be able to finagle $30,000, perhaps out of a diversity budget created from the lawsuit. In the end, we never heard from Hall again, but I was happy with how proactive Morty was in setting up and attending the meeting. Morty carried himself like a professional, which could only help us land sponsorship deals down the road. Of course, we needed money immediately if we were going to get Morty on the track any time soon.

It took a few months but, sure enough, money started trickling in during the spring and summer of '98. In April, Jill Gregory, manager of sponsorships at Texaco, informed Charles Watkins that the oil company was turning down the partnership opportunity with Wittnauer. Watkins, pleased that we had found an African-American driver, told my father Wittnauer was still interested in becoming Miller Racing's primary sponsor. After dangling that carrot in front of us, Watkins later said he would commit $25,000 if the pending UAW-GM show-car program came through. He told my father he didn't have the few hundred thousand dollars we needed to get Morty Buckles through a season at Lanier, and Wittnauer wasn't looking to do a full-fledged marketing or ad campaign behind us. It wasn't the extensive commitment we were looking for, but every sum of money helped.

Within a couple of weeks, UAW-GM approved our show-car program. UAW-GM wanted to display our Pontiac at Charlotte Motor Speedway, Michigan International Speedway, Atlanta Motor Speedway, New Hampshire Motor Speedway, and Phoenix International Raceway. UAW-GM also offered $125,000 in sponsorship money. The deal gave us a nice little injection of hope. Our debt had climbed to nearly $200,000, and GM's other offices weren't helping. I had just received a letter saying that Pontiac-GMC was no longer going to foot the bill for our Top Kick truck, effective immediately. The letter also stated that my father and I had exceeded our parts allotment by $3,000. This happened because Harry Turner at GM Motorsports had ordered extra parts for us and told us he would apply them to his division's budget, but in the end had handed the bill over to Pontiac without telling us. The biggest slap in the face was that the letter was signed by Reggie Armstrong, an African-American consumer merchandising manager for Pontiac-GMC who I had considered a friend; Reggie was a guest at my wedding. Some of my Detroit-area friends later told me they overheard him say the following to a group of African-Americans at a party: "How are those Millers going to get millions of dollars to compete with white folks in racecars?"

We now needed a truck to tow our trailer to the UAW-GM exhibitions, which started in a matter of days. After researching various options to lease or buy a new truck, we ended up leasing the Top Kick from the truck dealership in Charlotte where we picked it up. The dealership wanted $35,000. My father, now a pro at leveraging credit, spent three days calling leasing companies. He found one in Florida that dealt with other motorsports companies and was comfortable with our credit. We arranged a five-year lease. The truck was now ours. I just hoped we didn't hit any steep hills.

Our next order of business was signing a formal driver's contract with Morty Buckles, who had already started to race in the Late Model class at Lanier with the R&W power plant and spare Pontiac Grand Prix body that were left over from the previous year. Chad Talbott drafted the contract. Morty agreed to enter ten Saturday night races during the summer of 1998 for Miller Racing. Some of his toughest competitors would be racing up to thirty times in a season, but for the time being ten was all we could afford. Since Chad lived in the Atlanta area, he volunteered to keep an eye on Morty. This saved my father and me many trips down South.

It didn't take long for Morty to hit his stride. His meticulous driving style shot him into frequent top-ten finishes, sometimes into the top five. On one of the few trips we made to Lanier, my father and I met Dave Liniger Jr., the son of the track's owner. Liniger Jr. said Morty was a potential draw for African-Americans, and said he was thinking about ways to market Morty to African-Americans in the area.

While Morty tore up Lanier, my father and I finalized preparations on the Miller Racing-Wittnauer show car. We visited Motorsports Image, a paint shop in Mooresville, to plot the car's design. Like many of the other backyard racecar businesses in the Charlotte area, Motorsports Image was nestled in a nondescript lot off of a gravel driveway. There was also a small house on the property. A couple of stock cars, stripped down to their steel skeletons, sat outside the shop. There were about half a dozen more cars inside, where a small army of workers were grinding, blasting, sanding, and blowing with air and power tools. The chemical fumes and dust particles in the atmosphere nipped the nose and eyes. A gentleman named Mike Bonds took off his goggles and introduced himself to my father and me. I showed Mike the two renderings Jay Sylvester, a talented graphic designer in Niles, Ohio, had crafted in a matter of a few days. As we began discussing the red and white paint job, one by one the hum of each tool came to a halt. Within a few minutes, the shop fell silent. The workers approached my father and me and went through the Twenty Questions routine. The co-owner of the business, a guy by the name of Smitty, asked where we raced, who our driver was, and where we were from. He took a liking to us, especially when he found out my father used to drag race, as he was a drag racer himself. Smitty invited us over to his house for a barbecue he was hosting in his backyard the next day. We could also check out his street rod, he said. My father and I graciously declined, as we had to leave town that day.

Working with UAW-GM was a pleasant experience compared to GMSPO. Mark Kowalski, one of the coordinators for the motorsports exhibits, personally looked out for Miller Racing. He always made sure to position our display in the highly trafficked areas of each exhibit. He put us up in nice hotels, he double-checked our reservations, he took care of our meals. At the exhibits, UAW-GM employees welcomed our team with open arms. Many of the staffers were NASCAR fans, so they asked questions about Morty's latest progress and talked about going to see him if they were ever in Atlanta. The staff's enthusiasm trickled down to the throng of racing fans who stopped by our booth to read the placards we had posted about the history of African-Americans in motorsports and ask questions about our effort. Another participant on the tour who kept our spirits up was Oliver "Cool Breeze" Rivers, a friend of my father's childhood friend. My dad had recruited Oliver, a retired African-American bus driver from Philadelphia, to drive one of the UAW-GM tour buses. Oliver was suave and sartorial, hence his nickname. He dressed in fine clothing, wore a large diamond earring, and spoke in calm, measured tones. The UAW-GM staff loved him.

The highlight of the tour was the UAW-GM Quality 500 Winston Cup race weekend in early October. As the title sponsor, UAW-GM pulled out all of the promotional stops for the estimated 50,000 fans that were expected to visit the tent village over the course of the three-day weekend. At the entrance, UAW-GM staff members handed out over 30,000 posters, which were designed by renowned stock-car enthusiast and painter Sam Bass. The Miller Racing-Wittnauer International car sat near the center. Many of the African-American UAW-GM employees on hand bombarded my father and me with questions and words of encouragement. We heard things like: "It's about time." "I'm glad you guys are with us." "Let me get my camera." "Lord, Lord, Lord." "I'm telling everyone back at the plant." "You guys are pioneers." That Saturday evening, UAW-GM hosted its annual employee awards banquet in a tent behind the Hyatt in upscale South Charlotte. About three hundred employees and their loved ones attended. After various award presentations and feel-good speeches about the wonderful employee relationships forged at UAW-GM, Bernie Weber, a motorsports manager, took the stage to welcome Miller Racing to the UAW-GM family. Morty and Maria, who had driven up from Atlanta for the banquet, followed my father and me up to the stage. When Bernie introduced Morty the crowd went crazy. Upon hearing that Maria was Morty's crew chief and mechanic, the crowd got louder. When Maria walked off the stage, several women charged toward her to say hello. Morty was also bombarded with newfound fans. Mark Kowalski ran up to us and said, "Good job! Good job! You guys have something here!"

Toward the end of the night, I made my way over to Humpy Wheeler, who I had noticed a little earlier standing on the other side of the tent. He acted as if he didn't recognize me. I re-introduced myself.

"How's he doing on the track?" Wheeler asked when I told him about Morty.

"Morty's a top-five contender in Late Model Stock," I told him. "We just need more sponsorship."

"Say hello to your dad," he said curtly before walking away.

When we packed up on Monday morning, I saw a scene that would haunt me for years to come. As we loaded the trailer I noticed several commercial stake trucks coming down the access road toward us. The truck beds were packed with young African-American men. Many of them had rags wrapped around their heads, and they were all holding trash bags. It was the clean-up crew. Watching the young men picking up the white race fans' trash, I thought about the menial role these African-Americans were playing in one of NASCAR's big weekends and wondered how prevalent this scene was at tracks throughout the South. Like the stray, old African-American restroom attendant collecting tips in a pie tin at smaller tracks, these young men were relegated to the very margins of opportunity at one of the biggest NASCAR venues in America. Yes, the UAW-GM event showed the role of African-Americans in motorsports was evolving. But the groups of black bodies, sweating through ragged clothing in a field of refuse in the damp morning air, reminded me that the specter of segregation still loomed in the backdrop of everything we did. For all of our accomplishments, there was still a very long way to go until we could create more opportunities for black people at the track.

That fall, David Miller called my father to tell him about a black driver that was racing Legends cars just up the road in Greensboro. Chris Bristol, a twenty-one-year-old student at North Carolina A&T, was participating in the university's Intercollegiate Auto Racing Association (ICARA) program. A&T, along with UNC Charlotte, Duke, Virginia, South Carolina, and

North Carolina State, ran accredited engineering courses that allowed students to develop and race Legends cars against other schools in ICARA. Chris B.'s technical savvy and driving ability had helped earn A&T an ICARA championship. He was also a marketer's dream. He was tall, good-looking, and had a striking mane of dreadlocks. David had heard about Chris B. through Clay Hare, a renowned chassis man at Concord and a fixture on the Legends circuit. My father and I flew down to Greensboro to meet Chris B. in person. We were only more impressed. He told us how he had been interested in racing since age five and how his mother and stepfather supported his interest. In fact, his mother was a fan of IndyCar driver Bobby Rahal, whose shop was near the family's hometown of Columbus, Ohio. When he was eleven, Chris B. was racing 80cc motocross bikes, but as he grew older he started setting his sights on stock cars. He told us that even though North Carolina A&T was a Historically Black College and University (HBCU), the ICARA program had mostly white engineering students. In fact, a recent white graduate of the program had landed a $60,000-a-year job with Richard Childress Racing. Meanwhile, black graduates of the program tended to move on to manufacturing jobs outside of racing. Chris B. said part of that disparity was due to the fact that some African-American students in the program didn't put in as much time as the white students. These black students had no real aspirations of racing on a higher level. My father and I were disheartened by such news, as it almost gave credence to journalist Herman Hickman's idea that African-Americans weren't paying their dues at the lower levels of racing. At the same time, here was Chris Bristol, one of the crown jewels of the ICARA series, and no major team was offering him a job on par with what Childress offered the white graduate.

By the end of the month, Miller Racing signed Chris B. as a driver. He would race for us in Street Stock at Concord for the

1999 season. UAW-GM, as well as Charles Watkins of Wittnauer, was ecstatic that we had found a second African-American driver.

As usual, my father and I remained busy in the offseason. Before Christmas, I received an invitation to the upcoming Sports Summit, a gathering of sports-industry executives in New York City. Brian Z. France, the son of Bill France Jr. and NASCAR's vice president of marketing, was on the scheduled list of attendees. While I never did get to speak to Brian Z. France at the event, I did meet Andrew Craig, CEO of Championship Auto Racing Teams (CART). CART, akin to Formula 1, was an open-wheel series based in the US featuring both domestic and international drivers. Craig, a clean-cut Englishman, gave a compelling speech about the growth of CART over the years, replete with a PowerPoint presentation and action-packed video footage. I perked up when he told the room of 1,000 that CART was actively seeking increased minority participation, especially African-American drivers, owners, and mechanics. More minorities and women were essential if CART racing was going to grow in popularity, he said. I darted through the cluttered banquet hall toward the podium, stepping on toes, banging knees, and walking in front of a few TV cameras along the way. I apologized at each hurried misstep. As soon as the speech ended, I got in line behind three young white women in business skirts who also wanted to speak to Craig. When it was my turn, I introduced myself and told Craig I had an African-American driver ready for the Toyota Atlantic Series, CART's developmental league for burgeoning open-wheel drivers.

"What's his name?" asked Craig.

"Morty Buckles."

"I've heard of him. Here's my card. Call me next week for a meeting."

A few weeks later, my father and I flew into the Detroit Metro Airport and hopped in a rental car toward CART's headquarters in Troy, Michigan. While Miller Racing hadn't been involved in open-wheel racing since the '70s, we were excited about Craig's message at the Sports Summit. With CART's governing body behind us, we figured we might have an easier path toward sponsorship. If that were the case, my father and I would gladly straddle the line between stock-car and open-wheel racing. We knew Morty Buckles was seasoned enough to drive in either, and Chris Bristol was young enough that we could groom him for both. Of course, CART was much more expensive, which meant we would be looking for a deal in the area of $1 million a year.

A bright red open-wheel racer gleamed proudly in the eighth-floor lobby. Andrew Craig rounded the corner to greet us. "Gentlemen, I'm glad you came in to see us," he said in his British accent. "Follow me."

We sat on a black leather couch with a glass table in front of us. I pulled out the Miller Racing portfolio and gave Craig the usual spiel. Midway through my monologue, Roger Bailey, head of the CART-sanctioned Indy Lights Series, entered the room. Bailey had a heavy British accent as well. My father wowed the two Englishmen with his stories about traveling around the country with Benny Scott. I provided the visuals, leafing through a binder full of photos of African-American drivers in Formula Fords, Formula Super Vees, and Formula 5000s.

"By golly! You did all this stuff years ago!" cried Craig. "There's no question you can operate any type of race team. If I get you a Toyota Atlantic car and some engines, can you test a few African-American drivers?"

"Yes, we're ready," I replied.

As soon as we pulled out of the parking lot, my father and I started discussing drivers besides Morty and Chris B. that we could recruit for the proposed CART Toyota Atlantic test. By now, Bill Lester had been referred to us on multiple occasions. Lester had been racing competitively since the mid-'80s. He got his start in the SCCA Series in northern California, where he won the 1984 Rookie of the Year award and the GT-3 Regional Road Racing Championship in 1985 and 1986. By the '90s, he had graduated to SCCA's Trans AM series and had his sights set on driving in NASCAR. He had electrical engineering and computer science degrees from the University of California, Berkeley, and, from what we heard, had an excellent knowledge of mechanics. The only slight problem was that Bill was pushing forty. Still, we figured his years of experience would allow him to race in CART immediately.

I flew out to the Bay Area to meet with Lester and gauge his interest. He was serious about racing, so serious that he had quit his cushy job at Hewlett Packard in order to devote more time to driving. "I can't go back to corporate America," he said. "I can't sit behind a desk anymore. I'm a driver." He jogged every day in the Oakland hills to stay in shape, he said. He also spent hours on the phone each day calling NASCAR teams for possible driving opportunities, mostly to no avail. However, he was currently in talks with new team owner Ed Rensi. Rensi had also left a cushy corporate job—CEO of McDonald's—to devote more time to racing. Lester mentioned how Rensi had given him a $2,000 plane ticket to fly to the East Coast to test a stock car, a gesture he felt most African-American owners could not afford. Lester's skepticism came through even more when I invited him to the Toyota Atlantic test. He said he was interested in participating but did not want to sign any long-term contracts with us. I understood his apprehension. He had been around long enough to realize that most black race teams folded as quickly as they began. He wanted stability wherever he could find it.

Back in Virginia, my voicemail was loaded with messages. They were mostly from African-American drivers interested in the CART test. Apparently, every once in a while CART received calls from African-American drivers looking for team openings and sponsorship help. Once word of a driver's test spread, the phones started ringing off the hook. CART directed all of the interested parties to me. One driver to emerge from the flood of responses was David Francis Jr.

My father and I met David Francis Jr. in the lobby of the Palos Verdes Inn in Redondo Beach, California. At the time, he was working at a high-tech computer company in Southern California. He grew up in South Central Los Angeles, where he raced BMX bicycles at a young age and followed the career of his favorite driver, the late Brazilian F1 champion Ayrton Senna. Francis Jr. raced locally in a truck series before enrolling in the Skip Barber Racing School, the best open-wheel racing school in the country. The top-notch driver's education helped him win several races and a regional championship in the entry-level Skip Barber Formula Dodge Series. At the Dodge Series award banquets, competitors always gave him and his white girlfriend dirty looks. He still loved racing, though, and spoke intently about making a career in CART. He had already invested over $20,000 in racing, scrimping from the modest revenue his full-time job netted him, and dreamed about the day a sponsor would come knocking on his door. We invited him to our room and showed him our team presentation, which we had now digitized and placed on a CD to play on computers. "Where did you get this? Who did this?" he exclaimed. He watched in awe as I clicked through photos of Benny Scott next to the Formula 5000 racer Benny drove at the inaugural Long Beach Grand Prix, held close to Francis Jr.'s stomping grounds. I clicked on video interviews with Morty Buckles and Chris Bristol. "I didn't know, I didn't know," said Francis Jr. of all the black racers he was seeing before him. "I've only heard of Willy T. Ribbs. I didn't know African-American racing history was so rich." David was sold on the prospect of driving for us right then and there and asked about next steps. We told him to call Chad Talbott to sign a contract. He was excited, as other white teams had expressed interest in signing him, only to never follow up with a formal agreement. Within weeks, David was officially on board with Miller Racing Group (as we were now calling ourselves), and patiently awaited confirmation on the CART test.

In March of 1999, Chris Bristol got out to a fast start at Concord. He was racing the Pontiac Firebird David Miller had assembled to consistent top-ten finishes. By now, a few major changes had taken place at our home away from home. The Furrs sold the track, which they had already renamed Concord Motorsport Park, to the Laton family. Gary Laton had been a part-time driver in the NASCAR Busch Series Grand National division, but had recently retired after a horrific crash at Michigan International Speedway that nearly took his life. His brother David Laton was now the managing partner at Concord. It was sad saying goodbye to Yvonne and Henry Furr, as they had always been so welcoming and supportive. The Latons changed the names of some of the classes; the old Street Stock division, where Chris B. was racing, was now called Limited Stock. The other major change was that my father and I moved the team from shop No. 10 to shops No. 5 and No. 6, a switch that gave us a whopping 3,000 square feet. It was more costly, and my father and I were still paying back debt, but as the team continued to grow, we figured the move to a bigger space was necessary. The new digs lifted the spirits of David Miller, who seemed to be getting along with Chris B. really well. In fact, Miller Racing's team morale was as high as it had ever been. New drivers, new shop, new sponsor, a pending deal for a CART program, and the upcoming Rainbow/PUSH conference instilled everyone with a feeling of optimism. Our star was just coming into focus.

The momentum continued into May, when I attended a marketing forum held on the gargantuan Queen Elizabeth 2 cruise ship. A colleague of mine, Darren Marshall, suggested I make the trip to Manhattan for the two-day event. The QE2 party had helped Darren rake in over $4 million worth of business for his International Sports Licensing (ISL) agency. "You're anchored out at sea off the coast of New York City, talking to the top decision makers—one on one—in tuxedos," he told me. The $10,000 ticket was steep, but the opportunity to hobnob with executives from Pennzoil, McDonald's, Procter & Gamble, and countless other companies was too good to pass up. The QE2 event took place on the heels of the *Real Sports* piece and just before the Rainbow/PUSH conference. With the subject of African-Americans in motorsports now seeping into the public consciousness, I wanted to target companies that might be enthusiastic about our team's mission and our recent in-roads, regardless of whether or not they were already involved in motorsports. My main message: *now* was the time to act.

The weekend entailed hour upon hour of fine dining, cocktails, schmoozing, name-dropping, and delivering the Miller Racing Group–sponsorship plea. But I accumulated a stockpile of business cards, including one from an assertive blonde woman who scurried across the room to meet me.

"I saw you over here by yourself, and I was by myself," she said. "I have an appointment with you later. I'm Julie Walker with Procter & Gamble." Over the years, Tide, a P&G company, had backed NASCAR legends Darrell Waltrip and Ricky Rudd. She almost offered a bona fide sponsorship deal on the spot. She envisioned P&G's Gain brand as the sponsor for our car, in part because P&G marketed the ultrafragrant laundry detergent heavily toward African-Americans and Latinos. She also told me that P&G sold a lot of its products in Food Lion grocery stores, a retail chain that in 1995 brokered a deal to become "The Official Supermarket of NASCAR." Food Lion had been sponsoring the traveling NASCAR SuperFan Festival, an interactive, family-friendly event held at various stops along the Winston Cup tour.

Walker told me African-Americans were the largest consumers in many Food Lion stores in the Southeast. She wanted me to contact Gail Cox, who worked on P&G's Food Lion account.

When I spoke to Cox a few days later, she was excited about the idea of a show-car program. Cox was in the process of relocating from P&G's main headquarters in Cincinnati to a field office in Charlotte and wanted to meet with me after the Rainbow/PUSH conference. She wanted me to bring along some examples of what our car might look like with the Gain logo and color scheme. That day, I visited my local Food Lion and purchased a box of Gain. I dumped the detergent down the drain, carved out the logo from the empty bottle, and FedExed my crude handiwork to Jay Sylvester. I told Jay I needed Gain-friendly renderings of a Pontiac Grand Prix and a tractor-trailer rig. He said he would have the prototypes done in less than a week. To the chagrin of my wife, our kitchen smelled like Gain for two days.

As the Rainbow/PUSH conference in July drew closer, my father was on the phone from 7 a.m. until midnight, seven days a week. He fielded calls from black drag racers, stock-car and open-wheel drivers, and team owners from coast to coast, all fed up with corporate America continually denying them sponsorship. One driver he spoke to daily was Doc Watson, who raced in the amateur Automobile Racing Club of America (ARCA) stock-car series. Doc had limited sponsorship from a Philadelphia newspaper but felt he could do a lot better if he had more money behind him. My father empathized with Doc and the other callers and suggested they all get to Washington for the event. It would be an opportunity to meet and share stories with fellow African-Americans in motorsports as well as the big names that were scheduled to be in attendance, including Willy T. Ribbs, Malcolm Durham, Brian Z. France, NBA hall-of-famer Isiah Thomas, ex–Cleveland Cavalier Brad Daugherty, who had stake in a NASCAR Craftsman Truck team, and, of course, Rev. Jesse Jackson. Andrew Craig would also be there to unveil the CART African-American Driver Development program, which was now confirmed. The media was expected to be in full force. The collective narrative of frustrated, perseverant, proud African-Americans in motorsports was about to take the stage in our nation's capital. With the harsh realities of the past and present on display, the future for all of us was about to change. At least, that's what my father and I hoped.

When I arrived at the Omni Shoreham Hotel on the morning of July 1, at least twenty racecar transporters were lined up along the street. Crew members shook hands with crew members from other teams as they unloaded hot rods, stock cars, and sports cars. I saw license plates from Maryland, California, Georgia, Michigan, New Jersey, and North Carolina. Closer to the hotel entrance, teams were positioning their freshly cleaned racecars in a roped-off display area. TV reporters visited drivers and crew members to set up interviews.

One drag racer near the display area had his car's hood up, revealing a missing engine.

"Where's the engine?" I asked.

"I had to sell it so I could get here from California," he said. "I can't race it anyhow. I don't have a sponsor."

In the lobby, drivers and owners toted business portfolios. I caught bits and pieces of conversations about engines, clutches, tires, and debt. I found my father talking to Doc Watson and Leavy Morgan, a road racer from Detroit. My dad excused himself from the conversation and told me that we should head outside, as David and Kathy Miller were about to pull up. Sure enough, as we reached the sidewalk we saw David turning the GMC Top Kick and forty-four-foot Miller Racing Group trailer off of Connecticut Avenue onto Calvert Street. Before David could park, Malcolm Durham walked up to my father and said, "Hey Len, tell your driver he has to go up to Cleveland Avenue, then turn around." It was great to see Malcolm. He told us how he and his sons were building race engines out of their shop in Maryland, and how the family was struggling to find sponsorship for his sons, who were also drag racers.

David parked and hopped out of the truck with Kathy. They were both wearing Miller Racing Group T-shirts, which we made especially for the event. David also had his Miller Racing Group cap on and half a cigar in his mouth.

"This city drivin' is rough!" David said. "Cars tried to run me down on Connecticut Avenue."

"How do you feel now, white boy?" blurted out Doc Watson, who had stepped outside to check out our trailer. "You're the minority now." Doc chuckled.

"I feel all right. I'm with the Millers," replied David.

A tour bus, filled with elderly white people, parked next to us. The driver stepped out and said to Doc, "Hey, boy, you can't park here. This is for buses."

"Lenny, hold my hat," said Doc. He rolled up a copy of *USA Today* and wielded it in the direction of the bus driver, saying, "White cracker, who you callin' a boy? Going to jail doesn't bother me."

"Get out of my way," retorted the bus driver. "I can't park my bus." My father and I restrained Doc. It was muggy outside, and as I clasped Doc with all my might, I started to sweat through my pinstripe suit. Thankfully, before the jawing turned into fisticuffs, the bus driver walked away in disgust and told his passengers to exit from the bus's current parked position.

David backed the car out of the trailer. It was rush hour, and a few commuters rolled down their windows to ask what was going on.

"Is he into car racing now?" asked a woman in a BMW after I told her Rev. Jesse Jackson was hosting his annual sports conference. She told me she would watch the news that evening to see how the conference went.

David unhooked the winch cable on the front bumper, reeled it back on the spool, and asked if I wanted to drive the car over to the display area. Doc Watson bet me $100 to pull the car under the portico at the hotel entrance.

"Hold on to my suit jacket," I said.

With sweat soaking through my oxford shirt, I climbed through the window and nestled into the seat. I hit the starter switch and the car let out a turbocharged growl. David marshaled me backward a few feet so I could make the tight right turn up the hotel driveway cleanly. As I pulled underneath the portico, the car's roar reverberated off of the ceiling. A group of United Airlines flight attendants who were waiting for a shuttle bus looked around in horror, as if the building might collapse. A couple of bellhops eyed me with spite. I couldn't blame them. Even my ears started ringing. But boy, that pain felt good. (Doc never paid up the $100. To this day he still owes me.)

I hustled back toward the front entrance. The speeches were about to begin. In the lobby, some clusters of young African-Americans passed out flyers. I figured they were courting sponsorship, but the flyers told a story. One of the crude computer printouts, entitled "A Washington Redskins Motorsports Folly," lambasted some African-American players on the Washington Redskins who owned hot rods for purchasing engines from a white-owned shop. One portion of the flyer read:

> The African-American players have determined that African-American owned speed shops don't have the capability to build sophisticated Hot Rod or Street Rod motors [sic].

It went on to say that the popular white-owned shop ended up subcontracting the work back to the African-American–owned shop, because it was "the best machine shop in the DC area." The flyer listed the following hypotheses as to why the players opted for the white-owned shop:

A. Just self-hatred
B. Behavior carried-over from plantation times
C. The white coach told them where to go
D. They couldn't bring their wives to a black establishment (blonde syndrome)
E. All of the above

Whether or not any of the claims were true, the gentlemen handing out the flyer felt betrayed. Another leaflet blamed major companies like MBNA America, Hardee's, Coca-Cola, Pep Boys, and Texaco for consistently rejecting or shortchanging African-American racing programs while they concurrently supported white teams. The inflammatory literature left uneasy white folks with red faces, while many African-American readers just shook their heads.

The convention's main hall was packed. I saw at least twenty newspaper reporters and half a dozen TV cameras in the rear. At the dais on-stage, Willy T. Ribbs, Andrew Craig, Charles Farrell, Brian Z. France, and Brad Daugherty all started to settle into their seats. Chad Talbott waved me over to his seat. I also saw Tracy Belmear, one of Darren Marshall's African-American co-workers who worked on ISL's account with CART. I'd met Tracy on the QE2 back in May and we had been keeping in touch. A few days earlier, Tracy called to tell me that because CART didn't have any black employees they wanted him to stand up when all CART employees were asked to stand up. "I work for ISL," said Tracy with frustration. "CART doesn't have any African-American employees. He's going to make me a token in public to make CART look good. This is going to be embarrassing." It was unsettling that Tracy had been put in such an uncomfortable position by the CART folks.

Charles Farrell opened the speeches by talking about the unlevel playing field for African-Americans in motorsports. Willy T. Ribbs told his story about qualifying for the Indianapolis 500. When it was Andrew Craig's turn, he rolled out the plans for CART and Miller Racing Group to run a Toyota Atlantic test for three African-American drivers and indeed motioned for Tracy, my father, and me to stand up. When I sat down, an African-American in a pit crew uniform whispered in my ear, "At least somebody's trying to do something out here." Brian Z. France spoke about NASCAR's desire for diversity and announced NASCAR's pledge of $25,000 toward the Urban Youth Racing School, a new program in Philadelphia that offered inner-city kids the opportunity to learn about driving and maintaining racecars.

After Daugherty spoke, a door on the right side of the stage opened, and through it emerged a man dressed in a black safari-style shirt and black pants. It was Rev. Jesse Jackson. Front and center, Rev. Jackson pulled out a tiny, checkered flag and said, "Black and white makes up the checkered flag." The audience stood and applauded. "How can champions in racing be declared when everyone is not allowed to compete?" he asked. His speech, laced with sports history, case studies, and moving metaphors, challenged corporate America to join in the mission of diversifying NASCAR, a sport that was at once American and undemocratic, populist yet exclusive. His speech ended to rousing applause and he opened up the floor for questions. A woman from Maryland introducing herself as "Gee Whiz" said, "As a black female in drag racing, I'm unique. Oil companies at the drag strips acknowledge my uniqueness, but offer me one lousy case of oil. Why is that, people?" After an uncomfortable silence from the panel, Charles Farrell told Gee Whiz that Rainbow/PUSH would help her foster some corporate relationships, and that she should view the conference as a networking opportunity for such needs. Leavy Morgan asked, "Can't we get sponsorship for the adults that own racecars and are ready to go? I'm sick and tired of hearing about these go-kart programs for African-American youth that are really designed to snuff out the adults so corporations can escape from the real issues. The adults need sponsorship too."

Rev. Jackson ended the Q&A session and led everyone to the parking lot for some photo opportunities with the media. My father had hired a photographer, an African-American fellow recommended by Rainbow/PUSH, to follow us around and take pictures of the experience. As we mingled outside, my father noticed him eating a sandwich, with his camera dangling from his neck. "Hey, what are you doing, man?" my father yelled. "You need to get ready and take some pictures!" The photographer threw his sandwich in a greasy brown bag and sprang into action. The Rainbow/PUSH staffers placed Rev. Jackson in Malcolm Durham's drag racer. Camera flashes danced off of the exposed, chrome engine. Rev. Jackson posed for a few more photos alongside Willy T. Ribbs, Andrew Craig, and Brian Z. France and disappeared inside for lunch. The camerapeople and reporters switched their attention to some of the drivers milling about. A reporter from a Florida-based TV channel interviewed Doc Watson next to the Hills Brothers Coffee NASCAR Winston Cup racer he had borrowed from white owner Junie Donlavey. "I don't know," he repeated to the reporter's questions about why he thought he wasn't receiving the support he needed. "Sponsors just don't want to take a chance."

The day ended with lunch inside the grand banquet room. I sat at a table with Malcolm Durham and Andrew Craig, who couldn't stop gushing about the driver development program. "You're going to be very popular in a few days," he said. After lunch, as I stood with Tracy, Chad, and my father in the lobby, I noticed David and Kathy ogling Rev. Jackson as he made his grand exit, shaking hands and waving like the beloved politician that he was.

"I can't believe we got that close to Rev. Jackson!" exclaimed David like an excited teenager. "He looks bigger in real life."

"Mr. Miller, David and I see all kinds of people with you. I'm glad we got to get out of Concord," said Kathy. David and Kathy did some sight-seeing the day before, including a visit to the National Zoo. I asked where they had eaten lunch.

"I was freaked out," David said. "We saw Lebanese, Chinese, Vietnamese, Thai, and a lot of other funny stuff we couldn't even pronounce. When we saw those yellow arches, we were happy. We knew what McDonald's was." We all laughed. David and Kathy were out of their element in the city, but were taking the new place, people, and experience in stride.

After the conference, the media continued to cover the subject of African-Americans in motorsports. Through the fall, multiple newspapers previewed the forthcoming CART test. An article about Chris Bristol even surfaced in the *Greensboro News & Record*. Rainbow/PUSH promised to continue the dialogue with its corporate contacts. We hoped the buzz would land us a megadeal in the near future.

In the meantime, my father and I had to figure out how to keep both Chris B. and Morty on the track for the rest of the '99 season. The UAW-GM money had already gone toward paying off debt, and while we had some solid sponsorship leads, including the upcoming meeting with Gail Cox at P&G, we needed some funding fast. We managed to keep Chris B. afloat in the relatively affordable Limited Stock down at Concord. Morty, on the other hand, had been sidelined due to a lack of resources in the much more costly Late Model level and awaited our call. Randy McNulty, one of our allies at Concord who now operated out of shop No. 10, offered to rent us a lime green Pro truck on a race-by-race basis. It was a bit of a gamble, for, if Morty totaled the truck we would have to pay up to $25,000 to cover the crash damage. We asked Morty if he would be willing to foot half the bill for racing the truck at Concord. Morty agreed, and after crunching some numbers we calculated that Morty could enter six races. With the upcoming Gail Cox meeting scheduled for a Friday in Charlotte, I summoned David, Randy, and Morty to prep the truck for a race the following evening. That way, my father and I could meet with P&G and see both Chris B. and Morty race. If things went our way, we could land a sponsorship deal and have two black drivers win in the same weekend.

Cox met us in the lobby of the P&G field office and walked us back to a conference room. There, she introduced us to Kurt Frehner, a representative from a marketing firm that worked with P&G out in Cincinnati. I talked Frehner and Cox through our digital presentation, after which Frehner and Cox said they wanted to review the NASCAR All Pro schedule and possibly back us for the Busch Grand National Series. When I showed Cox the rendering of the Gain car, she smiled from ear to ear.

"We may want to create an event in front of a Food Lion store," said Cox. "Also, can you guys get a Hispanic driver and a female driver on your team too?"

I could see my father's expression change, as we both sensed P&G might try to sweep a series of diversity issues into our small effort. Still, I told Frehner and Cox that finding drivers of different backgrounds wouldn't be a problem.

"Good, good," said Cox. "I think we'll need all three to cover ourselves so the senior executives won't reject us. Hispanics and females are taking the forefront now." She told us the next step was setting up a meeting with Food Lion, which would happen in the next few weeks. Kurt gave us each his business card, assured us he would be in touch, and rushed out of the room to catch his flight back to Cincinnati.

My father and I hit the hotel to change out of our business suits and put on casual clothes for the track. David was working on the Firebird when we got to the shop. As soon as he saw us, he started talking about the experience in DC and how he was in awe of Rev. Jackson. "And that Doc Watson, boy. He doesn't take shit from anybody." David lit a cigar, stroked his bushy beard, and told us Chris B. was showing improvement on the track. However, David wanted to set some boundaries in the shop, as the precocious college grad wanted to hop under the hood any time he had the chance. "I know the kid is a mechanical engineer and everything," said David, "but I do the setups." David also told us that the lime green Pro truck was ready to race. "We may get two wins tomorrow night," he remarked. "With two black drivers in victory lane on the same night, Concord will never be the same."

My father and I left the track to meet Chris B. for dinner. Over fried chicken, macaroni and cheese, and string beans at Ryan's buffet in Concord, Chris B.—who addressed each of us as Mr. Miller—gave a different perspective on his relationship with David. He thought David was just an average mechanic, and guessed that David was holding on to many of the shop duties in fear that he may one day lose them to Chris B. He also felt emasculated by David on a regular basis. "Mr. Miller, David always makes me clean the shop with a broom or wipe down the car with a rag," he said. "When I tell him I want to evaluate our suspension setup, he gives me the silent treatment, Mr. Miller." I believed him. Chris B. had such an affable air about him that David may have seen an opportunity to assert himself as a manager. It's not an uncommon circumstance in the small-time stock-car garage, the crew chief flexing his supervisory status. On Cup teams, the crew chief had the second highest profile job next to the driver, coordinating the driver with the pit crew, the spotter, and the rest of the mechanical specialists on race days via radio. Just like the short track drivers, the local crew chiefs had aspirations of one day making it to NASCAR.

"Chris, you have to *demand* to play a more active role in mechanical duties," said my father. "We're not here every week, so you have to be more aggressive."

"Okay, I'll keep trying. But David is hard to work with, Mr. Miller."

Chris B. said he was adjusting to Concord's tricky tri-oval well, and that he looked forward to participating in the CART test. I suggested that he enroll in a class at Skip Barber Racing School to acclimate himself with driving an open-wheel car. He said he would call his mother in Ohio to set aside a few thousand dollars for the class.

The next morning, my father and I scarfed down a greasy breakfast at Shoney's and headed to Tiger Tom Pistone's parts store for some last-minute needs. We had grown accustomed to stopping by Tiger Tom's on race days. Located off of a dead end in a residential area, the place was like a NASCAR museum. Out front, he had old trailers and car carcasses littered about. Inside, he had row upon row of used suspension components, springs, fuel lines, pistons, starters, brake pads, alternators, generators, axles, and almost any other part a pit crew at Concord might need. While the place looked like a muddle of greasy metal, he and his daughter Lena had an extensive, organized inventory. Tiger Tom charged far less than some of the big-name retailers and extended us a generous credit line; without the financial leniency, we may have been out of luck for some races. He and Lena also filled us in on track gossip, free of charge.

"Hey, look who's here," said Tiger Tom. "I know you guys have some money. I'm broke. Look at this sandwich my wife made for me. It has no meat in it!" My father chuckled and pulled out his checkbook. Lena ran over and gave my father a long hug. I told her about both Morty and Chris B. racing that evening at Concord.

"You guys don't even live in North Carolina, and you do better than the local racers we see twice a week," she said.

We picked up everything on David's parts list and made our way back to the shop. Randy McNulty paid a visit and reiterated that he and David had the lime green truck in tip-top racing shape. "I've seen him drive at Lanier," Randy said about Morty. "Y'all got yourselves a driver."

Chris B. showed up in baggy pants and an oversized shirt. Morty pulled up with his family shortly thereafter. It dawned on my father and me that we would have about ten African-Americans gathered in the pits for the Saturday night races. I couldn't be certain, but that had to be some sort of record. The good ol' boys were giving us stares, but with an increased presence, I walked around with a greater sense of pride. Sure, we still had a long ways to go until we had more black folks at the track as owners, crew members, and fans. But today's assembly felt like progress.

Chris B. and Morty changed into their driver's suits and attended the 5 p.m. meeting. Randy towed the lime green truck with "U-Rent" painted on the sides into the pits. David finished up his work on the Firebird. As usual, it was hot and humid. My clothes stuck to my skin. The pits buzzed with the customary pre-race activity. The track announcer introduced the evening's schedule over the loudspeakers as engines roared to life. It was time to race.

No matter the outcome, we had already made history.

The Beginning of the End

13

In January of 2000, NASCAR began piecing together its Diversity Council. Founded by Brian Z. France in the wake of the Rainbow/PUSH conference, the Diversity Council was responsible for creating minority internships across all levels of stock-car racing—from drivers and mechanics to desk jobs at NASCAR's corporate headquarters—and facilitating sponsorship deals. France tapped retired jocks Joe Washington and Brad Daugherty to help assemble the collective, which would grow to include driver Bill Lester, Magic Johnson, and a few dozen others.

In the years to come, the Diversity Council never included Miller Racing in its master plan. In fact, many of its programs, most notably 2004's ballyhooed Drive For Diversity campaign, lured black drivers away from our teams and placed them with white-owned teams.

At first, the Diversity Council's initiatives, while small in scope, were just the kind of tangible changes we had long hoped to see. In April of 2000, Texaco, the sponsor for NASCAR vet Ricky Rudd at the time, announced that it would donate a Legends car and money to the same North Carolina A&T ICARA engineering program that produced Chris Bristol. Rudd's team, Robert Yates Racing, would also offer an internship to an A&T student. Dodge Motorsports followed suit later in the year by introducing a scholarship program that aimed to teach minorities about racing technology. Upon graduation, Dodge would look to place the scholarship recipients with a Dodge team. Dodge Motorsports also named Willy T. Ribbs as a driver for owner Bobby

Hamilton's NASCAR Craftsman Truck Series team. NASCAR itself inaugurated scholarships in association with the United Negro College Fund and Hispanic Association of Colleges and Universities. The Urban Youth Racing School started a driver development program, entering students in Super Mini Cup races along the East Coast, and would soon land sponsorship assistance from GM, EA Sports, Dale Earnhardt Jr., NASCAR.com, and Joe Gibbs Racing. Rev. Jackson, Charles Farrell, and company, who had been working the phones constantly to enlist more companies in the plight to diversify NASCAR, set up a series of meetings on Oct. 19, 2000 between Rainbow/PUSH and representatives from the Big Three automakers. Toward the end of year, Rainbow/PUSH also made significant headway with Dr Pepper as a potential sponsor for Miller Racing Group.

News of the Big Three meeting and the Dr Pepper possibility arrived at a time when some solid sponsorship leads went sour. Gail Cox at P&G put us through a series of hoops and hopeful conversations only to disappear on us.

Midway through the '99 season, Cox asked me to create some additional car designs bearing the logos of P&G's brands.

"I have a meeting with Food Lion," she told me over the phone. "I need a stock-car and trailer rendering with Pringles, Vicks NyQuil, Vicks DayQuil, Dawn, Dryel, Crisco, Sunny Delight, Febreeze, Crest, and Bounty. And put Food Lion on there, too."

"The car's going to look cluttered," I said.

"I know it's going to look crazy, but this is what I need."

I asked if she could send me the logos digitally via e-mail or CD.

"I don't have anything to give you," she responded, sheepishly. "How did you get the Gain logo?" I told her I cut the logo from an actual bottle, scanned it, and sent it to a graphic designer.

"I'm sorry about this," she said, "but you're going to have to buy all the products and get the labels off. Also, I know this is short notice, but I need you to have all this done in four days."

When my wife came home from work that day, I asked her to help me do a little grocery shopping. We drove to Food Lion and purchased all of the necessary products.

"Does Ricky Rudd or any other NASCAR team go through this?" asked my wife on the way home.

"This is a bunch of crap," I said, frustrated with the whole process. "We better get something out of this."

I laid all the products out on the kitchen table and grabbed a pair of scissors. I pulled the Crest toothpaste out of the box and cut out the logo. I slipped the plastic label off the Sunny Delight orange drink and cut out the logo. I had to use a clothing steamer to loosen the label on the bottle of Crisco cooking oil. The steamer didn't work on the Dawn label, so in a hurried moment I poured the liquid soap down the drain. Later, as I cleaned up, I made the mistake of turning on the faucet and leaving the room for a minute. When I returned, bubbles were spewing out of the drain and overflowed onto the kitchen floor. In my mind, I heard my wife's words over and over: "Does Ricky Rudd or any other NASCAR team go through this?" I drove the FedEx envelope of logos over to Dulles airport that evening to make sure Jay Sylvester would receive it the next day. Jay worked about twenty-four hours straight to turn around the renderings in the short four-day window.

A few months later, in September, Cox called to say that the P&G folks in Cincinnati weren't interested in sponsoring us. She said a Coca-Cola ethnic marketing representative she knew in Charlotte was interested in the team. Plus, a colleague from Wilton Connor, a consumer products packaging company, told her the company would consider creating some retail packaging with photos of Morty and Chris B. Of course, Wilton Connor had to obtain packaging contracts from brands interested in incorporating motorsports into their marketing plans.

"I can't promise anything, but we may have a chance," said Cox.

It sounded like a circuitous road toward another dead end. Before hanging up, she had another request.

"Can you get VIP tickets for Dave Cully of Wilton Connor Packaging, his wife, myself, and my husband Ira, for the UAW-GM Quality 500?"

The race, held at the recently renamed Lowe's Motor Speedway in Charlotte, was coming up in just a few weeks, and we had very limited access to VIP passes.

"I know this may be asking too much of you, but if we all could see your Wittnauer show car at the UAW-GM exhibit and see the race, we could get a feel for what you're doing."

"Gail, you can get into the exhibit free," I replied with a sigh. "And we'll do the best we can on the VIP tickets."

When I spoke to Dave Cully at the UAW-GM race he was friendly and sounded genuinely enthused about designing some packaging for us. But, as I suspected, he could only do so with the involvement of another company. In the end, Food Lion, Coca-Cola, and Wilton Connor never partnered with Miller Racing.

That UAW-GM race weekend wasn't a total loss, however. Our Wittnauer show car continued to garner interest from NASCAR fans, as did Morty, Maria, and Chris B., who, dressed in red-and-white Miller Racing Group shirts, sat at a table next to the car. At the end of the day on Saturday, Morty's and Chris B.'s arms felt limp from autographing over 1,200 UAW-GM posters. When we ran out of posters, fans wanted their jackets, seat cushions, umbrellas, shirts, and hats signed. One woman wanted her arm autographed. At times, up to 100 people were in line, including an African-American youth group whose members were in awe of Morty and Chris B. The youngsters had never seen an African-American stock-car driver in their lives, let alone two. In fact, that was the feedback we received from almost all of our visitors that weekend.

"They're like diamonds in the rough!" said Mark Kowalski of the buzz surrounding Morty and Chris B. "If they make it to Winston Cup, they'll change the sport."

I started chasing some of the other sponsorship leads that came out of the QE2 weekend. The first person I called was James Giffin, vice president of marketing for Lincoln Technical Institute, Inc. Lincoln Tech was a vocational school offering curriculums in air conditioning repair, computers, automobile mechanics, and other trades at campuses across the country. On the QE2, Giffin, who spoke a mile a minute, told me he was interested in partnering with Miller Racing because over a third of his school's students were African-American. Also, Lincoln Tech was already backing a Winston Cup driver.

"Geoff Bodine received an associate sponsorship from Lincoln Tech last year for 1 million bucks," he told me over the phone when I called to explain our current need for a sponsor. "All we got was a little decal on the car that no one could see with the car going 200 miles per hour."

I told him Lincoln Tech could have its name all over our car for far less than a million.

"Can I get a few appearances, too?" he asked. "Can I get some of the students to be interns on the team during an All Pro race?"

"You can have all of the above for much less than a million bucks," I assured him.

Giffin loved the idea and asked if we could meet with his marketing staff at Lincoln Tech's West Orange, New Jersey headquarters to outline the details of the program. He felt we could put a sponsorship plan into motion for the 2000 season.

We headed to New Jersey on a warm morning in late July. I showed Giffin and five other Lincoln Tech executives our digital presentation in an ultramodern conference room. While videos of

Morty Buckles and Chris Bristol played in the background, I talked up all the ways Miller Racing could be an attractive marketing vehicle at Lincoln Tech campuses. My father leafed through a flip chart that illustrated our targeted demographics and our plan for advancing an African-American driver up through the NASCAR ranks. Giffin reiterated to his colleagues that his predecessor had invested a million in Geoff Bodine for a barely noticeable decal, and that our team, if we remained competitive, could offer them far more visibility. Everyone nodded, and after some follow-up questions from the other executives, Giffin said Lincoln Tech would indeed sponsor us for the All Pro Series in 2000.

"Our minority students will like this," Giffin remarked to us on the way out. "You guys have two mechanical engineers as drivers. It will be perfect. Your crossover appeal is great. We'll have all this in writing in August."

We called Morty and Chris B. to tell them the good news. They were both relieved. So was David Miller.

"You and Senior are magicians," David told me over the phone. "Chris will win some races next year, and so will Morty." Team morale was high. Between the next check from UAW-GM and the newfound Lincoln Tech deal, we could conceivably put both drivers on the track in 2000 and provide enough resources for them to take the checkered flag. With Chris B. new to driving stock cars and Morty getting acclimated to a new vehicle at a new course, we knew they both needed extra track time to improve. More races meant more expenses. And there were still those good ol' troublemakers at Concord who tried to derail the dark-skinned newbies. One Saturday night at Concord, Morty was in second behind a woman in a red, white, and blue truck late in the race. During the last few laps they were door-to-door. Suddenly, as he made a move to pass, she sideswiped him, sending Morty into the wall and out of the race. After the race, Kathy Miller told us, "Two members of the winning truck team said that nigger wasn't going to win tonight." My father and I complained to Concord's new head honcho David Laton. He dismissed the incident as typical track behavior.

While we awaited confirmation from Lincoln Tech, I e-mailed some of my other QE2 contacts, all to no avail. Within days, I received negative responses from Kodak, ProLine, Stanley Tools, Purell, ConAgra, and Levi's. I was disappointed with the barrage of "no's," but I had faith in the Lincoln Tech deal. "We'll be all right," I told myself.

At the end of August, my father and I met with Giffin again in West Orange. "I just need to go over the numbers for NASCAR All Pro and what you think it would take to run Busch in two years," he said. "I will get all of this in contract form next week." Giffin and my father started to crunch numbers. I was happy to hear the word "contract."

The meeting lasted about forty-five minutes. As he walked us to the door, Giffin said, "Give me a call after the Labor Day weekend. I should be able to fax you a contract then. I'll mail you an original after we make sure we agree on everything."

I called after Labor Day weekend to touch base.

"James Giffin doesn't work here anymore," a secretary told me.

I started to feel lightheaded and nauseous. I gripped the phone tight.

"Where did he go? What happened?"

A new management group purchased Lincoln Tech; Griffin was let go over the weekend.

"Do you have his home telephone number?"

"No."

I asked her if she could transfer me to Cathy Lazzara, the marketing services manager we had met on our last trip.

"Hold on."

I left a frantic message on Lazzara's voice mail. Two hours later, she called back.

"What happened to James Giffin?" I asked.

"They terminated him over the weekend," she replied. "I don't know the details."

I told her about our pending sponsorship and asked her if she could find out if our program had been handed over to someone else. She offered to run down the hall to Giffin's former office to look for the Miller Racing Group proposal. She put me on hold for about five minutes. When she got back on the phone, the news wasn't good.

"Everything in his office is gone. I don't think I can help you at this point. Sorry."

I phoned my father to tell him Lincoln Tech was dead. "I can't believe this," he said. "I'll call Morty and Chris."

I had also kept in touch with another QE2 acquaintance, Helen Clark, who was the director of brand strategy for Texaco. When we met on the ship, I wasn't optimistic about a Texaco sponsorship since the oil company had passed on the opportunity to co-sponsor the Wittnauer show car only a few years prior. I called and e-mailed Clark periodically anyway, hoping that Texaco might come around in light of all the Rainbow/PUSH and CART buzz. Sure enough, in October of '99 she e-mailed me saying that Texaco had hired a new director of sponsorships, Michael Hargrave. Hargrave came from Anheuser-Busch and had a lot of experience working with NASCAR. I phoned him and we set up a meeting for the last week of October at the Texaco office in White Plains, New York. In the meantime, I tailored a comprehensive sponsorship proposal specifically for the Texaco/Havoline brand. I studied how Texaco marketed its products and its No. 28 Winston Cup car, which at the time was piloted by a promising young driver named Kenny Irwin. Texaco was also sponsoring Michael Andretti's CART team, Newman/Haas Racing. We had a couple of talented black drivers who were preparing for both stock-car and open-wheel racing. I figured we had a shot.

"Are you Lenny?" asked a female executive in the lobby of the Texaco headquarters in White Plains. Her heels had clicked along the floor the entire walk toward me. She extended her hand and said her name was Sheri Welte, assistant manager of sponsorships. She walked me through a maze of hallways and elevators and sat me down in a meeting room with a large, round table. Mike Hargrave walked in, shook my hand, and told me to cue up the presentation. The room got eerily quiet, as both Welte and Hargrave had serious looks on their faces. I connected my laptop to an extension cord and reached for the outlet, only to find out the cord would only reach if I sat my laptop at the very edge of the table. If someone sneezed, my computer would have plummeted to the floor. After my fifteen-minute presentation, Hargrave broke the silence.

"Where did you get that?" he asked in admiration. "That presentation is state of the art!" As I started to pull the marketing proposal out of my briefcase, Hargrave said, "I'm interested in Miller Racing Group, but I don't want to be the only sponsor. Do you have anyone else that's interested?"

"We're talking to Procter & Gamble," I said.

"I think Procter & Gamble would be a better sponsor for you because they have more brands," said Sheri Welte.

Huh? I thought to myself. Why are we discussing Procter & Gamble at Texaco?

"Well, I think Texaco can be a part of this, but I just don't want to be the only one on the car," remarked Hargrave. I started to talk about our longer-term goals, but Hargrave cut me off.

"Do you know Bill Lester?" he asked.

"Yes," I said.

"I met him a few years ago at a race. He's an impressive guy, but he's in his late-thirties, which is too old." I wasn't sure what to make of his assessment, as Lester didn't factor into our plan for sponsorship.

"Okay, give me your proposal and we'll look at it and get back to you within a week. We'll make a quick decision on this," said Hargrave.

I handed over the proposal and packed up my laptop. Sheri Welte shook my hand and said, "It was nice meeting you," then disappeared down the hall. I asked Hargrave if I could speak to Helen Clark. He said she was in a meeting but that I could leave a note in her office.

I continued to follow up with Hargrave through the holiday season. His response around Thanksgiving was, "We're still working on what direction we're going to go. I'll know something soon. Give me a call in two weeks."

About a week before Christmas, Hargrave told me, "We're not going to sponsor a team. We're going to sponsor engineering scholarships at African-American colleges."

My heart dropped to my stomach.

One of the engineering programs on Texaco's list was the North Carolina A&T ICARA Legends class. Miller Racing Group had Chris Bristol, an alumnus of the A&T ICARA program, ready to take a giant leap toward NASCAR. At that very moment, Texaco could have made Chris B. a poster boy for diversity in NASCAR and placed him, along with Miller Racing Group, on a path toward Winston Cup. But, apparently, Texaco wasn't ready to make that kind of full-on commitment. Instead, the petroleum company was content with the PR they would get for the handout to the HBCU. A few months later, my father bumped into Hargrave at a gala honoring the Texaco-A&T partnership. Hargrave sounded like he barely recalled my meeting with him up in White Plains. My father introduced Hargrave to Chris B., who was also in attendance. Hargrave shook his hand and excused himself from the conversation.

To compound our dead ends toward sponsorship, the CART program, after a promising start, blew up in our faces.

In the weeks following the Rainbow/PUSH conference résumés from African-American drivers, mechanical engineers, and crew members starting piling up at CART's offices. One résumé came from a fellow named Andrew Kelley, an open-wheel driver living in Hilliard, Ohio, who had been calling CART for nearly two years looking for some help finding a driving opportunity. Within minutes of speaking to him on the phone I knew Kelley was a natural fit. He was only twenty-six years old, yet he already had over twenty years of racing experience. In 1979, he won all thirteen races in a 25cc Midget Karting series, and as he worked his way up the karting ranks he amassed six series championships. As a teenager, he became the first African-American driver to win a Formula Mazda series race. He held a business degree from the Ohio State University and had started a nonprofit organization that taught inner-city kids about the variety of jobs in motorsports besides just driving. Despite his impressive credentials, he hadn't yet found a team or a sponsor to back him. I invited him to come out and meet my father and me at Summit Point Raceway in West Virginia, where Chris Bristol would be driving for the three-day Skip Barber Racing School session on July 18. It was a six-hour drive for Kelley. He would drive to Summit Point and back in the same day.

"Chris may be a better driver in this road racing than in stock-car racing," commented my father as we watched Chris B. practice at Summit Point from a gazebo-like shelter near the last turn. Chris B. downshifted awfully well for an open-wheel rookie and negotiated the twists, turns, and hills smoothly. On a complete 180-degree turn he slowed from 100 mph to 40 mph with ease, then exploded onto the straightaway at just the right moment. As his practice run progressed, his lap times got shorter and shorter.

"He's catching on quick," said one of the instructors next to us. "Definitely above average."

"Mr. Miller, I love this road racing," gushed Chris B. after the day's first session. "I love it. I hope you can get this Toyota Atlantic team together."

When Chris B.'s group was called out to the track again, my father and I noticed an African-American guy cutting across the parking lot toward us. It was Andrew Kelley. The three of us sat at a wooden picnic table in the shade. Kelley recalled his experiences getting denied sponsorship from places like Miller Brewing Company and Shell Oil—companies that had also turned us down along the way. On one occasion, an executive asked him to bring along his trophies to a meeting, to prove that he was indeed a real racecar driver. Kelley packed twenty of his first-place trophies, which he kept in a display case at home, in a duffel bag and lined up them one by one on the executive's desk. At the end of the meeting, the executive told Kelley, thanks, but no thanks. My father explained to Kelley that if he signed an agent's contract with Miller Racing Group we could represent him in such meetings. "We can deal with the problems, while you focus on driving." Kelley liked the idea of a support system. Within a couple of weeks, he was signed to Miller Racing Group.

In August, CART held separate press conferences to announce David Francis Jr. and Andrew Kelley as the first two drivers in the first Toyota Atlantic test session. Reporters were all over Francis Jr. on the day of his press conference, which was held before he raced on the Grand Prix circuit at Belle Isle in Detroit. On his own, David had reeled in $20,000 of temporary sponsorship from a Detroit radio station and MGM Grand Casino. With Belle Isle so close to downtown Detroit, a noticeable number of African-Americans were walking around the course. Some stopped dead in their tracks when they saw the young African-American man in a red driver's uniform. Others took photos. One woman wept. "He's breaking new ground," she said with tears in her eyes. "It has to be hard." Chad Talbott, who had grown fond of the open-wheel racing community's more international and upper-middle-class fan base, hoped a Miller Racing Group Toyota Atlantic team would materialize soon. "Open-wheel racing is for me," he said. "Get me on the wine and cheese circuit." In the months following the press conferences, national newspapers ran stories about David Francis Jr., Andrew Kelley, and the Toyota Atlantic test, as did *African Americans On Wheels* magazine, a publication put out by the multicultural multimedia company On Wheels, Inc.

My father and I were happy with the hype surrounding the CART program, but we were also skeptical about CART's commitment to Miller Racing and the driver development program. "While the test session does not guarantee the participant a drive with any particular team," read the press release announcing Andrew Kelley's participation, "the evaluation will help the driver as he/she seeks sponsorship and a drive in a race series." Amateur drivers like David Francis Jr. and Andrew Kelley needed years of high-level racing experience to hone their skills and make them more attractive to sponsors. A couple of test runs for PR purposes wouldn't cut it. Francis Jr. had shown how green he was at the Grand Prix race in Detroit, where he finished toward the back of the pack.

In September, Andrew Craig gave me a call. He sounded flustered.

"Lenny, is Miller Racing Group forcing drivers to sign an agent's contract with your team as a prerequisite for the CART African-American Driver Development Program?" he asked.

"No, we're not forcing anyone to do anything," I said.

"I received a call from Bill Lester," he told me. "He said he wants to be included in the program, but he would have to sign an agent's contract with Miller Racing Group first. Are you using this program to start a driver's representation agency?"

I recalled my preliminary talks with Lester, when he told me he didn't want to sign a contract binding him to Miller Racing

Group. I told Craig that was the last time I had spoken to Lester about racing and that I had never spoken to him about the CART test. I also explained that Andrew Kelley and David Francis Jr. had signed agent's contracts with us so we could help them find sponsorship, but these agreements had nothing to do with the CART test. Craig understood, but still had a hint of concern in his voice.

"How close are we to selecting the third driver?" he asked. I told him we were considering a couple of candidates with strong résumés, including drivers Steve Saunders and John Petiford, and that we would make a decision within a week. He asked me to call him as soon as we decided.

I made a conference call to my father and Chad to get to the bottom of why Andrew Craig had made such allegations about our dealings with Bill Lester. My father and Chad guessed that Lester was trying to bully his way into the development program. If my father and Chad were right, we would argue to keep Lester out of the test. We wanted younger drivers. Plus, we didn't want to include someone who was trying to circumvent us in the process.

Craig called a few days later. My father and Chad were right.

"Lenny, let's put Lester in the test to avoid friction from him," he pleaded with me. I said I would have to conference with our team attorney.

"Lester is a NASCAR driver, Andrew!" Chad exclaimed off the bat. "He's not going the open-wheel route. This will be a waste."

"Let's just put him in the car to avoid controversy," responded Craig. "He did pretty well in a NASCAR Busch car at Watkins Glen. David Francis Jr. struggled at the race in Detroit. He was almost last."

"The development program's objective is to evaluate talent so they can be groomed over time to become great drivers," I interjected. "African-American drivers don't get the same amount of track time as white drivers." I also expressed my concern about Lester's age.

"I'm the CEO and can do what I want," said Craig, who hadn't given us a valid reason to include Lester. All I could think was that Lester was trying to reap the benefits of an African-American driver program without dealing with the African-Americans involved.

"Then what do you need Miller Racing Group for?" I said, now heated. "Are we just a conduit so CART gets news clippings? What do we get out of all this?"

"Let's not get contentious, gentlemen," said Chad.

"I'm not getting contentious!" hollered Craig. He lowered his voice and said, "I'm putting Bill Lester in the test, but we won't announce it."

That was that, Lester was in the test. Chad and I called my dad to tell him. I was so disgusted I could barely speak to my own father. It was becoming evident that CART was using Miller Racing Group as a front for a feel-good PR campaign.

The Toyota Atlantic test, held at Buttonwillow Raceway in Southern California, became a formality. According to written evaluations by Precision Preparation, Inc., a motorsports team CART brought in to judge the talent, David Francis Jr., Andrew Kelley, and Bill Lester all proved to be capable open-wheel drivers. The evaluations were supposed to be used by CART to help the drivers find sponsorship, but CART never delivered.

I told Kelley and Francis Jr. that my father and I would help them find sponsorship, but we did not have the money to put them on the track. We would have given them a shot at stock-car racing, but they lived too far away from Concord and did not want to relocate. In the end, their racing careers stalled.

Bill Lester continued chasing his NASCAR dreams, and for a moment made it to the top. He followed in the footsteps of Willy T. Ribbs by signing to Bobby Hamilton's Craftsman Truck team, and raced competitively in the lower-tier NASCAR series for years. In 2006, at age forty-five, Lester entered two Cup races. He finished in the back of the pack in both.

In June of 2000, Andrew Craig was terminated as CEO of CART. In 2003, CART went bankrupt and morphed into the Champ Car World Series.

At the start of 2000, my father and I decided to devote all of our resources to racing Chris B. in the Limited Stock class at Concord. It was essential to maintain Chris B.'s progress in full-scale stock cars, since most of his experience was in the 5/8-scale Legends vehicles. UAW-GM renewed our show-car program, which gave the team some income, but it wasn't enough to include Morty in our plans for the year. He was simply too advanced to continue racing in the Pro Truck class at Concord, and we couldn't afford to sustain him for a full season in a higher class. We had barely enough money to pay rent for our shop at Concord through February. Plus, between Chris B. and Morty, Chris B. was younger and needed more track time before he could go much further in his career. Morty was disappointed that he wouldn't be racing with us in 2000, but agreed that a low-budget program would be a waste of time and resources. Once again, Morty would sit in Atlanta and await any updates on the sponsorship front.

The personal problems between David and Chris B. escalated through the first half of the 2000 season, which came to an abrupt, scary halt. Chris B. still complained that David wouldn't listen to his advice in the shop. When he did challenge David on a chassis setup, David would respond by leaving the shop for hours in a huff. Chris B. also said that David left the shop filthy and disorganized, a hint that the stock-car novice should pick up a broom. Chris B., admittedly intimidated by David Miller's backwoods persona, didn't have the gall to confront David on the conflict. Instead, he vented to friends, family, my father, and me. By June, the situation had spiraled to a point where the two barely spoke to each other. The tension led to Chris B. wrecking the Firebird in a Saturday night race. It was reminiscent of our past experiences with Chris Woods, Nick Smith, and Keith Van Houten, guys who let personality beefs devolve into costly, dangerous consequences. My father did his best to mediate, telling them both over the phone that we needed them to act like grown men.

One morning, I received a call from Chris B.'s mother, Gwen.

"Did you know that Chris B. had to go to the hospital yesterday?" she said. "He hit the wall practicing at Concord between turns one and two. He chipped a bone in his right foot." The injury required Chris B. to sit out for more than six weeks. Miller Racing now had no one on the track.

Our sponsorship search came to a similar standstill. In May, I attended the QE2 conference again; my dad paid for the ticket with money from his personal funds. For the most part, my spiel fell on deaf ears. Representatives of Columbia House, MGM Grand Casinos, Pennzoil-Quaker State, and America Online—companies that all sponsored auto racing in some capacity—slipped me business cards as quickly as they could and moved on to the next meeting. Kaye DeShields, manager of retail products and services for the US Postal Service, was intrigued, but warned me that USPS's marketing budget was tight. I told her I had seen their large hospitality tent at a NASCAR Winston Cup event at the Phoenix International Raceway. She said it was most likely an initiative from a western division, and asked me to follow up with her when she returned to her office in Washington. Craig Hudson, vice president of brand marketing for Harrah's Entertainment in Las Vegas, thought we had a good marketing plan, but told me all his company's auto-racing dollars were committed to A.J. Foyt. "Why don't you talk to the Indians?" he said, directing me to the Native American–owned casino in central North Carolina that Harrah's managed. When I asked him whom I might contact at the North

Carolina casino, he said he really didn't know anyone there. The rough sea conditions weren't helping my cause, either. During the first night, the ship pitched from side to side, making many attendees seasick. I felt fine, but nearly half my appointments on the second day were either late or failed to show up due to illness. John Crisci, event-marketing manager for Taylor Made golf equipment, showed up thirty minutes late for our breakfast, sick to his stomach. He spoke in incoherent sentences and barely spit out the fact that Taylor Made was considering a sponsorship of Winston Cup star Dale Jarrett, an avid golfer. Crisci said that a Cup sponsorship might be too steep for Taylor Made, though, and that a NASCAR endeavor with a lower price tag might be more attractive to his company. His face bright red, Crisci told me to call him in a couple of weeks before scurrying off to the bathroom. Midway through the event, I was sick at the fact that my dad had dropped $13,000 on the ticket.

I was eager to meet with Brown & Williamson Tobacco, though, as its Viceroy brand had sponsored Black American Racers, Inc. back in the mid-1970s. From the outset, I knew a stock-car sponsorship was unlikely. As a result of a 1998 settlement with the state's attorney general, the tobacco companies had to overhaul how they marketed and advertised to consumers. Over time, part of that change included a falling out with NASCAR, which, over the past decade, had made a full-throttle effort to cater to fans of all ages. (In 2003, R.J. Reynolds' Winston brand lost title sponsorship of the Cup series, paving the way for NASCAR to strike a title sponsorship deal with Nextel.) However, Brown & Williamson's Kool brand sponsored the CART Toyota Atlantic Series as well as CART's Team Kool Green; over the course of five years Brown & Williamson had given Team Kool Green more than $50 million. Kay Culliton, divisional vice president of marketing services and operations, arrived a few minutes early. I showed her old photos of Benny

Scott and told her about David Francis Jr. and Andrew Kelley. She was impressed and said she was confident a significant sponsorship program could be developed with Miller Racing Group. When I told her we needed $900,000 to compete in the CART Toyota Atlantic Series, she didn't bat an eye. At the end of our meeting, Culliton pulled out her business card and jotted down the names of people she was going to organize in Louisville for a meeting.

For weeks afterward, Culliton tried to orchestrate the meeting, and even had lunch with Chad Talbott, who was now living in the Louisville area, to discuss future plans. But the necessary congregation of Brown & Williamson executives never happened. In fact, her colleagues weren't returning her messages regarding Miller Racing Group. "I've told everyone that Brown & Williamson needs to jump on this opportunity, but I'm confused," she said about the lack of response she was getting. "I've never had this happen to me in my corporate career."

On the QE2, I received positive feedback from the reps from Knights Inn. Marilyn McHugh, vice president of marketing, and Jody Riina, director of marketing services for Knights Inn's parent company Cendant Corporation, sounded enthused by the Slim Jim All Pro Series plan and asked me to send a proposal to McHugh's office in Parsippany, New Jersey. As requested, I overnighted the proposal within a couple of days.

(My dealings with Riina and McHugh, Culliton, and, to a certain extent, P&G's Gail Cox, made me wonder if female executives might be more receptive to our plight. I imagined that many powerful businesswomen had to overcome chauvinist obstacles en route to success, and that they might have identified with our struggles.)

In mid-June, I dialed Jody Riina's number. A female voice said, "Barbara Levy."

I asked to speak to Jody Riina.

"Jody is no longer with Cendant. This is Barbara Levy, her replacement. Can I help you with anything?"

I recapped my conversation with Riina and McHugh on the QE2. Levy didn't know what I was talking about and suggested I call Marilyn McHugh. McHugh instructed me to resubmit the proposal to Robb Ford, who handled marketing projects for all of Cendant's brands. When I updated my father on the situation, he was just as befuddled as I was at yet another unfortunate twist of fate. "When I was young, people kept their jobs for years," he griped. "Now it's down to weeks."

Off the bat, Robb Ford sounded eager. Over the phone he praised a Knights Inn program that gave minority hotel franchise applicants special financing provisions. He was familiar with NASCAR and said he had already evaluated several high-dollar sponsorship proposals. "NASCAR fans are our customers, and your team is an economical way to get involved in the sport," he said.

I called Robb Ford at least once a week to follow up. He always assured me he would get back to me with news. "I'm working on it," he would say in an upbeat tone.

By August he stopped returning my calls. After September, I never heard from Robb Ford or Knights Inn again.

In the end, I followed up with everyone I met on the QE2 trip, but nothing materialized. I learned that phrases like "I'm working on it," "Use my name to contact so-and-so," "Follow up with my assistant," and "Send me an e-mail" were code for "We aren't interested."

In the fall, Charles Farrell called with uplifting news. He had brokered meetings with Ford, GM, and DaimlerChrysler (as it was now known after the 1998 merger) on October 19 at a hotel in downtown Detroit. Rev. Jackson would be in attendance, as well as Rick Wagoner, CEO of General Motors. At the time, all NASCAR Cup teams had an affiliation with one of the Big Three automakers (in 2007 Toyota started entering cars in Cup racing). The meetings in Detroit felt like a make-or-break moment for us. If Rev. Jesse Jackson could not get one of the Big Three to hop on board with us, who could?

I met my father and Al Anderson at Rainbow/PUSH's hotel suite in Detroit. Anderson, an old friend of my father's, ran a marketing services company in Atlanta and had been tapping his contacts for sponsorship leads. A man with a boom microphone in front of his mouth and a cell phone attached to his hip let me in through the suite's double doors. Inside, Rev. Jackson and his staff had set up a makeshift business center. I sat at a long, mahogany table where my father, Al Anderson, and Charles Farrell were using the armament of phones to communicate with various reps from the Big Three. I glimpsed Rev. Jackson in a separate room by himself, talking on a cell phone with his reading glasses on. About every ten minutes he would pop in to visit us at the table and ask questions about the team. "I have to meet with Rick Wagoner today," he said on one trip out. "I think I'm going to take you guys over there with me. Let me see." Morty and Chris B. eventually made it to the suite and anxiously waited to find out what was going to happen next.

"DaimlerChrysler will be here first," said Farrell. Daimler-Chrysler's reps were Bob Wildberger and Bill Tracy from Dodge Motorsports. After Wildberger and Tracy, we would meet with Gary Claudio from GM and Elliott S. Hall from Ford. Hearing the names did not give me much solace. Al Anderson had been in talks with Wildberger and Tracy about recruiting a Miller Racing Group driver for Dodge's Craftsman team, but there was a rumor floating around that Willy T. Ribbs had already been selected. My father and I had been working with Gary Claudio since '95, and I felt like we had plateaued with how far we were going to get with him. Elliott S. Hall, an African-American, was a former lobbyist for Ford in Washington and currently held the title of vice president of dealer development. As far as I knew, Hall did not make major decisions concerning Ford's participation in motorsports.

There was a light knock on the door of the suite. The staffer with the boom microphone let in Wildberger, Tracy, and an African-American gentleman who introduced himself as an employee of Dodge. Wildberger excitedly told us about Dodge Motorsports' diversity effort. Tracy chimed in to say that the team was already looking at Willy T. Ribbs and Bill Lester as possible Craftsman drivers. Morty and Chris B. looked on quietly.

"We're working with a guy named Al Anderson, too, who markets African-American drivers," said Wildberger.

"I'm Al Anderson," said Al, who was offended that the representatives hadn't remembered his name having just been introduced only minutes ago. "You guys are *not* working with me. You rejected my proposals over six months ago. You don't even know who I am. I'm sitting right next to you!"

Flustered, Tracy spit out, "Can Morty and Chris fly to Tennessee in three days for a test drive in Bobby Hamilton's truck?"

"Today is Friday, and you want them to be in Tennessee on Monday?" replied my father. "What time?"

"Seven o'clock in the morning," said Tracy.

"That's almost impossible," said my father. "Who's going to pay their expenses? We heard Willy T. Ribbs was already selected to be Dodge's driver for next season."

My father, Al, and I were angry. It was clear that Dodge's desire to include us was contrived. Sure, we could have scrambled to send Morty and Chris B. out to Tennessee on Monday and found a way to foot the bill, but to what end? So Dodge could take group photos of us all smiling in phony harmony for its diversity portfolio, only to tell us they did not have driving opportunities for us? We felt like an afterthought.

"Guys, we're not doing anything for Bobby Hamilton," said Al.

"Our minority program is ahead of everyone else's, gentlemen," said the African-American rep, implying that we were missing out on a golden opportunity. The three Dodge guys tossed their business cards on the table and told us to contact them by the end of the day if we changed our minds.

The meeting with Gary Claudio and another GM rep was also unproductive. "I know I can get you some parts," said Claudio. "I have to make a trip to Charlotte next month. I'll visit you so we can talk about your plans for next year."

We had heard it all before.

"I support Rainbow/PUSH and will do my best to help Miller Racing Group," said Claudio before making his way to the door with his coworker. The GM reps were in and out in less than twenty minutes.

As we prepared for our appointment with Ford, I noticed an African-American gentleman in a suit standing just outside the door of the suite. He whispered something to Charles Farrell then vanished.

"That was Elliott S. Hall. He forgot about our meeting and scheduled another meeting," Farrell informed us. "He'll have to cancel. He said he'll call me in New York."

"Isn't he in charge of dealerships at Ford?" I said. "I don't think he's the motorsports guy."

"I know, I know," said Farrell. "But that's who they sent."

Our high hopes for support from one of the Big Three were fast dissolving.

"I'm going over to see Rick Wagoner," announced Rev. Jackson when he emerged from his side room in an expensive business suit. "I want the drivers over there in one hour. You can walk. I'll be at the top floor." Wagoner's office was located on the top floor of the GM Renaissance Center, a massive, 5.5-million-square-foot business and retail complex on Detroit's riverfront. As we left the suite and headed for the elevators, Chris B. had a pouty look on his face.

"I hope we take the Dodge test," he said as we walked through the hotel lobby toward the exit.

"Chris, you don't have enough experience yet," said my father. It was the truth. Chris B. wasn't yet skilled enough for the Craftsman level.

"Besides, Bobby Hamilton isn't going to let us run anything," said Al Anderson. Morty agreed with our decision. Chris B. listened and nodded, but would not relent.

"Mr. Miller, I may not be the smartest man in the world, but we need to go to the Dodge truck test in Nashville," he said. "It's seat time." I understood his inclination to salvage what we could from the Dodge opportunity. He was young, he was hungry, he was competitive, and like the rest of us, he was tired of being told no. In his mind, while the offer may not have been ideal, it was better than no offer at all.

"Mr. Miller, help me understand," he repeated in bewilderment on our walk. "It's seat time, Mr. Miller. It's seat time."

At the Renaissance Center, a glass elevator overlooking Windsor, Ontario, and the Detroit River shot us up to the top floor. In the reception area, four of Rev. Jackson's lieutenants, seated around a circular table, nodded to us as we walked by. Wagoner's secretary led us down a large circular staircase to his office. Wagoner was sitting at the end of a long, rectangular wooden table, flanked by an entourage of African-American execs, as well as former Detroit Pistons basketball player Dave Bing. Rev. Jackson stood, smiled, and introduced everyone before we got down to business. Wagoner related our experiences to the plight of Tiger Woods and acted sympathetic to our cause. "Have you heard of Herb Fishel at GM?" I sat quietly and didn't bring up my one run-in with Fishel at the SAE Motorsports Conference, where his colleague Don Taylor shut down any prospects of a GM-Miller Racing partnership. The African-American execs initiated conversations with Chris B. and Morty. At one point, Rev.

Jackson started to chant, "We need money, Rick. We need money!" Wagoner asked a couple of general questions about our effort and wished Morty and Chris B. luck in their careers. Rev. Jackson thanked the GM execs for their time and told Wagoner he would be in touch. Before we set foot outside, Rev. Jackson said goodbye to us and rushed off to the airport with his entourage. We walked out of the Renaissance Center with nothing close to a sponsorship deal. All we could do now was hope that Rev. Jackson's follow-up calls and letters would persuade Wagoner and his staff to back Miller Racing Group.

For weeks Rainbow/PUSH tried to broker a second meeting between Wagoner and Rev. Jackson. The follow-up meeting never happened. Neither did the meeting with Ford's Elliott S. Hall.

Willy T. Ribbs indeed drove Bobby Hamilton's No. 8 Craftsman Truck for the 2001 season. He started twenty-three races and had an average finish of twenty-first place. It was his one and only season with the team. Bill Lester filled the spot the following season but did not fare much better with an average finish of nineteenth place. In 2003, Dodge pulled the plug on the program.

Within weeks of the Big Three meetings, we received a call from Dave Mackey, the owner of a marketing company named Pendine Motorsports. Pendine handled auto-racing initiatives for Dr Pepper in the US. For much of 2000, Rev. Jackson had been in talks with Jack Kilduff, the president of Dr Pepper, about a sponsorship. The soft drink company had backed Joe Washington and Julius Erving during their brief foray into NASCAR, and although the Washington-Erving effort folded, Dr Pepper was still looking to make a footprint in NASCAR, as well as market its brand to more African-Americans and other minorities.

Once he saw our operations in Concord, Dave Mackey didn't need much convincing. He loved my father's background in racing and Chris B.'s combination of youth, looks, and driving ability. A few days into the New Year, Mackey had a three-year contract ready for us to sign. It was the first time a sponsorship deal had materialized so quickly for us. Within the blink of an eye, our 2001 season had been salvaged.

We now had a different problem on our hands, however. For months, Chris B. had been acting more and more apathetic about the team. When Mackey and others from Pendine contacted him about signing the Dr Pepper contract, he didn't return their calls. The young driver still couldn't get over the fact that we had passed on the Dodge test. In the weeks following the Big Three meetings, Chris B. had stopped returning calls from Chad Talbott and my father. He had also had it with David Miller. "I'm done with that redneck, Mr. Miller, I'm done!" he told my father near the end of the 2000 season, after his foot had healed and he'd gotten back on the track at Concord in the Firebird. "I keep telling you, there's something wrong with that boy," said David Miller, who wasn't helping Chris B.'s morale by continually treating him like a subordinate. In the meantime, David had forged a relationship with a twenty-nine-year-old African-American driver named Reggie Primus, who was racing at dirt tracks down in South Carolina. Primus had a background in mechanical engineering, having taken coursework at the HBCU South Carolina State University. David bragged, "I've seen him run in the dirt. Reggie is going to be the man." My father and I were happy about the discovery and agreed to meet with Primus, but we weren't ready to replace Chris B. Primus wasn't experienced enough to drive in Late Model Stock and didn't have Chris B.'s mechanical skills. Plus, Mackey had been so enamored of Chris B. that our deal with Dr Pepper might have hinged upon our disgruntled driver's participation. Morty was down in Atlanta and still available to race. We decided that if Chris B. bailed, we would put Morty in the Dr Pepper car.

I left multiple messages for Chris B. My father called him. Chad called and e-mailed him. David, who hadn't seen him in days, said that Chris B. didn't believe Dr Pepper was going to follow through on its promise to us. "Mr. Mackey is just a consultant," posited Chris B. to David. "He's not Dr Pepper, the company. There's not going to be any sponsorship."

While Chris B. was MIA, a press conference announcing the Miller Racing-Dr Pepper partnership was planned for January 26 at the Rainbow/PUSH Wall Street Project summit in New York. Rainbow/PUSH asked us to have our show car with Dr Pepper signage ready to display on stage in the main hall. David and Kathy agreed to tow the show car up to the Big Apple for the event.

"Are you sure David can navigate around New York City without wrecking our trailer?" I asked my father.

"I've already thought of that," he replied. "I'm going to get Cool Breeze Rivers to meet David and Kathy on the New Jersey Turnpike to navigate for them. Cool Breeze knows the city by heart." Preparations for the press conference were coming together. All we needed was our driver.

One evening my father, Chad, and I were on a conference call discussing Chris B.'s attitude change when Chad excused himself to take another call. A minute later he returned, and told us in a panic, "That was Al Anderson. Chris called Dave Mackey and said he resigned from Miller Racing Group. Chris allegedly tried to take the Dr Pepper sponsorship to another agent. What do we do?"

"Let's put Morty in the Dr Pepper ride," I said without hesitation.

"Call Morty, Chad," my father said. "I can't believe this." My father was disheartened, as was I. We had invested time and money in Chris B., at a time when no other team was ready to make such a commitment. Now, he was not only quitting on us, he was trying to sabotage one of the few sponsorship offers my father and I would ever receive. Chris B.'s actions, like Bill Lester's during the CART fiasco, spoke volumes about the limited opportunities for African-American drivers and teams. Chris B. was so desperate for sponsorship that he was willing to backstab and betray if it meant a shot at money. Only a sliver of NASCAR's multi-billion-dollar pie was trickling down to its black participants, which triggered divisiveness and distrust rather than commiseration and unification.

Within minutes, Chad called us back.

"Morty's ready to go," he said. "He's stunned that Chris didn't take the opportunity."

Mackey approved Morty as the driver. Reams of documents and contracts laced with Chris B.'s name had to be amended accordingly. A few days later, Chad got a call from Chris B.'s lawyer asking us to release Chris B. from his agent's agreement with Miller Racing Group. Chad was happy to sever ties.

January 26, 2001 was a Friday, the last day of the Wall Street Project summit. The event was being held at the Sheraton Hotel near 57th Street and 7th Avenue in Manhattan. Chad flew in from Louisville. Al Anderson and Virgil Scott came from Atlanta. A contingent from Dr Pepper's management team, including Jack Kilduff, arrived from Dallas. David and Kathy Miller, who had driven up to New York with the new Dr Pepper show car a few days prior, stuck out like sore thumbs. David sported a worn T-shirt and an old, crinkled ACDelco cap. Kathy had never seen so many African-Americans in suits in her life. "Now I know how you all feel at Concord," she said. "I'm outnumbered now." Reggie Primus, who drove up with David and Kathy, was equally in awe. When I ran into Charles Farrell, he told me he had overheard folks buzzing about the unveiling of the Dr Pepper car. Our press conference was shaping up to be one of the most anticipated moments of the entire event, he said.

Over 1,000 people packed the main convention hall for the announcement of the Dr Pepper car. Rev. Jackson stood at the podium in the center of a long dais. About twenty-five TV cameras, perched on an elevated platform in the rear of the room, started to focus their lenses on the civil-rights activist, as well as our show car, which faced the audience at a 45-degree angle and still bore an opaque cover. About fifty more cameramen and dozens of reporters positioned themselves in front of the stage. Charles Farrell and another Rainbow/PUSH staff member hustled Morty onstage. Then, my father, Virgil Scott, Chad Talbott, and I were ushered in front of the covered show car, along with Jack Kilduff, Dave Mackey, and two other Dr Pepper executives.

Rev. Jackson launched into a speech about the long, hard road in front of African-Americans in racing and the importance of corporate sponsorship. As he segued into Dr Pepper's landmark association with Miller Racing, stage attendants slowly pulled the cover off the maroon and white No. 21. New-age music played over the loudspeakers and Dr Pepper coolers were wheeled onstage. Once the Dr Pepper logo on the hood came into full view, the crowd stood to applaud. Those of us onstage beamed at the rousing response and squinted at the eruption of flash bulbs and colorful stage lights. A couple of cameramen asked Morty to stand in various poses next to the car while he held a can of Dr Pepper. More dignitaries from Rainbow/PUSH, Dr Pepper, and other organizations jumped onstage to take part in the reverie. I was so overwhelmed by excitement I could hardly tell who was standing next to me and whose hand I was shaking. Hours later, as David, Kathy, and Reggie walked outside to begin the tricky task of getting the car off stage and back into the Top Kick, the trio was met by a mob of excited fans on the street. David handed out a few dozen Dr Pepper autograph cards with Morty on the front to several African-Americans and Puerto Ricans who said things like, "I hope he goes down there and beats those guys," and "About time they let a brother race, man!"

In the weeks that followed, *The New York Times*, *USA Today*, and various local TV stations picked up our story. My father's phone rang off the hook for interview requests. Fans in Virginia, North Carolina, and Pennsylvania stopped my father, me, and other members of the team in public to say hello and give words of encouragement.

For a brief moment, we all felt like movie stars.

We rode the wave of excitement right into the 2001 season. We purchased a Townsend Racing Products Late Model chassis and hired Rick Townsend himself as crew chief. As skilled as David was, Rick was an upgrade at the position. David took the changeover in stride and remained a dedicated member of the crew. Rick, David, and Morty worked day and night to prep the new No. 21. We raced at our home track of Concord, as well as South Boston Speedway in Virginia; Southern National Speedway in Kenly, North Carolina; Martinsville Speedway in Martinsville, Virginia; and the New River Valley Speedway in Radford, Virginia. We worked with a savvy public relations director named Stephanie Carroll, who coordinated media events and spearheaded a TV commercial featuring Morty for the New River Valley Speedway. Overall, the Dr Pepper funding allowed us to invest in better equipment and manpower, which translated into Morty consistently qualifying and often finishing in the top five.

The 2001 season wasn't a complete breeze, as our sponsorship instilled furious envy in track officials and competitors. At our home track of Concord, where the specter of the Furrs had fully disappeared, officials waved unwarranted red and yellow flags when Morty led races. On July 7, when Morty drove to victory at the Coastal Plains Speedway in Jacksonville, North Carolina, it felt like Flemington all over again.

Morty passed local track champion Mack Best on the last lap between turns one and two. On the observation deck of the Miller Racing Group trailer, Maria and Morty's mother and brother jumped up and down in anticipation. Mack Best rode Morty's rear bumper all the way down the backstretch into turn three.

Morty created just enough breathing room coming out of turn four and charged down the front stretch for the win. Everyone on our plot went crazy and ran over to meet Morty in the winner's circle. There, a third car, No. 99, which finished in third place, pulled alongside Morty. The driver of the No. 99 revved the engine to a piercing volume and shook his fist violently out the window. As I drew closer to the winner's circle, I heard the crew of the No. 99 car shouting threats at some of our team members. Maria ran over to Morty, who was taking down the window net to get out; the No. 99 car was so loud that Morty may not have known what was happening. Maria told him, "Stay in the car. There may be trouble." I turned around and saw ten raggedy misfits from the pits running toward the Dr Pepper car, with track officials and two police officers in tow. "I just want to protect my wife and mother if fighting breaks out," Morty told me through the window. The gate on the grandstand side of the track was now open, and as the team spotters came back over to the pit area I noticed our spotter, Ricky Dennis, shouting face to face with the spotter for the No. 99 car. Officials and police officers struggled to quash the mob, whose members were waving fingers at us and shouting racial epithets to anyone who was listening. Once the fracas died down, Morty climbed out of the car to receive the trophy. The track announcer hurried through the ceremony. The trophy queen was nowhere in sight. The track photographer, shaken from the near-riot, wasn't snapping any shots. A chorus of boos and expletives rained down from the grandstands.

Determined not to let our proud moment pass without documentation, I pulled out the small camera I had in my coat pocket and went to work. We had just taken our new Dr Pepper car to the winner's circle, a landmark achievement not only for us but for any African-American racers who understood our struggles to get there, and I'd be damned if I'd let the hecklers thwart us. I started directing the crew members into different poses and positions around the car. I pointed, instructed, and snapped, pointed, instructed, and snapped. I got down on my knees for some shots, took a few steps back for others. My dad acted as my security detail. He stood close by and scanned my surroundings. When I finished, I saw that security had forced the mob back into the infield. Through the glare of the bright lights, I saw fans in the grandstands still pointing at us. I heard them yelling, "You people go home! You people go home!" A little boy, no more than seven years old, had his face pressed up against the catch-fence on the front straightaway wall. "You people go home!" he shouted. "You people go home!" The police offered to escort us to our cars, but we declined. We wanted to walk out together like the other crews at Concord would: as a team.

The team, as it was currently constituted, would not last very long, though.

Once the 2001 season ended, we focused on entering Morty in the ARCA RE/MAX series for next season. ARCA RE/MAX had no affiliation with NASCAR, and its competition level was a few notches below Cup racing, but the amateur stock-car series would allow us to keep up Morty's track time at a relatively lower cost than NASCAR Late Model. ARCA RE/MAX held races at a mix of oval and dirt tracks, road courses, and bigger speedways like Pocono. Some NASCAR teams even scouted for drivers at ARCA RE/MAX races, which were often televised. It was a productive way to bide the team's time in between the handful of Late Model races we could afford.

My father and I reached out to our old friend Bobby Gerhart about forging a partnership for ARCA. Bobby lived close to my father, in Lebanon, Pennsylvania, and had been racing in ARCA on and off since 1988. He was one of ARCA's best, most consistent drivers. He frequently placed in the top ten and in recent years had won big races at Daytona and Talladega. The success had helped earn him sponsors, including a major deal with a

Michigan casino in 1998. We asked Bobby if he would be interested in entering Morty in the ARCA RE/MAX series as a joint venture between Miller Racing and Bobby Gerhart Racing. We wanted Bobby's name behind our effort, as we figured it would give Morty credibility in the eyes of ARCA officials and potential sponsors. We also knew that Morty had a great chance of quickly becoming one of the series's premier drivers, which could garner good PR for Bobby and his team. Bobby agreed to the partnership, provided my father and I footed the bill for Morty's start-up expenses, which included paying for his rookie testing and, if he passed, an ARCA license. All in all, the licensing process would total $40,000.

As soon as Morty got his ARCA license, we received a call from his lawyer in Atlanta. Morty wanted to break his contract with Miller Racing.

Morty's lawyer didn't give much of an explanation as to why Morty wanted to quit our team. The lawyer said something about Morty wanting to explore other driving opportunities. That was that. We didn't speak to Morty again.

Within a year, the two drivers who we believed could one day transform the very complexion of NASCAR walked away from Miller Racing. We had invested time, money, and emotional highs and lows in the development of Chris B. and Morty as the NASCAR superstars we knew they could be. We weren't prepared to lose both of them so suddenly. Chris B. and Morty not only left us with an irrevocable hole in our wallets, they left us with an unprecedented challenge, one that outweighed all the others: the doubt that my father and I could succeed as NASCAR team owners. For over a decade, one by one, we confronted the obstacles we knew we were going to face. The hustle for corporate dollars. The reticence from potential sponsors. The fickle ties to those companies that did back us. The open discrimination from rivals, track officials, and fans. The middling commitment from

NASCAR. The crashes. The debt. The specter of other failed black-owned efforts. The rejection from the black bourgeosie. The lack of understanding from our own family and friends. We knew our journey toward a lasting integration in NASCAR would be fraught with near-impossible difficulties. But, by the time Chris B. and Morty signed with Miller Racing, we felt like we had overcome damn near all of them. We had reached a plateau in our mission. We had a big-name sponsor in Dr Pepper; we had Rev. Jackson on our side. More and more Americans were finding out about our story and the stories of Wendell Scott, Willy T. Ribbs, and all the other great African-Americans who had been racing for nearly a century. Thanks to Jackie Robinson, Tiger Woods, and so many other trailblazing African-American athletes, we knew integration was possible. With NASCAR warming up to the idea, integration almost seemed imminent. We had fought off the inevitable weariness that came along with our undertaking. We felt battle-tested and ready to take black racing to a place where it had never been before.

But we were now left feeling like our dream was not to be.

14
Champions

For my father and me, our last days in stock-car racing were the most fun—and we spent them with a white driver behind the wheel.

Franklin Butler III came to us at a time when we had run out of black drivers.

Around the time we released Morty from his contract, David Miller told us about a twenty-four-year-old African-American kid name Shanta Rhodes, who was driving in Street Stock about an hour north of Concord. Shanta grew up in a poor rural town outside of Raleigh and started racing at East Carolina Motor Speedway in Robersonville. When I first met him, he was upbeat and courteous. He spoke excitedly about one day making it to NASCAR. Without other options for a driver, we put him in the Dr Pepper car for the 2002 and 2003 seasons. We planned on entering Shanta in Street Stock at Concord as well as two ARCA races. We painted a graphic with "Salute to Rajo Jack" on the hood to honor the late, great African-American driver.

While he showed potential a few months into the season, the Shanta Rhodes experience fast imploded. He became irresponsible with his work in the shop, and after a while stopped doing any maintenance duties. He became increasingly argumentative. He showed up hours late to practices and races; sometimes he wouldn't show up at all. We would call friends and family to try and track him down, but often nobody knew where he was. When we did find him, he would give nonsensical excuses about being stuck in traffic. We knew he was lying. We didn't have any proof, but my father and I suspected that he might have had a substance-abuse problem. The incident that ended his run with Miller Racing was a hit-and-run accident that he was involved in while he was driving our rig. We had to go to court; I even had a detective show up at my house in Virginia to serve me papers. Then, toward the end of 2003, he disappeared from the scene at Concord for good. As far as I know, no one at Concord ever heard from him again. It was a shame. He was a good kid who probably didn't have much direction as a youngster.

In addition to starting 2004 without a driver, our primary sponsor, Dr Pepper, severed ties with us. Some personnel changes occurred during 2003, and the new folks in sports marketing told us they wanted to focus on college football. Two of these newcomers, a pair of young black executives, had visited us during a racing weekend in Charlotte. They were fidgety the entire time and looked like they couldn't wait to get back on the plane. One of the execs was a fellow Morehouse grad. But it didn't matter. He, like the rest of his colleagues, didn't believe in us.

Another huge setback arrived back in July of '03, when, according to a *USA Today* article, NASCAR ended its donations to Rainbow/PUSH. The report came after months of mounting tension between the two parties. NASCAR, which had publicly gotten involved in various campaigns to support US troops overseas, didn't take too kindly to Rev. Jackson and Rainbow/PUSH members speaking out against the war in Iraq at various protests and rallies. Neither did Peter Flaherty, president of the conservative National Legal and Policy Center (NLPC). Flaherty made public a letter he sent to Bill France Jr. asking NASCAR to cut off its funding for Rev. Jackson's group. In response, NASCAR president Mike Helton made the following statement on April 23: "While we have supported the Rainbow Coalition's work on diversity issues, we do not endorse many of Reverend Jackson's political views or any other political views." Then, during a speech at the Rainbow/PUSH Coalition Conference in June, board member Bill Shack called NASCAR "the last bastion of white supremacy" in sports; NASCAR's chief operating officer George Pyne happened to be in the room. Weeks later, our friend Charles Farrell caught flack for using an inflammatory choice of words, too. In an interview for CNSNews.com, Charles was quoted as saying, "there is a perception that stock-car racing is a good ole boy's Southern redneck cracker sport." Shack's and Charles's comments, along with protests organized by Flaherty's NLPC group, generated bad PR for NASCAR and forced the France family to take some sort of action. While later reports made it unclear if and when NASCAR officially cut off funding to Rainbow/PUSH, one thing was for certain: the controversies created a rift between the two powerful groups, one that was never quite repaired.

With Rev. Jackson and Rainbow/PUSH no longer centerpieces of NASCAR's diversity initiatives, newly appointed chairman and CEO Brian Z. France launched the Drive for Diversity program in October of 2003. For starters, Drive for Diversity announced it would collect applications for minority drivers and crew members, test and select drivers for NASCAR's lower levels, and help set up drivers with Cup teams and potential sponsors. The short-term goal for the 2004 season was to get four drivers and twelve crew members paired with teams. One of the first teams to participate in the program was Joe Gibbs Racing.

It was no coincidence that Drive for Diversity was announced at a time when NASCAR was starting to see a steady decline in its TV ratings. In the midst of its mega deal with Fox and NBC, NASCAR needed to find ways to broaden its fan base. Suddenly, the idea of breaking a Tiger Woods into the sport sounded like a viable, if not necessary, business move. NASCAR also wanted to target the swelling Latin American market in the US, and aimed to recruit Latino drivers for Drive for Diversity. Plus, a sultry and talented twenty-one-year-old female open-wheel driver named Danica Patrick was just starting to make waves in the Toyota Atlantic series, proving that a woman could draw more attention to a sport than many of her male counterparts. "I think diversity is a long-term pursuit that will help make NASCAR more attractive to everyone," said Brian Z. France in the December 5, 2003 *Charlotte Observer* article entitled "A Plan for Diversity."

The promise of guaranteed spots with more established teams left us high and dry for potential black drivers. My father and I scoured short tracks across the Southeast, contacting racing friends to find out if they knew of anyone. When we did find a candidate, we couldn't present an offer that was more attractive than Drive for Diversity's. In NASCAR's new program, minority drivers saw the window of opportunity that had been shut for so long finally creak open. Big teams, including Joe Gibbs Racing and Bobby Hamilton Racing, created seats specifically for minority drivers. Companies like Domino's, Kodak, and Miller Brewing announced they would sponsor cars for the drivers. In May of '04, NASCAR named NBA hall-of-famer Magic Johnson as co-chairman of a new Executive Diversity Steering Committee, which aimed to not only increase diversity in NASCAR's teams and workforce but also expand the audience. In Johnson, NASCAR now had a successful African-American businessman and one of the friendliest faces in all of sports as one of its diversity ambassadors.

The roster of all-star participants helped Drive for Diversity scoop up newcomers like Joe Henderson III, a teenager out of Tennessee with a ton of upside, as well as some more familiar faces: Bruce Driver, Chris Bristol, Morty Buckles, and Reggie Primus. In the cases of Chris B. and Morty, the promise of making it to Cup racing via Drive for Diversity led them to forsake any of their previous ties to Miller Racing Group. At the 2005 Association For Diversity In Motorsports (AFDIM) awards dinner held at Lowe's Motor Speedway, my father received a lifetime achievement award. Chris B. was asked to give a speech at the event. To a crowd of about four hundred folks, Chris B. spoke about his background in racing and his aspirations of following in the footsteps of Wendell Scott. Standing at the podium, looking at my father, my mother, and me in the eyes, he never once mentioned Miller Racing. When it came to Morty, his bio on Morty-Buckles.com referred to racing at Concord, driving in a Dr Pepper Late Model car, and working with ARCA champion Bobby Gerhart. Nowhere on the site does Miller Racing factor into Morty's stock-car racing narrative. In an interview for the February 27, 2006 issue of *ESPN The Magazine*, entitled "Door-to-Door," Morty said, ". . . some people didn't give me a break here or there." Granted, he was more referring to white teams passing on him because of his skin color. Still, it was as if the black team that indeed gave him a break had never existed. The disregard of our effort to help launch the careers of Chris B. and Morty hurt. We gave these guys track time, we helped them get sponsorship, we connected them with Rainbow/PUSH and other high-profile organizations, and the support had blown up in our faces. We now faced the reality that NASCAR's pool of prospective African-American drivers wanted nothing to do with us. Pretty soon, Chad Talbott, Bobby Norfleet, and Donald "Doc" Watson were the only black people involved in stock-car racing that communicated with us on a regular basis.

NASCAR, apparently, wanted nothing to do with us either. On the same evening AFDIM honored my father, three or four NASCAR representatives who where in attendance on behalf of the Diversity Council left the banquet room when my father rose to accept his award. They didn't return until he finished his acceptance speech. A rumor soon circulated that a NASCAR official told Wayne Clapp, AFDIM's founder and executive director, that honoring Leonard W. Miller was a big mistake. We learned sometime later that NASCAR withdrew further donations to AFDIM. We weren't sure if NASCAR administrators dismissed us based on our one-time ties to Rev. Jackson and Rainbow/PUSH, or if they felt guilty about poaching our potential drivers for Drive for Diversity while excluding us as owners. What we did know was that, after fifteen years of trying to put some color onto the gravel and into the pits of NASCAR, we were pariahs.

By the time we met Franklin Butler in the spring of '04, my father and I were on the verge of giving up stock-car racing for good. Herman Gantt, the Miller Racing's devoted crew chief who stuck it out with us during the last rocky days in the Dr Pepper car, had known Franklin for a while. Herman was a fixture on the Late Model scene up and down the east coast and had seen Franklin race many times over the years. Franklin hadn't raced much of late, but Herman said he was skilled, affable, and worth meeting.

Herman was right. Franklin and his family turned out being some of the warmest, most open-minded people my father and I had ever met in racing. He and his father ran an insurance company outside of Richmond. Franklin III graduated from Randolph-Macon College in Ashland, Virginia, where he was a football star. His family had supported his love of racing ever since he was a teenager. His father used to race. His younger brother, Brandon, raced stock cars in the Southeast. In person, Franklin reminded me a bit of former US senator and ex-presidential candidate John Edwards. Franklin exuded confidence, Southern charm, and liberal ideals. He empathized with our struggles of trying to make it in NASCAR, as he had never been able to crack Cup racing himself. On multiple occasions, teams passed on him in favor of someone who had higher friends or family with the team. Such is the dynastic nature of how so many of NASCAR's driving opportunities are decided. Franklin was capable enough to make it to Nextel Cup, he just never had the inside track like others. When we told him we were pretty much broke, Franklin volunteered to race for free. He loved stock-car racing and missed heading out to the track every weekend, he said.

Eager to get back on the track ourselves, my father and I devised a plan that could keep Franklin racing from week to week. Franklin was overqualified for Late Model, which meant, barring crashes, we could bank on him finishing in the top five or higher. We signed a contract with him stipulating that 60 percent of our operational budget would come from Franklin's winnings. The purses for Late Model in our region ran in the vicinity of $500 to $1,500. As long as Franklin placed in the top three of a race, we would generate enough money to purchase tires and fix crash damage for the next race. The type of agreement we had with Franklin was unusual for Late Model since the purses are so low; it was more prevalent in Craftsman Truck Series and higher. Franklin agreed. When Herman found out Franklin was on board, he followed Franklin's lead and offered to stay on as crew chief for no pay.

We stripped the car of Dr Pepper signage, packed up all of our tools and equipment at Concord, and relocated to Old Dominion Motor Speedway in Virginia. Old Dominion hosted Late Model races that were part of the NASCAR-sanctioned Dodge Weekly Series. The track was close to my house, which meant I could keep an eye on things with minimal travel expenses.

We couldn't have asked for a more welcoming reception. Owner Steve Britt and general manager Hayne Dominick were the fairest track operators we had met since the Furrs. They assured us we wouldn't encounter any sort of discrimination under their watch, as they wanted people of all colors and creeds to feel right at home. In fact, Eric Stewart, the cornrowed African-American track employee who had greeted me at Old Dominion almost fifteen years earlier when I was looking for Tom Rice, was now the speedway's highest-ranking official. More African-American staffers worked in the concession stands. Steve and Hayne made sure to play a mixture of pop, country, and Motown music. From the grandstands to the pits, there wasn't a rebel flag in sight. The attempt at an inclusive atmosphere worked, as families of all shades and backgrounds sat alongside each other on Saturday nights and cheered on their favorite drivers. If NASCAR was looking for a successful model of how to integrate, the stock-car empire didn't need to look much further than Old Dominion.

Franklin got off to a dominant start in the 2005 season, winning race after race. While my father and I contributed small amounts of cash, our latest makeshift crew of volunteers and moral supporters were the ones who really kept us going from week to week. Herman became the heart and soul of the team. The Scottish-Irish Virginian carried himself like an impassioned war general. He was quiet yet competitive, refusing to give up on a race under the most adverse circumstances. Like my father, Herman grew up racing hot rods as a teenager. He never once thought about quitting the sport he loved most.

Herman's never-die attitude trickled down to the other members of the crew, namely Dave "Chico" Creasy, a former member of Sprint Cup driver Hermie Sadler's pit crew, and Tommy "Thumper" Zapo. Chico and Thumper were masters at working quickly and efficiently in the pits. When we ran out of parts or needed an extra hand, crew members from other teams pitched in without hesitation. Nathanial "Hollywood" Gheen, a mechanic at Old Dominion, stopped by our plot often to offer his technical savvy. Herman's friend Judee Smith handed out tools, contributed a few dollars for concessions, and always offered words of encouragement. My father liked to tell Judee that if she'd been around during the 19th century, she would have been a pioneer woman right up there with Susan B. Anthony. Sam Beaty, a car owner at Old Dominion, provided key parts at critical moments. On one occasion, after a solid qualifying run by Franklin, it looked like we were done for the night due to a malfunctioning carburetor. Sam, whose driver had qualified for the same race as Franklin's, stepped up and loaned us a $700 four-barrel carburetor. Franklin won the race, besting Sam's driver in the process. Days later, my dad told the story to Hiliary Holloway, a black friend of his in Philadelphia. Hiliary was so inspired that he donated $1,000 to cover the cost of a replacement carburetor for the next race. Every Saturday night of the 2005 season, Jack Blake, another fixture in the pits at Old Dominion, prepared special meals for the crew. It was the first time we ever had a cook on the team. He grilled chicken, ribs, and hamburgers. As if Jack's culinary blessings weren't enough, Franklin's family members often dropped off more food before finding a spot in the infield to cheer on their guy.

Thanks to the confluence of hard work, altruism, and Franklin's ability, Franklin won the 2005 Dodge Weekly Series Late Model championship at Old Dominion, making Miller Racing the first black-owned team in history to win a title on a NASCAR-sanctioned level. Officials at Old Dominion honored us at the end-of-the-year awards banquet. There was music, food, and dancing. Both Franklin and my father gave speeches. Metropolitan Auto Racing Fans (MARF), an association of over 10,000 DC-area racecar aficionados, acknowledged our achievements at an awards ceremony. Franklin received two awards from MARF: one for his accolades on the track, another for being the most popular driver in the region. Herman Gantt received an award for his outstanding mechanic work, and my dad earned the Dennis Lindsey Memorial Award for his dedication and contributions to the sport of auto racing.

We never did receive recognition from NASCAR, however. In fact, some of our inside sources at NASCAR told us that a packet we sent to Daytona Beach containing documentation of our championship ended up in the garbage. Regardless of whether or not the tale of the trashed gratitude was true, the fact of the matter is that no NASCAR official ever contacted my father or me to congratulate us on our accomplishment.

Despite the lack of recognition from NASCAR, the 2005, 2006, and 2007 seasons at Old Dominion were the most satisfying in all my years of stock-car racing. We were winning. The team members not only got along, they enjoyed working with one another. Rival crews accepted us in the pits and veered away from conflicts both on and off the track. We continued receiving acknowledgment from entities outside of NASCAR, like in January of 2006, when Quartermasters Racing Team (QRT), a Maryland-based drag-racing team with members of all skin colors, invited Franklin and his family to the annual awards banquet. QRT president Stan Proctor wanted to honor Franklin for his outstanding driving achievements. An audience of six hundred, the majority being African-American drag racers and fans, gave Franklin, his wife Angela, his mother Becky, and about a dozen other Miller Racing team members unbridled applause.

To my father, the years with Franklin at the helm hearkened back to the 1950s, when he served in the US Third Army's Direct Automotive Field Support Company. The company, which performed emergency repairs on jeeps and trucks under battlefield conditions, was comprised of several stock-car and drag-racing enthusiasts. My dad remembers vividly how all members of the company, regardless of racial differences, came together to fix cars for a greater cause: the United States of America. Many of the soldiers were proud Southerners, sporting tattoos of the rebel flag on their arms. Some even had relatives in the Ku Klux Klan. My father and the other black soldiers in the company probably would have been disgusted by these good ol' boys under almost any other circumstance. But under the auspices of fighting for country, the soldiers set aside personal beliefs and biases to work together on cars. With time, the good ol' boys in the company respected the mechanical aptitude and fortitude of my dad and the other black soldiers, as those qualities were what bound everyone in the company together. My father, who would return from his tour of duty to blast his customized 1940 Ford convertible hot rod down the streets of North Philadelphia, always remembered those days in the US Third Army's Direct Automotive Field Support Company as testament to the fact that it was possible for lovers of auto racing to look past their differences. At Old Dominion, my father and I worked alongside racers who shared different political ideals, some of whom were anti-gun control, anti-welfare, or had lingering prejudice in their consciousness, and we were still given the opportunity to thrive. And we did just that, thrive. We were still tight on money. We still didn't have a sponsor. We still had the longer-term aspiration of getting more African-Americans onto pit road. But now, we were champions. And it felt good.

After one Saturday night of racing, Judee motioned for my dad to join her behind our trailer and said, "Mr. Miller, the teams around here say you're not a nigger, but a real man."

I'm not sure I'd call the sentiment a victory—yet. Maybe, one day, as an African-American driver revs up his or her engine at the beginning of the Daytona 500, we will be able to call it a start.

THE END

A BRIEF HISTORY OF BLACK ACHIEVEMENTS IN MOTORSPORTS

1910

OCTOBER 25: Boxer Jack Johnson races against top-ranked white driver Barney Oldfield at a track in Sheepshead Bay, Brooklyn. The American Automobile Association, which does not allow black drivers to enter its events, refuses to sanction the race.

1923

Driver Dewey "Rajo Jack" Gatson begins racing in an unsanctioned, barnstorming racing circuit in Southern California. In the ensuing years, he races under the alias Jack DeSoto, claiming his background is Portuguese.

1924

AUGUST 2: Driver Charlie Wiggins and local entrepreneur William Rucker organize the inaugural Gold and Glory Sweepstakes in Indianapolis, the first major auto-racing event open to black drivers.

1934

MAY 30: As the riding mechanic for driver Deacon Litz, Bobby Lee Wallace—passing for white—becomes the first African-American to compete in the Indianapolis 500.

SEPTEMBER: Dewey "Rajo Jack" Gatson wins a 200-mile sprint-car race at Silver Gate Speedway in San Diego.

1947

Former Gold and Glory Sweepstakes driver Joie Ray becomes the first African-American to receive a racing license from the American Automobile Association.

1949

MAY 30: Black sprint-car owner and driver Mel Leighton tries to enter the Indianapolis 500. He is turned away due to his skin color.

1955

JULY 31: Driver Elias Bowie starts thirty-first in a NASCAR race at Bay Meadows Speedway in San Mateo, California. He is the first African-American driver to start a Cup-level race.

1956

FEBRUARY 26: Driver Charlie Scott, a member of the African-American racing organization Atlanta Stock Car Club, makes his one NASCAR appearance in a Grand National race at the Daytona Beach road course. He finishes nineteenth.

1957

Drag racer Malcolm Durham starts competing at Easy Street Dragstrip in Newton Grove, N.C.

1959

Drag racer Eddie Flournoy starts competing in the Los Angeles area.

1963

Malcolm Durham wins races against drag-racing heavyweights Dave Strickler and Bill Jenkins in a '63 Chevy he nicknames Strip Blazer.

DECEMBER 1: Driver Wendell Scott edges out white driver Buck Baker in a 100-mile race at Speedway Park in Jacksonville, Florida, for a victory. Scott becomes the first (and, as of the publication date of this book, the only) black driver to win at NASCAR's Cup level.

1966

OCTOBER 30: Wendell Scott finishes sixth in NASCAR's Cup standings with 21,702 points, only 1,250 points behind third-place finisher Richard Petty.

1970

AUGUST 19: With drag racer Kenny Wright in the driver's seat, the Miller Brothers Team wins the Fourth Annual New Jersey State Championship in the National Hot Rod Association's V-Stock class.

1971

JULY 15: Driver George Wiltshire starts twenty-ninth in a NASCAR Cup race at Islip Speedway in New York.

1972

Driver Benny Scott wins the Sports Car Club of America's Formula A Southern Pacific Division championship.

JULY 15: Leonard W. Miller, a part-owner of Vanguard Racing, Inc., enters driver John Mahler in the Indianapolis 500. Miller is the first African-American owner to enter a driver in the Indianapolis 500.

1973

Leonard W. Miller, Wendell Scott, Malcolm Durham, and Ron Hines found Black American Racers Association.

Driver Randy Bethea beats legend Darrell Waltrip for pole position in a Late Model Sportsman event at the Nashville Fairgrounds Speedway.

Former Gold and Glory Sweepstakes driver Sumner "Red" Oliver becomes IndyCar's first black mechanic.

1975

MAY 25: Randy Bethea starts thirty-ninth in NASCAR's World 600 race at Charlotte Motor Speedway.

SEPTEMBER 28: Benny Scott and Black American Racers, Inc., qualify for the inaugural Long Beach Grand Prix. Scott finishes in eleventh place.

1976

Benny Scott and Leonard W. Miller are inducted into the Black Athletes Hall of Fame.

1977

Driver Willy T. Ribbs races Formula Ford cars in Europe and wins the Dunlop Championship.

Richard Pryor stars in *Greased Lightning*, a movie based on the life of Wendell Scott.

1980

African-American driver James "Jim" Graham wins two lower-level NASCAR races in a car sponsored by Coors Beer.

1990

African-American owner Thee Dixon fields a car for white NASCAR Cup driver Mike Skinner.

1991

MAY 26: Willy T. Ribbs becomes the first African-American to enter the Indianapolis 500, in a car part-owned by Bill Cosby.

African-American driver Tuesday Thomas, a woman, drives in her first truck race at Augusta Speedway in Georgia.

1995

Driver Chris Woods wins Rookie of the Year honors in the Late Model class at Concord Motor Speedway.

1999

APRIL 22: Wendell Scott is inducted into the International Motorsports Hall of Fame.

APRIL 25: Motorcyclist Antron Brown wins his first NHRA Pro Stock Motorcycle event; he goes on to amass sixteen wins over ten seasons.

JUNE 27: Driver Bill Lester starts twenty-fourth in a NASCAR Busch Series race at Watkins Glen International in New York.

2000

APRIL 22: Drivers Bobby Norfleet and Bill Lester enter a Craftsman Truck Series race at Portland International Raceway, the first time two African-Americans have competed in the same NASCAR race.

JUNE 11: Owner Jim Logan and his team, Logan Racing, enter a car in an Indy Racing Northern Lights Series race at Texas Motor Speedway.

2001

JANUARY 26: Dr Pepper announces it will sponsor Miller Racing Group with driver Morty Buckles behind the wheel.

Mechanic and former driver Tim Shutt is promoted to crew chief for a Joe Gibbs Racing Busch Grand National team. Shutt is the first black crew chief in one of NASCAR's top series.

2002

MAY 26: Driver George Mack becomes the second black driver after Willy T. Ribbs to qualify for the Indianapolis 500. Mack finishes seventeenth. Mack's car is owned by African-American entrepreneur Marc Laidler, founder of auto-customization company 310 Motoring.

2004

OCTOBER 6: Teenage driver Chase Austin is signed to Hendrick Motorsports' driver development program.

2005

Driving for Miller Racing Group, white racer Franklin Butler III wins the Dodge Weekly Series Late Model championship at Old Dominion, making Miller Racing the first black-owned team in history to win a title in a NASCAR-sanctioned competition.

2006

JANUARY 23: Teenage driver Marc Davis signs with Joe Gibbs Racing through

NASCAR's Drive for Diversity program. Later that year, Davis wins six races in the Limited Late Model division at Hickory Motor Speedway in North Carolina.

JULY 16: Drag racer J.R. Todd becomes the first African-American to win an event in the NHRA's Top Fuel class.

2007

APRIL 28: Motocross rider James Stewart wins the American Motorcyclist Association (AMA) Supercross title, the first African-American to do so. The following year he wins the AMA Motocross National Championship with a perfect record (only the second rider in history to go undefeated), and in 2009 he wins his second AMA Supercross title.

JUNE 2: Dewey "Rajo Jack" Gatson is inducted into the National Sprint Car Hall of Fame.

2008

MARCH 30: After switching from motorcycles to dragsters earlier in the year, Antron Brown becomes the only driver in NHRA history to win races in both the Top Fuel and Pro Stock Motorcycle classes.

NOVEMBER 2: British open-wheel racer Lewis Hamilton becomes the first black driver (and youngest ever) to win a Formula One World Championship.

2009

OCTOBER 10: Antron Brown breaks the national speed record in Top Fuel (319.60 mph).

Index

About the Authors

LEONARD T. MILLER is a second-generation African-American auto racing team owner, the president of Miller Racing Group, Inc, and a twenty-one-year veteran commercial airline pilot. He has fielded teams in NASCAR, ARCA, and INEX under the Miller Racing Group banner with sponsorships from Dr Pepper, General Motors, Sunoco, and Lincoln Electric. In 2003, Miller was awarded the "Trailblazer Award" by the Quartermasters Drag Racing Team for his contribution to the development of African-American racecar driving in motorsports from 1993 to 2003.

Miller's father, Leonard W. Miller, entered a team in the 1972 Indianapolis 500 and is in the Black Athletes Hall of Fame. At the Old Dominion Speedway in Manassas, Virginia, in 2005, the Millers became the first African Americans to win a track championship in NASCAR's Weekly Racing Series, with Franklin Butler as their driver.

ANDREW SIMON is a writer and editor living in Brooklyn, New York. For over a decade he has covered music, sports, and pop culture for Rolling Stone Press, *VIBE*, *Complex*, and *ESPN The Magazine*.